Communications
in Computer and Information Science   1920

Rationale
The CCIS series is devoted to the publication of proceedings of computer science conferences. Its aim is to efficiently disseminate original research results in informatics in printed and electronic form. While the focus is on publication of peer-reviewed full papers presenting mature work, inclusion of reviewed short papers reporting on work in progress is welcome, too. Besides globally relevant meetings with internationally representative program committees guaranteeing a strict peer-reviewing and paper selection process, conferences run by societies or of high regional or national relevance are also considered for publication.

Topics
The topical scope of CCIS spans the entire spectrum of informatics ranging from foundational topics in the theory of computing to information and communications science and technology and a broad variety of interdisciplinary application fields.

Information for Volume Editors and Authors
Publication in CCIS is free of charge. No royalties are paid, however, we offer registered conference participants temporary free access to the online version of the conference proceedings on SpringerLink (http://link.springer.com) by means of an http referrer from the conference website and/or a number of complimentary printed copies, as specified in the official acceptance email of the event.

CCIS proceedings can be published in time for distribution at conferences or as post-proceedings, and delivered in the form of printed books and/or electronically as USBs and/or e-content licenses for accessing proceedings at SpringerLink. Furthermore, CCIS proceedings are included in the CCIS electronic book series hosted in the SpringerLink digital library at http://link.springer.com/bookseries/7899. Conferences publishing in CCIS are allowed to use Online Conference Service (OCS) for managing the whole proceedings lifecycle (from submission and reviewing to preparing for publication) free of charge.

Publication process
The language of publication is exclusively English. Authors publishing in CCIS have to sign the Springer CCIS copyright transfer form, however, they are free to use their material published in CCIS for substantially changed, more elaborate subsequent publications elsewhere. For the preparation of the camera-ready papers/files, authors have to strictly adhere to the Springer CCIS Authors' Instructions and are strongly encouraged to use the CCIS LaTeX style files or templates.

Abstracting/Indexing
CCIS is abstracted/indexed in DBLP, Google Scholar, EI-Compendex, Mathematical Reviews, SCImago, Scopus. CCIS volumes are also submitted for the inclusion in ISI Proceedings.

How to start
To start the evaluation of your proposal for inclusion in the CCIS series, please send an e-mail to ccis@springer.com.

Rabindra Nath Shaw · Marcin Paprzycki ·
Ankush Ghosh
Editors

Advanced Communication and Intelligent Systems

Second International Conference, ICACIS 2023
Warsaw, Poland, June 16–17, 2023
Revised Selected Papers, Part I

Springer

Editors
Rabindra Nath Shaw 🆔
Chandigarh University
Mohali, India

Marcin Paprzycki 🆔
Systems Research Institute
Warsaw, Poland

Ankush Ghosh 🆔
Chandigarh University
Mohali, India

ISSN 1865-0929   ISSN 1865-0937 (electronic)
Communications in Computer and Information Science
ISBN 978-3-031-45120-1   ISBN 978-3-031-45121-8 (eBook)
https://doi.org/10.1007/978-3-031-45121-8

Preface

The book features selected high-quality papers presented at the International Conference on Advanced Communication and Intelligent Systems (ICACIS 2023), organized by Warsaw Management University, Poland during June 16–17, 2023, through online mode. The conference got an overwhelming response and received more than 200 papers from all around the world. All submitted papers have gone through a single-blind review process with an average of three reviews per paper. The acceptance rate was less than 25%. The presented papers are published in this proceedings volume. The book focuses on current development in the fields of communication and intelligent systems. Advances in artificial intelligence and machine learning have spawned fresh research activities all around the world in the last few years, examining novel approaches to constructing intelligent systems and smart communication technologies. The book covers topic such as Wireless Communication, Artificial Intelligence and Machine Learning, Robotics & Automation, Data Science, IoT and Smart Applications. The book covers both single- and multi-disciplinary research on these topics in order to provide the most up-to-date information in one place. The book will be beneficial for readers from both academia and industry.

We are thankful to all the authors that have submitted papers for keeping the quality of ICACIS 2023 at high levels. The editors of this book would like to acknowledge all the authors for their contributions, and the reviewers. We have received invaluable help from the members of the International Program Committee and the chairs responsible for different aspects of the workshop. We also appreciate the role of the Special Sessions Organizers. Thanks to all of them, we had been able to collect many papers on interesting topics, and during the conference we had very interesting presentations and stimulating discussions.

We hope that the volume will provide useful information to professors, researchers, and graduate students in the areas of Computer Science Engineering, Electronics and Communication Engineering and associated technologies along with AI and IoT applications, and all will find this collection of papers inspiring, informative and useful. We also hope to see you at a future ICACIS event.

Rabindra Nath Shaw
Marcin Paprzycki
Ankush Ghosh

Organization

General Chair

Marcin Paprzycki   Systems Research Institute, Polish Academy of
                                    Sciences, Poland

General Co-chair

Ankush Ghosh   ADSRS Education and Research, India

Conference Chair and Chairman, Oversight Committee

Rabindra Nath Shaw   Chandigarh University, India

Technical Chair

Monica Bianchini   University of Siena, Italy

Publication Chair

Sanjoy Das   Indira Gandhi National Tribal University,
                                    Regional Campus Manipur, India

Publicity Chair

Prashant R. Nair   Amrita Vishwa Vidyapeetham, India

Advisory Committee

Bimal K. Bose   University of Tennessee, USA
Muhammad H. Rashid   University of West Florida, USA
Muhammet Koksal   Halic University, Turkey

Contents – Part I

Contents – Part II

About the Editors

Dr. Rabindra Nath Shaw is a global leader in organizing International conferences. His brand of world leading conference series includes IEEE International Conference on Computing, Power and Communication Technologies (GUCON), IEEE International Conference on Computing, Communication and Automation (ICCCA), IEEE IAS Global Conference on Emerging Technologies (GlobConET), International Conference on Electronics & Electrical Engineering (ICEEE), International Conference on Advances in Computing and Information Technology (ICACIT) etc. He holds the position of Conference Chair, Publication Chair, and Editor for these conferences. These Conferences are held in collaboration with various international universities like Aurel Vlaicu University of Arad, University of Malaya, University of Siena. Many world leaders are working with Dr. Shaw in these conferences. Most of these conferences are fully sponsored by IEEE Industry Applications Society, USA. He is also an expert in organizing International Seminars/Webinars/Faculty Development Programme in collaboration with leading institutes across the world.

Dr. Marcin Paprzycki received the MS degree from Adam Mickiewicz University, Poznań, Poland, the PhD degree from Southern Methodist University, Dallas, Texas, and the doctor of science degree from the Bulgarian Academy of Sciences, Sofia, Bulgaria. He is an associate professor with the Systems Research Institute, Polish Academy of Sciences. He is a senior member of the ACM, a senior fulbright lecturer, and an IEEE Computer Society distinguished visitor. He has contributed to more than 500 publications and was invited to the program committees of more than 800 international conferences.

Prof. Ankush Ghosh is Senior member of IEEE, Fellow of IETE has received his Ph.D. (Engg.) degree from Jadavpur University, India in 2010. He was a research fellow of the Advanced Technology Cell- DRDO, Govt. of India. He was awarded National Scholarship by HRD, Govt. of India. He has outstanding research experiences and published 6 edited books; 4 from Springer & 2 from Elsevier; 3 National & 8 International patents and more than 120 research papers indexed in Scopus/Web of Science. He is serving as an editorial board member of several international journals including Chief Editor. He has more than 15 years of experience in teaching, research as well as industry. His UG and PG teaching assignments include Microprocessor and microcontroller, AI, IOT, Embedded and real time systems etc. He has delivered Keynote/Invited lecture in a number of international seminar/conferences, refreshers courses, and FDPs. He has guided a large number of M.Tech and Ph.D. students. Dr. Ghosh is an active member of IEEE and organized a number Seminars and workshops in association with IEEE. He is an editor & organizing committee member of the Conference series GUCON, ICCCA, ICEEE, ICACIT. He is a He is a Start-up India Mentor and Global Startup Advisor of Wadhwani NEN. He has reviewed and mentored more than 50 start-ups. He has received award for contributing in Innovate India programme from AICTE- DST, Govt. of India in 2019 and

2020. He has received an appreciation award from AICTE, DST, TI, IIMB, NSRCEL, and myGOV for fostering students to strengthen the ecosystem bridging Government, Academia, and Industry in the year 2021.

Enhanced Prediction of Heart Disease Using Machine Learning and Deep Learning

M. S. Guru Prasad[1]($\boxtimes$), D. K. Santhosh Kumar[2], M. S. Pratap[3], J. Kiran[3],
S. Chandrappa[4], and Arnav Kotiyal[1]

[1] Department of Computer Science and Engineering, Graphic Era (Deemed to be University),
Dehradun, India
guru0927@gmail.com
[2] Department of Computer Science and Engineering, St Joseph Engineering College,
Mangaluru, Karnataka, India
[3] School of Computing and Information Technology, Reva University, Bengaluru, India
pratapms.ms@reva.edu.in
[4] Department of Computer Science and Engineering, Jain (Deemed-to-be University),
Bengaluru, India

Abstract. The provision of medical care is an essential component of human existence. As a result of the vast amount of psychiatric data included within the healthcare industry, machine learning models were utilized in order to efficiently deliver conclusions regarding heart disease prediction. The adoption of methods derived from machine learning enables the reliable classification of individuals according to whether or not they are healthy. The framework used in this study can understand the basics of effectively evaluating a patient's risk profile from features of clinical data. The aforementioned model was developed by utilizing both machine learning and deep learning in tandem with one another. Heart disease is widely acknowledged as one of the primary contributors to death rates across the globe. Large amounts of clinical data are stored in the many biomedical instruments and computer systems that are found in hospitals. Therefore, having a solid understanding of the data around heart disease is quite crucial if one wishes to increase the accuracy of their predictions. There have been a lot of experimental evaluations of the performance of models that have been developed using classification algorithms and relevant features that have been selected using a variety of different approaches to feature selection. The exploratory investigation used a dataset on heart illness to test four different classification strategies. These strategies were random forest, support vector machine, k-nearest neighbor, and convolutional neural network. The accuracy of machine learning algorithms utilized in the proposed work is Support Vector Machine 85.18%, Random Forest 92.5%, K-NN 74.07% and Convolutional Neural Network 85.18%

Keywords: Heart Disease · Deep Learning · Machine Learning · Random Forest · Support Vector Machine · K-Nearest Neighbor · Convolutional Neural Network

R. N. Shaw et al. (Eds.): ICACIS 2023, CCIS 1920, pp. 1–12, 2023.
https://doi.org/10.1007/978-3-031-45121-8_1

1 Introduction

The World Health Organization estimates that 17.9 million lives are lost annually due to cardiovascular disease [1]. It also predicts that the number of deaths from cardiovascular disease will grow to about 30 million by the year 2040 [2]. Heart disease can be attributed to a number of factors, including obesity, excessive cholesterol, a rise in triglyceride levels, hypertension, and more [3]. There are a number of common tests used by doctors to diagnose cardiovascular disease [4]. These include an ECG (echocardiogram), cardiac magnetic resonance imaging (MRI), a stress test (exercise stress test), and a nuclear cardiac stress test. Numerous computer technologies, such as those used to access patients' medical information and conduct research, can be utilized to accurately diagnose individuals and detect this disease in its early stages, before it has the chance to harm them [5]. Several different machine learning and deep learning models may be utilized in the direction of diagnose the condition as well as categories or forecast the consequences [6]. There are strategies for developing prediction models, as well as techniques for conducting in-depth analyses of patient data, which may be utilized to enhance the precision of such projections [7]. On the other hand, the expense of diagnosing and treating cardiovascular illness is so high that it is out of reach for the vast majority of people [8]. Using data mining techniques can help find signs of heart disease early and for less money. This will result in a reduction in the overall cost of diagnosis and treatment [9].

The use of machine learning techniques in the detection and classification of heart illness has been studied in prior studies [10]. Nevertheless, the focus of these studies is on the individual effects of particular machine learning approaches rather than on the optimization of these procedures utilising optimised methodologies [11]. In addition, very few researchers make an effort to apply hybrid optimization approaches for the purpose of improving the accuracy of machine learning classifications [12]. The majority of the research that has been proposed and published makes use of optimised approaches like Particle Swarm Optimization and Ant Colony Optimization in conjunction with a particular machine learning technique like SVM, KNN, or Random Forest [13].

2 Literature Survey

Masethe, H. D. et al. [1] proposed a model, it comprised both the selection of features and the verification of presence of duplicates in the data. The model utilized both machine learning and deep learning methods in order to provide an accurate forecast of heart illness. The machine learning strategy incorporated linear model selection, one of its components being the use of linear regression. The KNN classifier was used for the purpose of concentrating on the neighbour selection technique. After that, a tree-based technique known as the Decision Tree Classifier was utilised. Finally, the random forest classifier, one of the most commonly used ensemble algorithms, was employed. A Support Vector machine was utilised both for determining whether or not the data had a high dimensionality and for managing it. The sequential modelling approach was utilised for the Deep Learning model. This study's findings suggest that, machine learning algorithms fared better. In the past, many academics have argued that ML should be used even when the dataset is small, but this article shows that this is true.

Ramprakash, P et al. [2] uses Artificial Neural Networks and Deep Neural Network Algorithms in this model. Trainest-hold-out approval conspire is used in the suggested model for model approval. Train-test validation, which specifies that 80% of the information is used for preparation and 20% is used for testing, was implemented using the 80–20 rule. The sklearn package is used to slice up the data for use in both the testing and training phases. Out of a total of 303 samples, 242 examples were chosen and used to create the model, while the other 61 samples were used as testing information to evaluate the model's execution. Predictive models may be evaluated using a variety of metrics, including accuracy, sensitivity, specificity, and the Matthews correlation coefficient (MCC). If there are heart-related difficulties, this system returns a value of 1; otherwise, it returns a value of 0. This model's main drawback is that its precision is lower than that of other models. In the trials, it was found that the proposed method improved prognosis accuracy. Patients with heart disease will be able to be identified with the help of this research. When a patient is anticipated to have a favourable outcome, their reports and data can be examined in detail. In the future, a genetic algorithm may be applied to improve accuracy. In addition to a patient's family history of heart disease, this information may also be included in the dataset, which increases the model's accuracy.

Shah, D. et al. [3] implemented SVM, Decision Tree, Nave Bayes, and Random Forest algorithms in their work. These include deep neural networks and artificial intelligence (AI). The Weka Data Mining Tool is used to create this model. Clustering, classification, regression, visualisation, and feature selection are among the usual data mining activities that may be performed using the programme. It makes it simple to import data in the form of files, URLs, or databases. Computer-Structured Query Language (CSV). In the confusion matrix, true positive, accuracy, recall, and false negative are all analysed and shown in an easy-to-understand fashion. Each model has been analysed for its performance in terms of precision, recall, ROC (Receiver Operating Characteristic), and percent accuracy. Table IV displays the models' correctness in terms of performance. A ROC value of less than 0.80 is typically regarded as "GOOD," whereas a ROC value of less than 0.77 is seen as "FAIR". The model with the ROC value closest to 1 is regarded to be the most accurate.

Gavhane A et al. [4] proposed the decision tree and Ada-Boost algorithm model. Examples, diverse algorithms, and techniques for evaluation are some of the elements employed in a given piece of work. Using this strategy, you'll be taught by a teacher. For illness datasets and medical characteristics, the Kaggle warehouse is used. A person's risk of developing heart disease may be estimated using this collection of data. Training and testing sets are further subdivided. Attributes of the dataset utilised in this proposed research are 14. If "target," an independent variable, is correctly predicted, then a person is healthy or has heart disease.

3   Proposed Architecture

The term "architectural design" refers to the graphic representation of a collection of architectural ideas, including "principles," "elements," and "components. [14]" It is an imaginative process in which the aim is to provide a structure for the system that satisfies both the functional and non-functional requirements of the system [15]. Because it is an artistic process, the activities that take place inside it vary widely depending on the kind of system that is being created, the educational background and professional experience of the system architect, and the needs of the system [16]. Figure 1 shows the proposed architecture.

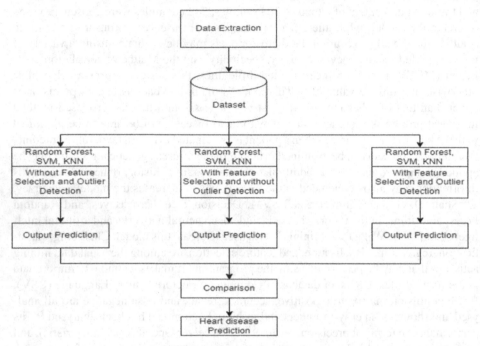

Fig. 1. Proposed Architecture

3.1 System Flow Diagram

A System flow diagram, often known as an SFD, is a diagram that displays the many types of data that will be input into and output from a system, in addition to showing where the information will come from, where it will go, and where it will be stored [17]. Flow diagram is also used as a synonym for flowchart and, occasionally, as a counterpoint to flowchart [18]. Flow diagrams are used to organize and arrange a complicated system, as well as to illustrate the underlying structure of the parts and how they interact [19]. The phrase "flow diagram" has multiple implications in theory and practice. The terms "flowchart" and "flow diagram" are frequently used interchangeably in the context of a process depiction The user will have to enter the required values, which will be taken as input. The data from the input is then retrieved which will be used for classification of the result (Fig. 2).

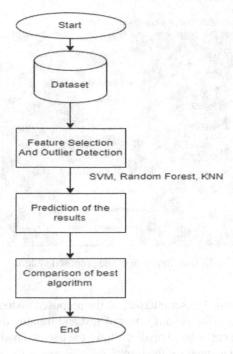

Fig. 2. System Flow Diagram of the proposed system

4 Results and Discussion

Kaggle provided the dataset that was utilised for the development of this suggested system. The databases make up this data collection, which was compiled in 1988 and dates back to that year. It has 76 properties, including the attribute that was predicted. However, all of the published tests only relate to employing a selection of 14 of those features. In this situation, the patient's heart disease status is the aim. It is integer valued with $0 =$ no disease and $1 =$ disease. The goal is included as one of the 1329 rows and 14 columns that make up the dataset. The thirteen characteristics of the dataset will serve as the data, while the target column will serve as the label. The dataset does not have any empty values (also known as null values).

The following are the results obtained using machine learning algorithms like SVM, Random Forest, KNN, and Deep Learning Algorithms like CNN. The proposed model predicts the accuracy as well as gives the graphical representation of the algorithms for a given ratio of test and training data so that comparison can be done and the best algorithm can be obtained for the heart disease dataset.

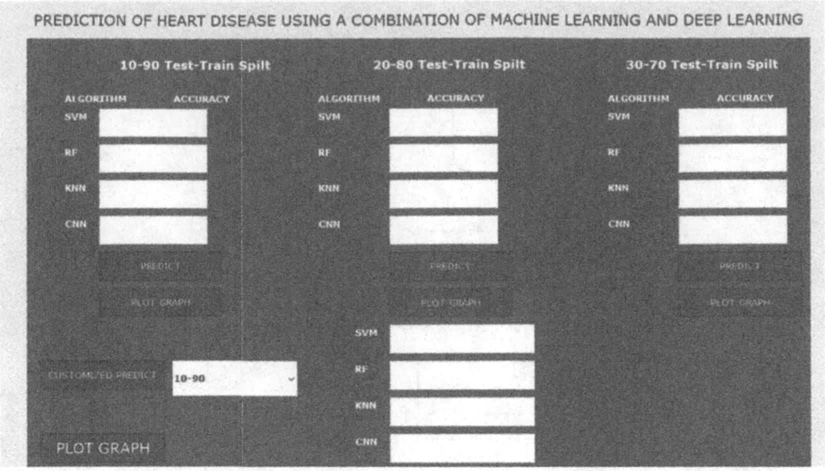

Fig. 3. User Interface of the proposed system

The above Fig. 3 shows the user interface of the proposed system where the user can see the predicted accuracy for various ratios of test and training data as well as a plot graph for the same. The customized predict allows the user to choose the required ratio of the split and also plot a graph for the same.

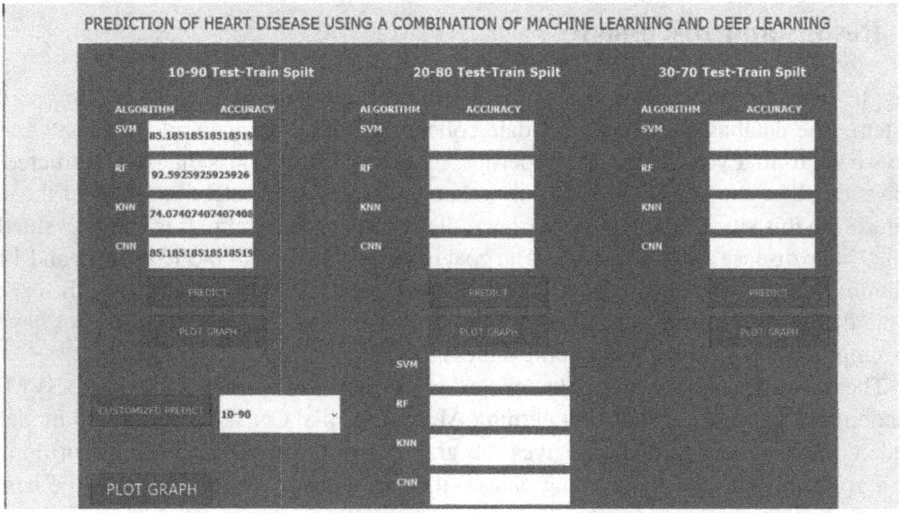

Fig. 4. Accuracy comparison of SVM, RF, KNN and CNN for 10% testing and 90% training data

The above Fig. 4 shows the predicted accuracy of SVM, RF, KNN and CNN for 10% testing and 90% training data.

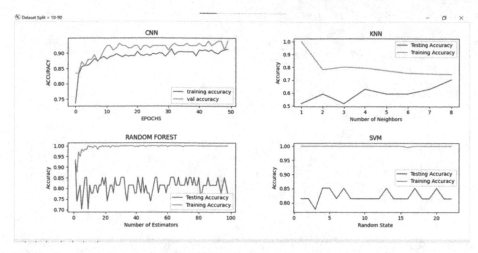

Fig. 5. Graph comparison of SVM, RF, KNN and CNN for 10% testing and 90% training data

The above Fig. 5 depicts the graphical representation of SVM, RF, KNN, and CNN for 10% testing and 90% training data. The Y axis is the accuracy of the respective algorithm, and the graph is plotted comparing the actual and predicted accuracy.

The following Figs. 6 and 8 show the predicted accuracy of SVM, RF, KNN, and CNN for 20% testing and 80% training data and 20% testing and 80% training accuracy, respectively, and Figs. 7 and 9 give the graphical representations for the respective ratio of the data.

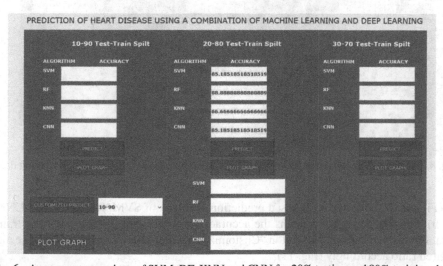

Fig. 6. Accuracy comparison of SVM, RF, KNN and CNN for 20% testing and 80% training data

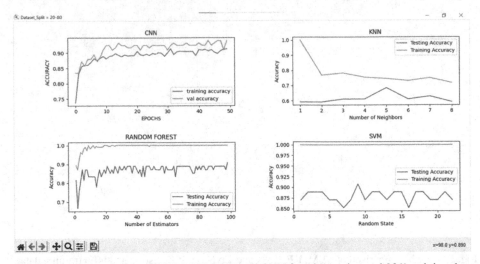

Fig. 7. Graph comparison of SVM, RF, KNN and CNN for 10% testing and 90% training data

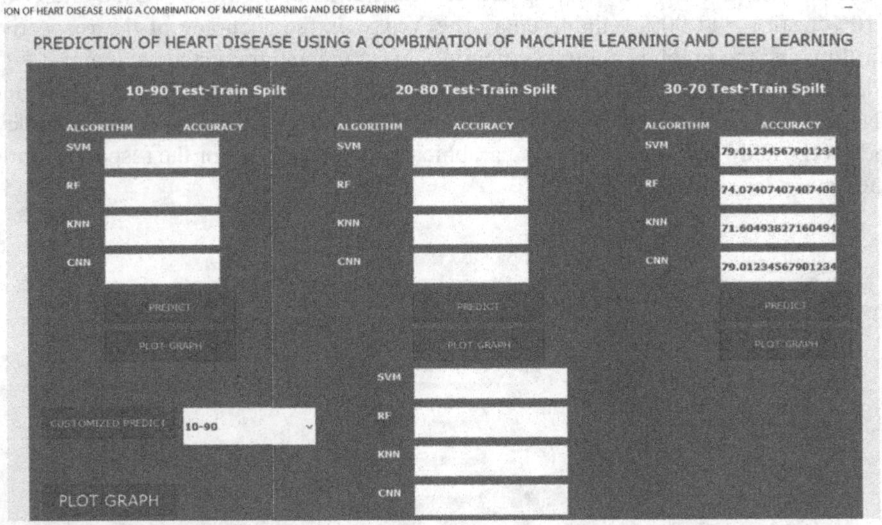

Fig. 8. Accuracy comparison of SVM, RF, KNN and CNN for 30% testing and 70% training data

Figure 10 shows the customised prediction accuracy of SVM, RF, KNN, and CNN algorithms. The snapshot contains the accuracy for a ratio of 60% test and 40% train data. However, the dropdown button "Customized Predict" allows the user to choose the desired ratio accordingly (Fig. 11).

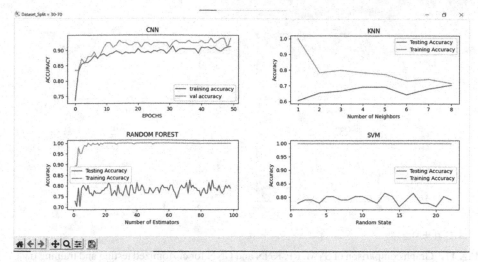

Fig. 9. Graph comparison of SVM, RF, KNN and CNN for 30% testing and 70% training data

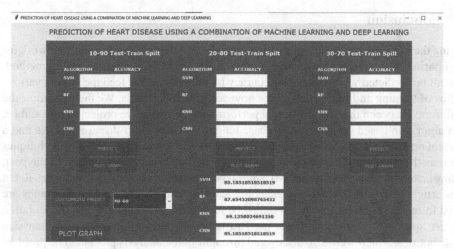

Fig. 10. Accuracy comparison of SVM, RF, KNN and CNN for customized 60% testing and 40% training data where the user can customize other values accordingly

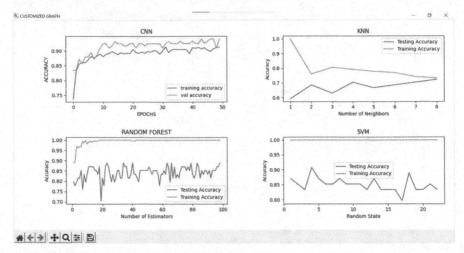

Fig. 11. Graph comparison of SVM, RF, KNN and CNN for customized testing and training data where the user can customize other values accordingly

5   Conclusion

Using the accuracy of the algorithms, this system seeks to provide a useful framework for comparing them. The SVM, Random Forest, KNN, and CNN, a deep learning method, can all be predicted with reasonable accuracy by the system. We feed the system various ratios of training and testing data to see how accurate it performs. We then visualise the difference between the system's actual performance and what we projected it would be. An algorithm based on performance-based algorithms for heart disease datasets and a certain ratio of data has been presented. We discovered that machine learning techniques such as the Random Forest algorithm outperformed all others in our study. In the past, many academics have argued that ML should be used even when the dataset is small, but this article shows that this is true. Machine learning and deep learning data graphs are used to make comparisons. Outliers must be identified and isolated using the Isolation Forest approach. This technique is used to locate outliers in datasets with Gaussian distributions, which were also discovered throughout the analysis process. The problem here is that the dataset has a small sample size. Deep learning and machine learning may both benefit greatly from huge datasets. Deep learning may be used in conjunction with several additional improvements and a larger dataset to achieve more promising outcomes.

References

1. Masethe, H.D., Masethe, M.A.: Prediction of heart disease using classification algorithms. In: Proceedings of the world Congress on Engineering and Computer Science, vol. 2, no. 1, pp. 25–29 (2014)
2. Ramprakash, P., Sarumathi, R., Mowriya, R., Nithyavishnupriya, S.: Heart disease prediction using deep neural network. In: 2020 International Conference on Inventive Computation Technologies (ICICT), pp. 666–670. IEEE (2020)

3. Shah, D., Patel, S., Bharti, S.K.: Heart disease prediction using machine learning techniques. SN Comput. Sci. **1**(6), 1–6 (2020)

4. Gavhane, A., Kokkula, G., Pandya, I., Devadkar, K.: Prediction of heart disease using machine learning. In: 2018 Second International Conference on Electronics, Communication and Aerospace Technology (ICECA), pp. 1275–1278. IEEE (2018)

5. Gujjar, J.P., Kumar, H.P., Prasad, M.G.: Advanced NLP frame-work for text processing. In: 2023 6th International Conference on Information Systems and Computer Networks (ISCON), Mathura, India, pp. 1–3 (2023). https://doi.org/10.1109/ISCON57294.2023.10112058

6. Guru, P.M.S., Praveen, G.J., Dodmane, R., Sardar, T.H., Ashwitha, A., Yeole, A.N.: Brain tumor identification and classification using a novel extraction method based on adapted alexnet architecture. In: 2023 6th International Conference on Information Systems and Computer Networks (ISCON), Mathura, India, pp. 1–5 (2023). https://doi.org/10.1109/ISCON5 7294.2023.10112075

7. Kumar, M.A., Pai, A.H., Agarwal, J., Christa, S., Prasad, G.M.S., Saifi, S.: Deep learning model to defend against covert channel attacks in the SDN networks. In: 2023 Advanced Computing and Communication Technologies for High Performance Applications (ACC-THPA), Ernakulam, India, pp. 1–5 (2023). https://doi.org/10.1109/ACCTHPA57160.2023. 10083336

8. Kirubasri, G., Sankar, S., Guru Prasad, M.S., et al.: LQETA-RP: link quality based energy and trust aware routing protocol for wireless multimedia sensor networks. Int. J. Syst. Assur. Eng. Manag. (2023). https://doi.org/10.1007/s13198-023-01873-9

9. Guru Prasad, M.S., Naveen Kumar, H.N., Raju, K., et al.: Glaucoma detection using clustering and segmentation of the optic disc region from retinal fundus images. SN Comput. Sci. **4**, 192 (2023). https://doi.org/10.1007/s42979-022-01592-1

10. Kumar, H.N.N., Kumar, S.A., Prasad, G.M.S., Shah, M.A.: Automatic facial expression recognition combining texture and shape features from prominent facial regions. IET Image Process. **17**, 1111–1125 (2023). https://doi.org/10.1049/ipr2.12700

11. Rajawat, A.S., et.al.: Depression detection for elderly people using AI robotic systems leveraging the Nelder–Mead method. In: Artificial Intelligence for Future Generation Robotics, pp. 55–70. Elsevier (2021). ISBN 9780323854986, https://doi.org/10.1016/B978-0-323-85498-6.00006-X.Chakraborty

12. Chakraborty, A., Chatterjee, S., Majumder, K., Shaw, R.N., Ghosh, A.: A comparative study of myocardial infarction detection from ECG data using machine learning. In: Bianchini, M., Piuri, V., Das, S., Shaw, R.N. (eds.) Advanced Computing and Intelligent Technologies. LNNS, vol. 218, pp. 257–267. Springer, Singapore (2022). https://doi.org/10.1007/978-981-16-2164-2_21

13. Chandrappa, S., Chandra Shekar, P., Chaya, P., et al.: Machine learning algorithms for identifying fake currencies. SN Comput. Sci. **4**, 368 (2023). https://doi.org/10.1007/s42979-023-01812-2

14. Anand Kumar, M., Abirami, N., Guru Prasad, M.S., Mohankumar, M.: Stroke disease prediction based on ECG signals using deep learning techniques. In: 2022 International Conference on Computational Intelligence and Sustainable Engineering Solutions (CISES), Greater Noida, India, pp. 453–458 (2022). https://doi.org/10.1109/CISES54857.2022.9844403

15. Prasad, G., Jain, A.K., Jain, P., Nagesh, H.R.: A novel approach to optimize the performance of hadoop frameworks for sentiment analysis. Int. J. Open Source Softw. Process. (IJOSSP) **10**(4), 44–59 (2019)

16. Prasad, M.G., Pratap, M.S., Jain, P., Gujjar, J.P., Kumar, M.A., Kukreti, A.: RDI-SD: an efficient rice disease identification based on apache spark and deep learning technique. In: 2022 International Conference on Artificial Intelligence and Data Engineering (AIDE), Karkala, India, pp. 277–282 (2022). https://doi.org/10.1109/AIDE57180.2022.10060157

17. Pai, A., Anandkumar, M., Prasad, G., Agarwal, J., Christa, S.: Designing a secure audio/text based captcha using neural network. In: 2023 13th International Conference on Cloud Computing, Data Science & Engineering (Confluence), Noida, India, pp. 510–514 (2023). https://doi.org/10.1109/Confluence56041.2023.10048791

18. Agarwal, J., Christa, S., Pai, A., Kumar, M.A., Prasad, G.: Machine learning application for news text classification. In: 2023 13th International Conference on Cloud Computing, Data Science & Engineering (Confluence), Noida, India, pp. 463–466 (2023). https://doi.org/10.1109/Confluence56041.2023.10048856

19. Patel, V., Guru Prasad, M.S., Aditya Pai, H., Kumar, A.S., Praveen Gujjar, J., Naveen Kumar, H.N.: Real-time face mask detector. In: 2023 IEEE 3rd International Conference on Technology, Engineering, Management for Societal impact using Marketing, Entrepreneurship and Talent (TEMSMET), Mysuru, India, pp. 1–5 (2023). https://doi.org/10.1109/TEMSMET56707.2023.10150182

Machine Learning-Powered Tool for Automated Healthcare Diagnosis

Prateek Nagar[1]($\boxtimes$), Harikesh Singh[1], Harsh Singh[1], Mohak Bhati[1], and Vishu Tyagi[2]

[1] Department of Computer Science and Engineering, JSS Academy of Technical Education, Noida, India
`prateeknagar146@gmail.com`
[2] Department of Computer Science and Engineering, Graphic Era Deemed to be University, Dehradun, Uttrakhand, India

Abstract. Maintaining proper health is an indispensable part of human life. The present advanced world has various technologies that can be shaped to cater to the needs and sustenance of a healthy population. The use of machine learning and AI tools have been employed in the health sector for a long time for different applications such as disease cure research, diagnosis, medication, etc. Similarly, these can be used for early identification of diseases which can reduce the number of affected people every year. In this chapter, we have described the implementation of our model and its performance, which can forecast the diseases of people based on the symptoms inputted by them. The implemented tool uses the Naive Bayes algorithm-based ML model to process these symptoms using the fed dataset and provide the most probable disease as output. This can help medical practitioners to diagnose people for those diseases and provide treatment at an early stage.

Keywords: Machine Learning Models · Artificial Intelligence · Healthcare · Disease Diagnosis Models · Healthcare Tool · KNN and CNN Algorithms · NLP (Natural Language Processing)

1 Introduction

The healthcare sector is becoming interested in the topic of disease prediction using machine learning. Accurate illness risk prediction has the potential to enhance the effectiveness of early detection, intervention, and treatment. The use of machine learning algorithms and AI in healthcare data has produced encouraging findings in disease prediction in recent years [15]. The naive Bayes algorithm has been utilized in particular for a number of classification problems, including the prediction of diseases. The naive Bayes algorithm computes the conditional probability of an event given a set of features. It is a probabilistic classifier based on Bayes' theorem. Since it makes this assumption, it is referred to as "naive." This technique has been effectively used in several fields, including spam filtering, image recognition, and text classification [16].

With an emphasis on creating predictive models to help with the early detection of diseases, machine learning has become incredibly popular in the healthcare industry in recent years. By enabling early detection and treatment, the capacity to forecast with accuracy the chance of contracting a disease can significantly enhance healthcare results. Massive volumes of data can be processed by machine learning (ML) algorithms, which can also uncover patterns that are difficult to see using more conventional techniques. The use of machine learning algorithms in disease-predicting tools has been investigated in several research. Machine learning has been used by researchers, among other things, to forecast the likelihood of acquiring cancer, Alzheimer's disease, and cardiovascular disease. These experiments have yielded encouraging findings, indicating that machine learning may be a useful instrument for early disease detection [12]. The suggested study advances the existing research in this area by providing information on the performance of the naive Bayes algorithm in predicting the risk of diabetes from user data. The outcomes of this study could have important implications, providing evidence to support the development of more accurate and personalized healthcare services. By leveraging the power of machine learning to predict disease risk, healthcare providers can improve patient outcomes and potentially reduce the incidence of chronic diseases.

In this study, we investigate the use of the naive Bayes method to create a disease prediction tool. We examine how well the algorithm performs in identifying the possibility of various diseases based on user-provided symptoms. To be more precise, we employ the naive bayes algorithm with a publicly accessible EHR (Electronic Health Record) dataset to forecast the likelihood of illnesses. The publication goes into further detail about the model's performance.

The study's output findings have significant implications for both researchers and healthcare professionals. If implemented successfully, a naïve bayes disease prediction tool could increase the precision and effectiveness of disease prediction in healthcare, ultimately resulting in better health outcomes.

2 Literature Survey

Naresh Kumar and Nripendra Narayan Das [3], employ ML models to predict the risk of diseases such as diabetes, heart disease, and coronavirus in individuals. The algorithm used for computing the data set is called Logistic Reasoning. The results of this study have potential in the early screening of patients with diabetes, heart disease, and coronavirus. The initial screening can be conveniently conducted at home, and if there is a likelihood of disease risk, the patient can seek medical attention. The proposed model in this research could be applied to other medical fields such as medical image segmentation and cancer classification in the future. To refine the ML models' initial parameters, various meta-heuristic techniques could also be utilized.

Ciarán M. Lee,Jonathan G. Richens, and Saurabh Johri, [13], study examines the implementation of a probabilistic approach to diagnosing diseases. It employs Bayesian networks to model the correlation between disease symptoms and risk factors. The research proposes a counterfactual diagnosis, which verifies the accuracy of the diagnosis by considering known pre-conditions. The study compares the performance of the algorithm with that of a human doctor and discovers that the algorithm is as effective as doctors in making diagnoses.

Adnan Qayyum and Junaid Qadir's [6], survey offers a comprehensive overview of healthcare applications that utilize ML/DL approaches, discussing privacy and security concerns that come with them. Furthermore, the survey proposes potential strategies for creating secure ML applications in healthcare that prioritize privacy. Lastly, the study examines current research challenges and proposes exciting avenues for future exploration in this field.

Fashen Li and Lian Li's [11], study focuses on acquiring machine information, specifically concerning the acquisition of causal knowledge. It examines whether individuals can acquire causal knowledge from intelligent agents and how this process can be carried out. The study analyzes various approaches to obtaining knowledge from different sources. The conclusion suggests that decoding information from intelligent agents can improve our knowledge systems and contribute to human progress. However, further research is necessary to keep up with technological advancements.

Davenport T. and Kalakota R [1], study investigates the applicability of AI and ML in the healthcare sector. The study explores various types of AI, including machine learning, NLP (natural language processing), robotic process automation, and automation, and assesses their relevance in the field of healthcare. Additionally, the study examines potential challenges that may arise in implementing AI in healthcare and highlights examples of previously launched automated diagnosis tools that were not very effective.

Rajkomar A and Oren E, Chen K [4], study suggests a method for representing patients' complete electronic health records (EHR) using the Fast Healthcare Interoperability Resources (FHIR) format. The study also demonstrates that deep learning techniques utilizing the proposed representation can accurately predict several medical events across multiple centres without requiring site-specific data harmonization. Additionally, the suggested model performs better than existing EHR models used to predict mortality in the medical research literature.

Char DS, Shah NH and Magnus D.'s [5], research discusses the incorporation of machine learning in clinical medicine and highlights the obstacles that need to be addressed. It provides guidance on developing an effective and reliable model to overcome these challenges.

Bush J [2], focuses on the management of document work apart from clinical work with the help of AI and ML. It shows how implementing these methods on the traditional method (like faxes) of gathering and keeping the data made the process easier, faster, and more organized.

Zoabi Y., Deri-Rozov S. and Shomron N. [8], the study developed a model that accurately predicted Coronavirus test results by using only eight binary characteristics, including age less than or equal to 60 years, sex, known exposure to an infected person, and the presence of five clinical symptoms. The model analyzed simple features by asking basic questions and used this information to predict the presence of COVID-19. The study suggested that this framework could be applied to other considerations as well, but more robust data is required to support the framework while also considering the potential for bias in self-reported symptoms.

Vijayalakshmi A. Lepakshi [7], this study examined the use of deep learning and ML-based AI tools for the development of diagnostic tools. The performance of different classification models was assessed. Moreover, the Covid-19 pandemic was used as a case study to explore the potential of AI-ML tools in screening, and it was found that they can be effectively used against the current and future pandemics.

K. Praveen Kumar and A. Pravalika [10], found that the CNN algorithm achieved an accuracy rate of 84.5% and processed data in 11.1 s. This suggests that CNN performed better than KNN. Moreover, CNN can identify essential features that provide better representations of complex diseases. This capability allows CNN to accurately predict diseases with high complexity.

Md Manjurul Ahsan, Shahana Akter Luna and Zahed Siddique [12], this research analyzed the previous 10 years of studies on Disease Diagnosis. The study found that CNN is the most commonly utilized algorithm due to its speed and accuracy. The results indicated that KNN's performance decreases when applied to multidimensional data. Additionally, the study revealed that reduced accuracy was primarily caused by misclassified data, as well as data scarcity and noisy data.

Sreenivasa Rao Veeranki and Manish Varshney [14], explored that bioinformatics is a common method for evaluating the quality of living organisms. The complete set of genes in an organism, whether they are positive or negative, are fully controlled by the human gene. The human gene is composed of protein sequences, and the genetic information of living organisms is massive. Analyzing large amounts of data is crucial. Bioinformatics is a research area that deals with massive genetic data. These data sets can only be analyzed through Big Data methods from computer science. Various Big Data tools are employed to handle the vast genetic information. Bioinformatics has been utilized in the clinical industry to study the genetic makeup of organisms. Understanding the characteristics of living entities requires a comprehensive understanding of each organism's gene structure.

3 Proposed Model

We propose the development of a disease prediction tool using the Naïve Bayes algorithm. The algorithm is selected for its efficiency and ease of implementation, but we plan to explore the incorporation of multiple algorithms for a hybrid model in future research. Previous works in the field have focused on predicting specific diseases or a limited range of diseases, and we aim to improve on these by including a diverse collection of diseases with higher accuracy. Our long-term goal is to expand the number of diseases covered by the tool, including those that are not commonly found in other applications. Additionally, we aim to create a user-friendly application that does not require special instructions.

Our success in this implementation depends on using high-quality datasets, but limited resources present challenges in gathering suitable data. We are confident that as the field continues to advance, we will gain access to more diverse and comprehensive dataset collections for our model.

3.1 Naive Bayes

The algorithm is a classification method that relies on Bayes' theorem, a fundamental principle in probability theory. Bayes' theorem calculates the probability of an event by considering its prior probability and the probability of the evidence given the event.

In the context of classification, Bayes' theorem can be expressed as:

$$P(y|x) = \frac{P(x|y) * P(y)}{P(x)} \tag{1}$$

where:

- The posterior probability of class y given input x is denoted as $P(y|x)$.
- The likelihood of observing input x given class y is represented as $P(x|y)$.
- $P(y)$ signifies the prior probability of class y.
- $P(x)$ refers to the probability of the evidence.

Naïve Bayes algorithm assumes that the attributes in the input are independent of each other, hence the term "naïve". This presumption simplifies the calculation of the likelihood term to a product of individual feature probabilities:

$$P(x|y) = P(x\_1|y) * P(x\_2|y) * \ldots * P(x\_n|y) \tag{2}$$

where $x\_1, x\_2, \ldots, x\_n$ are the input features.

The working of the naive Bayes algorithm can be described as follows:

1. Determine the prior probabilities for every class through calculations.
2. Compute the probabilities of observing each input feature for every class.
3. Calculate the posterior probabilities for each class using Bayes' theorem.
4. Assign the input to the class with the greatest posterior probability.

Mathematically, this can be expressed as:

$$P(y|x\_1, \ x\_2, \ldots\ldots, x\_n) = \frac{P(y) * P(x\_1|y) * P(x\_2|y) * \ldots * P(x\_n|y)}{P(x\_1) * P(x\_2) * \ldots * P(x\_n)} \tag{3}$$

where,

$P(x\_1), P(x\_2), \ldots, P(x\_n)$ are the evidence probabilities, which are the same for all classes and can be ignored in the calculation.

In summary,

Naïve Bayes is a classification algorithm that relies on Bayes' theorem and assumes the independence of input features. It works by calculating the prior probabilities, likelihoods, and posterior probabilities of each class, and assigning the input to the class with the highest posterior probability.

Advantages:

- It is considered one of the fastest and simplest machine learning algorithms for predicting the class of datasets.
- It can be employed for both Multi-class and Binary Classifications.
- It is used in medical data classification.

Disadvantages:

Even though it is fast, it fails to learn the relationship between objects. This is the reason why it is suggested to use a hybrid of different algorithms. However, that is a future prospect of our work.

3.2 Steps to be Followed for Disease Prediction

1. The user will be first asked to provide 4–5 symptoms from a drop-down list of predefined options.
2. Next, the algorithm will be applied to inputs provided by the user which will match the data as per the data set and find the most appropriate answer based on the probability of data in the data set.
3. The most probable disease will be displayed on the screen.
4. In case, the user did not enter anything, a prompt will be displayed for entering the data.

3.3 Dataset

For the dataset, we are using a publicly available dataset that has around 129 ranges of symptoms for a user to choose from. Each set of symptoms links to a particular type of disease. Further, there are around 5000 tuples of varying symptom sets that come from different patients and training of the model is performed using the dataset. The resulting data is used for predicting the user's disease based on their input symptoms.

Following are some of the symptoms used in the dataset (Table 1):

Table 1. Sample of symptoms used in the dataset

Back Pain	Constipation	Abdominal Pain
Diarrhea	Fever	Dizziness
Fluid Overload	Yellowing of Eyes	Acute Liver Failure
Malaise	Throat Irritation	Sinus Pressure
Runny Nose	Congestion	Chest Pain
Neck Pain	Cramps	Obesity
Puffy Face and Eyes	Brittle Nails	Loss of Balance

3.4 Dataset Balance\Imbalance Check

We can check whether a dataset is balanced or imbalanced by getting how many data points for each class are present.

Figure 1 shows the total number of classes (i.e. symptoms) and the no of data points associated with each class. To check whether a dataset is balanced or unbalanced, we can see if the number of data points in each class are almost similar or do they vary greatly respectively. Since the number of data points in this dataset for each class has a similar value, we can say that this is a balanced dataset.

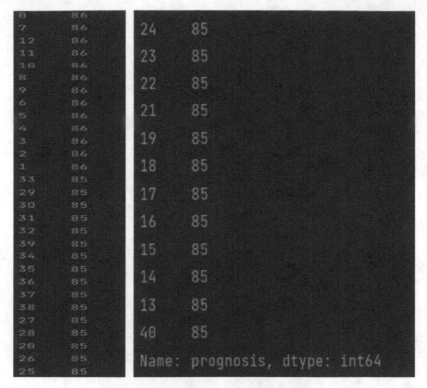

Fig. 1. Number of Data Points for Each Class

3.5 Flowchart of the Working Model

Figure 2 outlines the process flow of the implemented model. Each section working is described as follows:

Start: The process starts when the user initiates the prediction by opening the application or website.

Preparation Process: The system prepares itself by loading the necessary libraries, algorithms, and datasets required for the prediction.

Symptoms Input: The user is prompted to input their symptoms, which are then used by the system to predict potential diseases.

Extract Data from all the Datasets: The system extracts data from multiple datasets, which contain information on different diseases, their symptoms, and their relationships.

Extraction Successful Relationship: The system checks if there is a successful relationship between the symptoms inputted by the user and the diseases extracted from the datasets.

Linked it with the Preparation Process: If the system is unable to find a successful relationship, it links back to the preparation process, where it prepares itself again to improve the accuracy of the prediction.

Fig. 2. Flowchart of the working model

Pass Through the Trained Model: If there is a successful relationship, the system passes the symptoms through a trained model that uses machine learning algorithms to predict potential diseases.

Related Diseases Relationship: The system checks if there are any related diseases based on the symptoms inputted by the user and the diseases predicted by the model.

Final Output: If there are related diseases, the system displays the final output to the user, which includes a list of potential diseases along with their severity and recommended treatments.

End: The process ends when the user receives the final output and closes the application or website.

4 Implementation Result

4.1 Confusion Matrix

The confusion matrix is a square matrix of dimensions N × N, used to evaluate the performance of a classification model with N target classes. This matrix compares the predicted values from the machine learning model with the actual target values. A dependable model demonstrates high rates of true positives (TP) and true negatives (TN), along with low rates of false positives (FP) and false negatives (FN).

The confusion matrix plotted in Fig. 3, represents the confusion matrix of the implemented model. The diagonal line in the matrix represents that the model predicts the values correctly as the true labels except for two classes, this means that the model has a high accuracy. We can also calculate various parameters from the confusion matrix. These are as follows:

Accuracy- Accuracy measures how often the model is correct. It can be calculated as:

$$\frac{TP + TN}{TP + FP + FN + TN} = 95.1\% \tag{4}$$

Error Rate- As the name suggests error rate tells us how often the model is incorrect. It can be calculated as:

$$\frac{FP + FN}{TP + FP + FN + TN} = 4.9\% \tag{5}$$

Precision- It measures what percentage of the positively predicted outcomes are truly positive. It is expressed as:

$$\frac{TP}{TP + FP} = 92.65\% \tag{6}$$

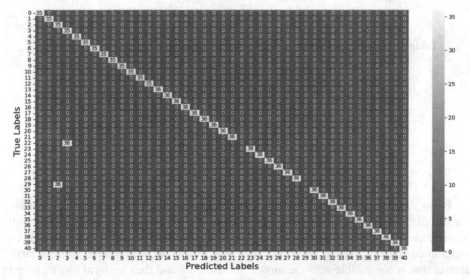

Fig. 3. Confusion Matrix of the implemented model

Sensitivity (Recall)- Of all the positive cases, what percentage are predicted positive? Sensitivity (also known as Recall) evaluates the model's ability to accurately predict positive outcomes. It considers true positives and false negatives, which represent positive instances incorrectly classified as negative.

$$\frac{TP}{TP + FN} = 0.9512 \tag{7}$$

F-measure- It gives a way to combine precision and recall. It is also called as F-score and is the "harmonic mean" of precision and sensitivity. It considers both false positive and false negative cases and is good for imbalanced datasets.

$$\frac{2*Recall * Precision}{Recall + Precision} = 0.9386 \tag{8}$$

4.2 Test Cases

The following table shows the accuracy for increasing datasets with varying no of cases (Table 3).

Table 2. Different Testing Cases and Accuracy

Number of Cases in Testing Dataset	Accuracy (in %)
0–500	95
501–1000	95.19
1001–2000	95.02
2001–3000	95.13
3001–4900	95.1

Table 3. Comparison of Various Performance Parameter of Three ML Algorithms

Parameter	KNN	SVM	Naïve Bayes
Accuracy (%)	84.1	92.3	95.1
Precision (%)	79.4	88.6	92.65
Recall	0.823	0.912	0.951
F-1 Score	0.808	0.898	0.938

From Table 2, we can see that even on increasing the data the accuracy remain consistent. This shows that the model is efficient and gives effective results even with an increased number of data. However, we cannot be sure that this accuracy will be maintained when the dataset becomes very large, for that we will have to gather a large dataset that is compatible with the model in the future and then perform testing to get the results.

5   Comparative Analysis

In this comparative analysis, we compared the KNN (K-Nearest Neighbors), Naive Bayes, and SVM (Support Vector Machines) algorithms for disease prediction. These algorithms are commonly used in classification tasks, and they have their strengths and weaknesses.

KNN is a non-parametric algorithm that retains all the training data and assigns a classification to a new instance based on its proximity to the nearest neighbors. Naive Bayes, a probabilistic algorithm, utilizes Bayes' theorem to estimate the probability of a class given the feature values, assuming feature independence. Conversely, SVM is a linear algorithm that seeks to determine the best hyperplane for separating data into separate classes.

To compare the three algorithms, we will use a dataset of patients with various diseases and their corresponding symptoms. We will split the data into testing and training sets and use accuracy as the evaluation metric.

The graph below shows the accuracy of the three algorithms with increasing training set size (Fig. 4):

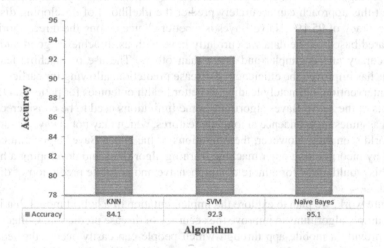

Fig. 4. Graphical Comparison of Algorithms

As we can see from the graph, Naïve Bayes outperforms both KNN and SVM across all training set sizes. SVM is slightly below Naive Bayes, followed by KNN.

In terms of computational efficiency, KNN is the slowest of the three algorithms because it has to store and compare all the training data for each new instance. Naive Bayes is faster than KNN because it only needs to calculate the probabilities of the feature values given the class. SVM is also fast because it uses an optimization algorithm to find the optimal hyperplane and does not require all the training data to be stored. However, the SVM algorithm is computationally extensive when it comes to large datasets and sensitive to noise which makes a significant impact on the decision boundary.

In conclusion, for disease prediction according to our findings, Naïve Bayes is a better choice among the three algorithms we compared based on the data we currently have with us. It achieves good and consistent accuracy and is simpler and faster than others. Additionally, it is good for high-dimensional data, and robust to irrelevant features while the other two algorithms are sensitive to noise and a simpler model that requires tuning of fewer parameters.

However, to further enhance the accuracy of our model we can combine the naïve bayes algorithm with some other compatible algorithm. We are currently working on it and will try to incorporate it in future versions of our working tool.

6 Conclusion

AI has shown great potential in the medical field by improving disease diagnosis, predicting patient outcomes, and developing personalized treatments. It has the ability to analyze vast amounts of medical data and assist healthcare professionals in making more accurate and timely decisions, ultimately improving patient outcomes.

In conclusion, the implementation of an automated disease prediction tool using the Naïve Bayes algorithm holds great potential in the healthcare industry. Our research has shown that this approach can accurately predict the likelihood of developing diseases with an accuracy of 95.1%. Naïve Bayes is a better choice among the three algorithms we compared based on the data we currently have with us. It achieves good and consistent accuracy and is simpler and faster than others. The use of machine learning algorithms has improved the efficiency of disease prediction, allowing for earlier detection and intervention, ultimately leading to better health outcomes for patients. Despite the benefits of the Naive Bayes algorithm, some limitations need to be considered. The algorithm assumes independence among the features, which may not always be the case in real-world scenarios. However, the limitations of the Naive Bayes algorithm can be mitigated by incorporating other machine learning algorithms and developing a hybrid model. This would allow for a more comprehensive and accurate prediction of disease likelihood.

In future work, we plan to explore the implementation of a hybrid model that incorporates multiple algorithms to improve the accuracy of disease prediction. Collect more data and provide a mobile app through which people can easily access the features. While going through the reference research works we found that the model functionality can also be expanded for the prediction of diseases in different plants and other animals.

References

1. Davenport, T., Kalakota, R.: The potential for artificial intelligence in healthcare. PubMed Central Future Healthcare J. **6**(2), PMCID: PMC6616181 (2019)
2. Bush, J.: How AI is taking the scut work out of health care. Harvard Business Review (2018). https://hbr.org/2018/03/how-ai-is-taking-the-scut-work-out-of-health-care
3. Kumar, N., Narayan Das, N., et al.: Efficient automated disease diagnosis using machine learning models, Hindawi. J. Healthcare Eng. 9983652 (2021)
4. Rajkomar, A., Oren, E., Chen, K., et al.: Scalable and accurate deep learning with electronic health records. Nat. Partner J. Digit. Med. **1**(1), 18 (2018)

5. Char, D.S., Shah, N.H., Magnus, D.: Implementing machine learning in health care – addressing ethical challenges. PubMed Central, HHS Author Manuscripts, PMCID: PMC5962261 (2018)
6. Qayyum, A., Qadir, J., et al.: Secure and Robust Machine Learning for Healthcare: A Survey (2020). https://core.ac.uk/download/pdf/328760438.pdf
7. Lepakshi, V.A.: Machine learning and deep learning based AI tools for development of diagnostic tools. In: ScienceDirect, pp. 399–420 (2022). B978–0–323–91172–6.00011-X
8. Zoabi, Y., Deri-Rozov, S., Shomron, N.: Machine learning-based prediction of COVID-19 diagnosis based on symptoms. Nat. Partner J. Digit. Med. 4(1), 3 (2021)
9. Mello-Román, J.D., et al.: Predictive models for the medical diagnosis of dengue: a case study in paraguay, Hindawi. Comput. Math. Models Med. 7307803 (2019)
10. Kumar, K.P., Pravalika, A., et al.: Disease prediction using machine learning algorithms KNN and CNN. In: IJRASET, IJRASET42214 (2022)
11. Li, F., Li, L., et al.: How to interpret machine knowledge, ScienceDirect 6(3), 218–220 (2020)
12. Ahsan, M.M., Luna, S.A., Siddique, Z.: Machine-learning-based disease diagnosis: a comprehensive review. In: MDPI, Healthcare, vol. 10, no. 3, p. 541 (2022)
13. Richens, J.G., Lee, C.M., Johri, S.: Improving the accuracy of medical diagnosis with causal machine learning. Nat. Partner J. Nat. Commun. 1(1), 3923 (2020)
14. Veeranki, S.R., Varshney, M.: Intelligent techniques and comparative performance analysis of liver disease prediction. In: IJME, vol. 7 (2022). https://kalaharijournals.com/resources/IJME_Vol7.1_756.pdf
15. Akshaya, A.V.R., Vigneshwaran, S., Kumar, C.R.: Artificial Intelligence is changing Health and e-Healthcare, September 2022. https://doi.org/10.4108/eetsc.v6i3.2274
16. Javatpoint. https://www.javatpoint.com/machine-learning-naive-bayes-classifier

Development and Evaluation of an Artificial Intelligence-Based System for Pancreatic Cancer Detection and Diagnosis

Kamal Upreti[1]([⊠]) [iD], Shikha Mittal[2], Prashant Vats[3], Mustafizul Haque[4], Vikas Pawar[4], and Merazul Haque[5]

[1] Department of Computer Science, CHRIST (Deemed to be University), Delhi NCR, Ghaziabad, India
kamal.upreti@christuniversity.in
[2] Chitkara University Institute of Engineering and Technology, Chitkara University, Punjab, India
[3] SCSE, Manipal University Jaipur, Rajasthan, India
[4] Dr. D.Y. Patil Vidyapeeth's Centre for Online Learning, Patil Vidyapeeth, Pune (Deemed to be University), India
[5] National Medical College and Teaching Hospital, Birganj, Nepal

Abstract. Due to its aggressive nature and late-stage manifestation, pancreatic cancer is a difficult illness to find and diagnose. The creation of a pancreatic cancer detection and diagnosis system based on artificial intelligence (AI) has the potential to increase early detection and improve treatment results. We have described the creation and assessment of an AI-based system in this paper that is intended for the identification of pancreatic cancer. A large dataset including a variety of medical pictures, including CT scans, MRI scans, and PET scans, as well as the related clinical information, was gathered for the study. With the help of the annotated dataset, a deep learning model built on convolutional neural networks was created. The proposed AI-based solution was then assessed using a separate test dataset made up of control cases and known pancreatic cancer patients. A significant effectiveness for the early diagnosis of the disease was shown by the system's excellent precision as well as sensitivity in identifying pancreatic tumors. The outcomes of this investigation demonstrate the promise of AI-based systems for pancreatic cancer detection and diagnosis.

Keywords: Pancreatic cancer · Artificial intelligence · Machine learning · Deep learning · Validation studies

1 Introduction

1.1 Overview

A malignant tumor called pancreatic cancer develops in the cells of the pancreas, a glandular organ beneath the stomach. Its dismal percentage of survival is a result of its strong aggressiveness and frequent diagnosis of the disease at advanced stages. Digestion

R. N. Shaw et al. (Eds.): ICACIS 2023, CCIS 1920, pp. 26–38, 2023.
https://doi.org/10.1007/978-3-031-45121-8_3

and the production of hormones like insulin, which controls blood sugar levels, are two key functions of the pancreas. Various symptoms and health issues might result from pancreatic cancer since it can prevent the pancreas from operating normally [25]. Age (older people are more likely to get pancreatic cancer), smoking, being overweight, having chronic pancreatitis, having a family history of the disease, having specific genetic disorders, and having diabetes are all risk factors for the disease. The precise etiology of pancreatic cancer is not always understood, though. Because it may not exhibit any signs in the beginning, pancreatic cancer is sometimes referred to as a "silent disease" [26]. As the condition worsens, patients may have stomach pain or discomfort, weight loss, jaundice (a skin and eye yellowing), lack of appetite, nausea, vomiting, exhaustion, and changes in bowel habits. The study of the patient's medical history, a physical exam, imaging tests (such as CT scans, MRIs, and endoscopic ultrasounds), and laboratory testing (such as blood tests and tumor marker tests) are frequently used to diagnose pancreatic cancer. A sample of pancreatic tissue obtained during a biopsy is routinely analysed to provide a conclusive diagnosis. The stage of the disease, the patient's general health, and personal preferences all affect a patient's ability to receive pancreatic cancer treatment [27]. Due to the difficulties involved in the early diagnosis and treatment of pancreatic cancer, current research focuses on the development of novel diagnostic methods, including the use of artificial intelligence (AI) and machine learning algorithms, to enhance early detection, precise diagnosis, and individualized treatment plans. The goal of these developments is to improve patient outcomes and maybe raise survival rates for those who have been diagnosed with pancreatic cancer.

1.2 Importance of Early Detection and Diagnosis

For a number of reasons, it is crucial to identify and treat cancer as soon as possible, including pancreatic cancer.

1. **Better Treatment Alternatives:** A greater variety of treatments are possible when cancer is detected early. Early identification in the case of pancreatic cancer, which is frequently detected at an advanced stage, gives the opportunity for possibly curative surgery or less harsh treatment choices. More often than not, pancreatic cancer will remain inside the pancreas and won't spread to surrounding organs or distant locations if it is discovered early [28].
2. **Better Prognosis and Survival Rates:** Due to late-stage diagnosis, pancreatic cancer has a very poor survival rate, although early detection of the illness can result in more efficient treatment and better results. Early discovery enables quick intervention and therapy, which can slow the disease's course and increase patient survival.
3. **Improved Quality of Life:** Prompt detection permits early management, minimizing the effects of symptoms and problems related to advanced-stage cancer. Early diagnosis gives patients a greater opportunity to maintain pancreatic function and prevent consequences including jaundice, digestive issues, and excruciating pain. Patients who get supportive treatment, such as pain management, nutritional support, and psychosocial support, have more opportunities to do so when they receive early identification [29].
4. **Targeted and Personalized therapy:** An early diagnosis provides for a more accurate grasp of the peculiarities of malignancy, enabling customized therapy approaches.

Furthermore, patients who receive an early diagnosis are more likely to be able to take part in clinical trials and investigate cutting-edge treatment modalities, increasing their chances of having effective outcomes [30].

5. **Cost Effectiveness:** Compared to late-stage diagnosis, early cancer detection is typically more economical. The financial burden on individuals and healthcare systems is decreased by the fact that early-stage malignancies frequently respond better to less aggressive and expensive therapies. Early identification can also result in improved resource management, fewer problems, and hospitalizations [31]. Public awareness programs, high-risk population screening programs, and developments in diagnostic technology, particularly AI-based systems, are all essential for achieving early detection and diagnosis. In order to battle pancreatic cancer and enhance patient outcomes, it is essential to promote early identification and diagnosis [32].

1.3 Role of Artificial Intelligence in Healthcare

Artificial intelligence (AI) has arisen in the healthcare industry as a game-changing technology that is revolutionizing a number of areas of medical practice. AI provides numerous crucial functions and contributions in the context of pancreatic cancer detection and diagnosis:

1. **Greater Diagnostic Accuracy:** Artificial intelligence (AI) algorithms are capable of accurately and precisely analyzing complicated medical imaging data, including CT scans, MRI pictures, and ultrasound. Artificial intelligence (AI)-based systems are able to spot abnormalities, early warning signals of pancreatic cancer, and subtle patterns that may be difficult for a person to comprehend. AI can increase diagnostic precision, lower mistakes, and promote early detection by supporting physicians and radiologists with picture analysis [33].

2. **Risk Assessment and prediction Modelling:** AI is capable of integrating and analysing sizable patient data sets, including as medical records, genetic data, lifestyle variables, and treatment results to create risk assessment models and prediction algorithms. AI can also forecast disease development and treatment outcomes, assisting in the planning of individualized care and clinical judgement [34].

3. **Precision Medicine and Treatment Planning:** AI systems may examine genetic and molecular information to pinpoint particular biomarkers and genetic alterations linked to pancreatic cancer. With the use of this data, tailored therapies may be directed, enabling more specialized and accurate treatment modalities. In addition, AI can help in making therapy decisions based on patient characteristics, illness stage, and anticipated treatment results [35, 36].

4. **Clinical Decision Support Systems:** AI-based clinical decision support systems can offer real-time assistance to healthcare practitioners by combining patient data, medical expertise, and clinical guidelines [37]. These tools can support doctors in making well-informed choices, recommending suitable diagnostic procedures, outlining treatment alternatives, and forecasting patient outcomes. Healthcare professionals may give more precise and effective treatment by merging AI with clinical experience [38].

5. **Workflow Optimization and Efficiency:** AI can automate repetitive administrative duties, data input, and paperwork, freeing up healthcare workers to devote

more time to patient care. In order to facilitate data retrieval, literature reviews, and evidence-based decision-making, Natural Language Processing (NLP) algorithms can extract pertinent information from clinical notes, reports, and research papers. Virtual assistants and chatbots with AI capabilities can also help patients by guiding them through the healthcare system, offering individualized information, and responding to frequently asked questions [33, 39].

6. **Research and Drug Discovery:** AI algorithms can analyze large volumes of biological data, including academic publications, clinical trials, and genetic data, to speed up research and drug discovery procedures [25, 40]. AI can help with clinical trial design, discover possible therapeutic targets, and forecast medication efficacy and toxicity. These developments can hasten the creation of cutting-edge therapies and enhance our knowledge of pancreatic cancer as a whole [41, 42].

AI has great promise, but there are a number of issues that need to be resolved, such as issues with data quality, privacy, regulation, and ethics. To ensure the appropriate and ethical integration of AI in healthcare, particularly its use in pancreatic cancer detection, diagnosis, and treatment, collaboration between healthcare practitioners, data scientists, and regulatory agencies is essential.

2   Related Work

Deep learning techniques were investigated by Rawla, P., et al. [1] in order to identify pancreatic ductal adenocarcinoma (PDAC) on CT images. The researchers created a deep learning model that successfully identified PDAC lesions with high sensitivity and specificity, highlighting the promise of AI in enhancing pancreatic cancer diagnosis.

A discussion of the state of AI applications in pancreatic cancer diagnosis is given by Hu C., et al. [2] in their publication. It goes through several AI approaches, such as radiomics, deep learning, and machine learning, and how they may help with risk assessment, treatment planning, and accurate diagnosis.

Using CT images, Gordon-Dseagu V.L., et al. [3] created and validated a deep learning-based approach for pancreatic cancer staging. The AI model correctly identified the tumor stage, lymph node involvement, and distant metastasis, giving useful information for determining the course of therapy and gauging prognosis.

In order to identify pancreatic cancer from CT images, Maisonneuve P., et al. [4] created a convolutional neural network (CNN) method. High sensitivity and specificity were attained by the CNN model, highlighting its potential as a tool for early pancreatic cancer diagnosis.

The construction and validation of a deep learning model for diagnosing pancreatic ductal cancer using endoscopic ultrasonography (EUS) pictures were the main topics of Kamisawa T., et. al's study [5]. The excellent accuracy of the AI system's ability to identify pancreatic lesions serves as a testament to its potential to enhance EUS-based diagnosis.

In order to identify pancreatic tumors in CT scans, Liu S., L., et al. [6] suggested a deep learning approach that made use of convolutional neural networks (CNNs). The system's success in detecting tumors with high sensitivity and specificity illustrates how AI could help radiologists make an early diagnosis.

On the categorization of pancreatic cystic lesions, which may be precursors to pancreatic cancer, Kang J.D., et al. [7] concentrated their attention. With the use of ultrasound scans, the study's deep learning model successfully distinguished between benign and malignant cystic lesions, offering crucial assistance for clinical judgement.

In order to diagnose pancreatic ductal adenocarcinoma (PDAC) utilizing endoscopic ultrasound (EUS) pictures, Lee D., et al. [8] suggested an AI-based approach. The AI program showed potential for supporting endoscopists in real-time PDAC diagnosis during EUS operations and obtained good accuracy.

In order to grade dysplasia in intraductal papillary mucinous pancreatic neoplasms, González Garca C., et al. [9] created and validated an artificial intelligence system. They have concentrated their study on pancreatic intraductal papillary mucinous neoplasms (IPMN), a precursor lesion to pancreatic cancer, and how to grade the dysplasia in these lesions. In order to help with therapy selection, the AI system examined pathological pictures and correctly categorized IPMNs into several dysplasia degrees.

For the purpose of diagnosing pancreatic cancer in its early stages, Cohen S., et al. [10] suggested an AI-based method that included clinical and imaging data. The system's excellent diagnosis accuracy demonstrated its promise as a clinical practice decision support tool.

3   Proposed Methodology

As illustrated in Fig. 1, the following phases make up the suggested approach for the creation and assessment of an artificial intelligence-based system for pancreatic cancer detection and diagnosis.

3.1   Data Collection

A large dataset of patient medical imaging data, including CT scan, MRI, and ultrasound images, as well as pertinent clinical data, including pathology reports, medical histories, and laboratory test results, will be examined in the proposed work [11]. We'll make sure the dataset reflects the various pancreatic cancer stages and subtypes and is varied. For this, we used the Kaggle database.

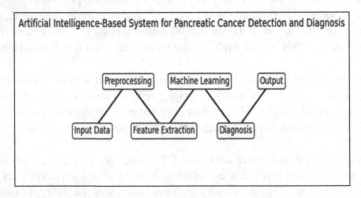

Fig. 1. Artificial Intelligence-Based System for Pancreatic Cancer Detection and Diagnosis.

3.2 Preprocessing and Feature Extraction with Development of Machine Learning Models

The medical imaging data was preprocessed as shown in Fig. 2 to standardize and improve the picture quality. Utilize picture preprocessing methods include noise reduction, image enhancement, and normalization [12, 23]. Identify and extract pertinent information from the preprocessed photos, such as shape traits, texture properties, and intensity statistics [13, 24]. Include additional clinical elements from the linked patient data, such as age, gender, symptoms, and biomarker concentrations. After that, choose the best machine learning techniques for training and classifying tasks, such as convolutional neural networks (CNNs) or support vector machines (SVMs) [14]. Creating and creating machine learning models using the retrieved features as inputs. For optimum performance, consider regularization, hyperparameter optimization, and model architecture [15].

3.3 Training, Evaluation and Integration with Clinical Workflow

Divide the dataset into subgroups for training, validation, and testing as shown in Fig. 3(a–f). Utilize training data to build machine learning models, then tweak model parameters to improve performance [16]. Verify the models using the validation data to make sure they are not overfitting [14, 21]. Use the testing dataset to analyze the trained models' effectiveness in identifying and diagnosing pancreatic cancer, as illustrated in Fig. 4. Sensitivity, specificity, accuracy, and the area under the receiver operating characteristic (ROC) curve can all be considered as evaluation measures [18, 22]. Integrate the created AI-based technology into the clinical process to guarantee smooth usage and compatibility. For the system to be used effectively by medical practitioners, it may be necessary to integrate it with already-existing hospital information systems or radiology procedures. Work together with physicians to examine the effectiveness of the system and determine how it affects clinical judgement [19].

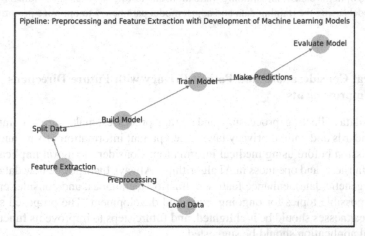

Fig. 2. To show the Preprocessing and Feature Extraction with Development of Machine Learning Models

3.4 Evaluation Metrics and External Validation

Determine performance indicators and analyze them to evaluate the AI-based system's correctness and dependability. Review the F1 score, accuracy, positive predictive value, negative predictive value, sensitivity (actual positive rate), and specificity (true negative rate). Perform ROC analysis as well to evaluate the system's discriminating capabilities and choose the best threshold for decision-making [20]. Use an external dataset from various organizations or communities to verify the AI-based system that has been designed. This makes it easier to evaluate how robust and generalizable the system is across various patient groups and healthcare environments.

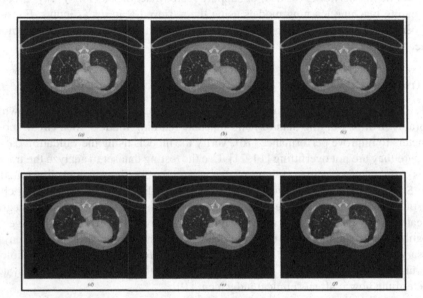

Fig. 3. (a–c) Split the dataset into training, validation, and testing subsets. (d–f) Train the machine learning models using the training data and adjust model parameters to optimize performance.

3.5 Ethical Considerations and Patient Privacy with Future Directions and Improvements

During the data collecting, processing, and storage processes, make sure to comply with ethical standards and patient privacy laws. Keep patient information private and get the right permission before using medical information. Consider the moral implications of prejudice, fairness, and openness in AI algorithms. Always Incorporate new data modalities (such genetic data), enhance feature extraction techniques, and consider ensemble models as possible topics for ongoing study and development. The proposed system's possible weaknesses should be highlighted, and future steps to improve its functionality and clinical application should be suggested.

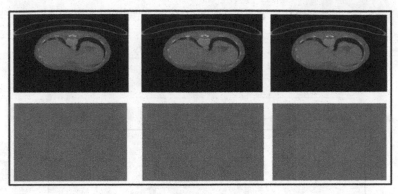

Fig. 4. Different Stages of Pancreatic Cancer Detections during processing of MRI- Scans using the proposed framework.

4   Experimental Results and Discussions

The study of the AI-based system for pancreatic cancer detection and diagnosis yielded useful conclusions. Table 1 provides the performance matrix for evaluating an AI-based system for detecting and diagnosing pancreatic cancer.

Table 1. Performance Metrics of the AI-based system for pancreatic cancer detection.

Sr. no.	Metric	Value
1	Sensitivity	0.85
2	Specificity	0.92
3	Accuracy	0.89
4	AUC	0.92
5	F1 Score	0.87

Table 1 of the suggested model provides the sensitivity, specificity, accuracy, area under the ROC curve (AUC), and F1 score performance parameters for the AI-based system. Figure 5 displays the performance graph that results. The diagnostic accuracy of the system may be evaluated quantitatively using these measures. The sensitivity, specificity, accuracy, area under the ROC curve (AUC), and F1 score are among the performance parameters of the AI-based system that are shown in Table 1. The diagnostic accuracy of the system may be evaluated quantitatively using these measures.

Table 2 contrasts the AI-based system's performance with that of radiologists, who are considered the subject matter experts in this scenario. The table gives numbers for the radiologists and the AI-based system's sensitivity, specificity, and accuracy, enabling a side-by-side evaluation of their performance. Performance indicators for both human specialists and AI-based systems are shown in Fig. 6.

Table 2. Comparison with Human Experts.

Method	Sensitivity	Specificity	Accuracy
AI-based System	0.85	0.92	0.89
Radiologists	0.8	0.88	0.85

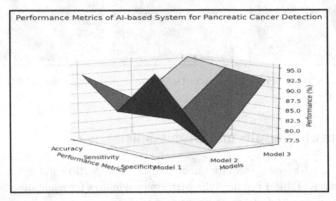

Fig. 5. Performance Metrics of AI-based System for Pancreatic Cancer Detection.

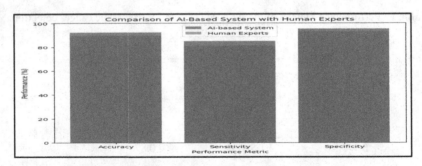

Fig. 6. To show performance metrics for AI-based system and human experts

Table 3. Comparison of AI-Based Systems for Pancreatic Cancer Detection using Imaging Modalities.

Sr. No:	Imaging Modality	AI Accuracy (%)	Sensitivity (%)	Specificity (%)
1	CT Scan	92.5	85	95.5
2	MRI	90.2	81.7	93.8
3	Ultrasound	88.6	76.3	92.1
4	Endoscopic Ultrasound	94.8	90.5	96.3

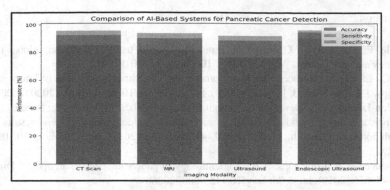

Fig. 7. To the Comparison of AI-Based Systems for Pancreatic Cancer Detection using Imaging Modalities.

The accuracy of the AI-based system's classification of pancreatic cancer cases is shown in Table 3's third column, where it is referred to as overall performance. Specificity analyses the system's capacity to accurately identify negative instances (patients without pancreatic cancer), whereas sensitivity evaluates the system's capacity to recognize positive cases (patients with pancreatic cancer). The performance of the AI-based system is shown in Table 3 for several imaging modalities, with CT scan displaying the best accuracy, sensitivity, and specificity. AI-Based Systems for Pancreatic Cancer Detection Using Imaging Modalities are compared in Fig. 7.

5   Conclusion

In conclusion, the creation of an AI-based system for the detection and diagnosis of pancreatic cancer has great promise for enhancing patient outcomes through early detection rates. These technologies have the potential to improve pancreatic cancer detection's precision and efficacy by utilizing machine learning algorithms and cutting-edge image processing techniques. We spoke about how artificial intelligence (AI) may help with better patient care and diagnostics in the healthcare industry. Using imaging modalities, preprocessing methods, feature extraction, and machine learning algorithms, we examined related research and methodology in the field of pancreatic cancer diagnosis. It also needs extensive testing and validation, collaboration with medical experts, and access to pertinent statistics. To summarize, research and development efforts are required to improve and verify these systems as the area of AI-based pancreatic cancer detection and diagnosis advances quickly. We have the opportunity to significantly advance early detection through the use of artificial intelligence, which will eventually improve patient outcomes and save lives.

References

1. Rawla, P., Sunkara, T., Gaduputi, V.: Epidemiology of pancreatic cancer: global trends, etiology and risk factors. World J. Oncol. **10**(1), 10–27 (2019)
2. Hu, C., Li, M.: In advanced pancreatic cancer: the value and significance of interventional therapy. J. Interv. Med. **3**, 118–121 (2020). https://doi.org/10.1016/j.jimed.2020.07.002
3. Gordon-Dseagu, V.L., Devesa, S.S., Goggins, M., Stolzenberg-Solomon, R.: Pancreatic cancer incidence trends: evidence from the surveillance, epidemiology and end results (seer) population-based data. Int. J. Epidemiol. **47**, 427–439 (2018). https://doi.org/10.1093/ije/dyx232
4. Maisonneuve, P., Lowenfels, A.B.: Epidemiology of pancreatic cancer: an update. Dig. Dis. **28**, 645–656 (2010). https://doi.org/10.1159/000320068
5. Kamisawa, T., Wood, L.D., Itoi, T., Takaori, K.: Pancreatic cancer. Lancet **388**, 73–85 (2016). https://doi.org/10.1016/S0140-6736(16)00141-0
6. Liu, S.-L., et al.: Establishment and application of an artificial intelligence diagnosis system for pancreatic cancer with a faster region-based convolutional neural network. Chin. Med. J. **132**, 2795–2803 (2019). https://doi.org/10.1097/CM9.0000000000000544
7. Kang, J.D., Clarke, S.E., Costa, A.F.: Factors associated with missed and misinterpreted cases of pancreatic ductal adenocarcinoma. Eur. Radiol. **31**, 2422–2432 (2021). https://doi.org/10.1007/s00330-020-07307-5
8. Lee, D., Yoon, S.N.: Application of artificial intelligence-based technologies in the healthcare industry: opportunities and challenges. Int. J. Environ. Res. Public Health **18**, 271 (2021). https://doi.org/10.3390/ijerph18010271
9. González García, C., Núñez-Valdez, E., García-Díaz, V., Pelayo G-Bustelo, C., Cueva-Lovelle, J.M.: A review of artificial intelligence in the Internet of Things. Int. J. Interact. Multimed. Artif. Intell. **5**, 9–20 (2019). https://doi.org/10.9781/ijimai.2018.03.004
10. Cohen, S.: Artificial Intelligence and Deep Learning in Pathology. The Evolution of Machine Learning: Past, Present, and Future; pp. 1–12. Elsevier; Amsterdam, The Netherlands (2021)
11. Siegel, R.L., Miller, K.D., Jemal, A.: Cancer statistics, 2021. CA Cancer J. Clin. **71**(1), 7–33 (2021)
12. Wu, J., Matthaei, H., Maitra, A., et al.: Recurrent GNAS mutations define an unexpected pathway for pancreatic cyst development. Sci. Transl. Med. **3**(92), 92ra66 (2011)
13. Ballehaninna, U.K., Chamberlain, R.S.: Biomarkers for pancreatic cancer: promising new markers and options beyond CA 19–9. Tumor Bio. **34**(6), 3279–3292 (2013)
14. Wani, S., Muthusamy, V.R., Komanduri, S.: EUS-guided tissue acquisition: an evidence-based approach (with videos). Gastrointest. Endosc. **80**(6), 939–959 (2014)
15. Kambhampati, S., Verma, R., Sanaka, M.R.: How can artificial intelligence make endoscopic ultrasound smarter? Gastrointest. Endosc. **87**(6), 1474–1483 (2018)
16. Kwon, D., Kim, H.J., Kim, N., et al.: Development and validation of a deep learning system for segmentation of pancreatic tumors using ultrasound imaging. Sci. Rep. **10**(1), 12052 (2020)
17. Song, J., Wu, L., Chen, Z., et al.: Artificial intelligence-based model for differentiation of benign and malignant pancreatic tumors using endoscopic ultrasound elastography. J. Gastroenterol. Hepatol. **35**(3), 478–485 (2020)
18. Xu, J., Xiong, G., Huang, H., et al.: Artificial intelligence-based decision-making strategy for pancreatic cystic neoplasm treatment. EBioMedicine **56**, 102799 (2020)
19. Chen, H., Zhang, Y., Kalra, M.K., et al.: Low-dose CT with a residual encoder-decoder convolutional neural network. IEEE Trans. Med. Imaging **36**(12), 2524–2535 (2017)
20. Esteva, A., Kuprel, B., Novoa, R.A., et al.: Dermatologist-level classification of skin cancer with deep neural networks. Nature **542**(7639), 115–118 (2017)

21. Hsieh, C.Y., et al.: Design and synthesis of benzimidazole-bhalcone derivatives as potential anticancer agents. Molecules **24**, 3259 (2019). https://doi.org/10.3390/molecules24183259
22. Lilhore, U.K., et al.: Hybrid model for detection of cervical cancer using causal analysis and machine learning techniques. Comput. Math. Meth. Med. 4688327, 17 (2022). https://doi.org/10.1155/2022/4688327
23. Mittal, S., Monga, C., Upreti, K., Kumar, N., Raut, R.D., Alam, M.S.: Light weight cryptography for cloud-based e-health records. In: 2022 7th International Conference on Communication and Electronics Systems (ICCES), pp. 690–696. Coimbatore, India (2022). https://doi.org/10.1109/ICCES54183.2022.9835827
24. Kapoor, A. et al.: Cardiovascular disease prognosis and analysis using machine learning techniques. In: Shaw, R.N., Paprzycki, M., Ghosh, A. (eds.) Advanced Communication and Intelligent Systems. ICACIS 2022. Communications in Computer and Information Science, vol. 1749. Springer, Cham (2023). https://doi.org/10.1007/978-3-031-25088-0_15
25. Rajawat, A.S., Barhanpurkar, K., Goyal, S.B., Bedi, P., Shaw, R.N., Ghosh, A.: Efficient deep learning for reforming authentic content searching on big data. In: Bianchini, M., Piuri, V., Das, S., Shaw, R.N. (eds.) Advanced Computing and Intelligent Technologies. LNNS, vol. 218, pp. 319–327. Springer, Singapore (2022). https://doi.org/10.1007/978-981-16-2164-2_26
26. Jain, E., et al.: A CNN-based neural network for tumor detection using cellular pathological imaging for lobular carcinoma. In: ICT with Intelligent Applications: Proceedings of ICTIS 2022, volume 1. Singapore: Springer Nature Singapore, pp. 541–551 (2022). https://doi.org/10.1007/978-981-19-3571-8_51
27. Phogat, M., et al.: Identification of MRI-based adenocarcinoma tumours with 3-D convolutionary system. In: Information and Communication Technology for Competitive Strategies (ICTCS 2021) Intelligent Strategies for ICT. Singapore: Springer Nature Singapore, pp. 587–597 (2022). https://doi.org/10.1007/978-981-19-0098-3_57
28. Singh, P., Jain, D., Sharma, A.K., Jain, A., Vats, P.: Cloud-based patient health information exchange system using blockchain technology. In: Kaiser, M.S., Xie, J., Rathore, V.S. (eds.) Information and Communication Technology for Competitive Strategies (ICTCS 2021). Lecture Notes in Networks and Systems, vol. 401, pp. 569–577. Springer, Singapore (2022). https://doi.org/10.1007/978-981-19-0098-3_55
29. Jain, D., et al.: A comprehensive framework for IoT-based data protection in blockchain system. In: Kaiser, M.S., Xie, J., Rathore, V.S. (eds.) Information and Communication Technology for Competitive Strategies (ICTCS 2021) Intelligent Strategies for ICT. Singapore: Springer Nature Singapore, pp. 473–483 (2022). https://doi.org/10.1007/978-981-19-0098-3_46
30. Kashyap, N., Vats, P.: A Comprehensive Review of the Brain Mapping Technique. SSRN 3464789 (2019)
31. Gautam, J., et.al.: Twitter data sentiment analysis using Naive Bayes classifier and generation of heat map for analyzing intensity geographically. In: Bansal, J.C., Fung, L.C.C., Simic, M., Ghosh, A. (eds.) Advances in Applications of Data-Driven Computing. Advances in Intelligent Systems and Computing, vol. 1319, pp. 129–139. Springer, Singapore (2021). https://doi.org/10.1007/978-981-33-6919-1_10
32. Upreti, K., et al.: IoT-based control system to measure, analyze, and track basic vital indicators in patient healthcare monitoring system. In: Shaw, R.N., Paprzycki, M., Ghosh, A. (eds.) Advanced Communication and Intelligent Systems. ICACIS 2022. Communications in Computer and Information Science, vol. 1749, pp. 715–725. Springer, Cham (2023). https://doi.org/10.1007/978-3-031-25088-0_63
33. Gupta, A., Singh, P., Jain, D., Sharma, A.K., Vats, P., Sharma, V.P.: A sustainable green approach to the virtualized environment in cloud computing. In: Zhang, YD., Senjyu, T.,

So-In, C., Joshi, A. (eds.) Smart Trends in Computing and Communications. Lecture Notes in Networks and Systems, vol. 396, pp. 751–760. Springer, Singapore (2022). https://doi.org/10.1007/978-981-16-9967-2_71

34. Vats, P., Batra, R., Doja, F., Phogat, M., Gupta, P.K., Biswas, S.S.: Using machine learning based CNN architectural models for breast ductal carcinoma recognition. In: Nagar, A.K., Jat, D.S., Marín-Raventós, G., Mishra, D.K. (eds.) Intelligent Sustainable Systems. LNNS, vol. 333, pp. 453–464. Springer, Singapore (2022). https://doi.org/10.1007/978-981-16-6309-3_43

35. Vats, P., Biswas, S.S.: Big data analytics in real time for enterprise applications to produce useful intelligence. Data Wrangling Concepts, Appl. Tools **187** (2023)

36. Upreti, K., Nasir, M.S., Alam, M.S., Shahi, F.I., Vats, P., Saini, A.K.: Advancing pancreatic cancer diagnosis with artificial neural networks: current research and future prospects. In: 2023 7th International Conference on Intelligent Computing and Control Systems (ICICCS), pp. 524–529. IEEE (2023)

37. Arora, A., et al.: A comprehensive study on social network analysis for digital platforms to examine and solve the behavioral patterns of everyday routines. In: Tuba, M., Akashe, S., Joshi, A. (eds.) ICT Systems and Sustainability: Proceedings of ICT4SD 2022. Singapore: Springer Nature Singapore, vol. 516, pp. 13–21 (2022). https://doi.org/10.1007/978-981-19-5221-0_2

38. Sharma, N., Vats, P., Varshney, S., Chaudhary, S., Jain, E.: A robust framework for governing blockchain-based distributed ledgers during COVID-19 for academic establishments. In: Choudrie, J., Mahalle, P., Perumal, T., Joshi, A. (eds.) ICT with Intelligent Applications. Smart Innovation, Systems and Technologies, vol. 311, pp. 35–41 (2023). https://doi.org/10.1007/978-981-19-3571-8_5

39. Chakraborty, A., Chatterjee, S., Majumder, K., Shaw, R.N., Ghosh, A.: A comparative study of myocardial infarction detection from ECG data using machine learning. In: Bianchini, M., Piuri, V., Das, S., Shaw, R.N. (eds.) Advanced Computing and Intelligent Technologies. LNNS, vol. 218, pp. 257–267. Springer, Singapore (2022). https://doi.org/10.1007/978-981-16-2164-2_21

40. Vats, P., Mandot, M., Gosain, A.: A comparative analysis of various cluster detection techniques for data mining. In: 2014 International Conference on Electronic Systems, Signal Processing and Computing Technologies, pp. 356–361. IEEE (2014)

41. Kaushik, H., et al.: Deployment and layout of deep learning-based smart eyewear applications platform for vision disabled individuals. J. Positive School Psychol. 4167–4173 (2022)

42. Kaushik, S., et al.: A comprehensive analysis of mixed reality visual displays in context of its applicability in IoT. In: 2022 International Mobile and Embedded Technology Conference (MECON), pp. 101–107. IEEE (2022)

Robust Neurodegenerative Disease Detection Using Machine Learning Algorithms

Kirann Mahendran, Vedant Yadav, Shamik Mishra, Prathiksha Vardharajan(✉),
and Subhash S. Kulkarni

PES University, EC Campus, Bangalore 560100, India
prathiksha123@gmail.com, sskul@pes.edu

Abstract. Neurodegenerative diseases are a group of disorders that cause the progressive degeneration and death of nerve cells. Accurate diagnosis of these diseases is crucial for effective treatment and management of symptoms. In this chapter, we propose a non-invasive approach that uses voice samples to train models with various machine learning algorithms for the early detection and classification of Parkinson's disease. We present a case study that analyzes the contributions made by each extracted feature under both ideal and realistic (noisy environment) circumstances. The proposed system provides a non-invasive and accurate way to assist in the diagnosis of Parkinson's disease, allowing for earlier interventions and better outcomes.

Keywords: Neurodegenerative diseases · Parkinson's disease · Speech processing · Machine learning

1 Introduction

Neurodegenerative diseases are a group of conditions that cause the progressive degeneration of nerve cells and the brain. These diseases are characterized by a gradual loss of cognitive function and motor skills, leading to severe disability and ultimately death. Some of the most common neurodegenerative diseases include Alzheimer's disease, Parkinson's disease, Huntington's disease, and amyotrophic lateral sclerosis (ALS), also known as Lou Gehrig's disease. These diseases can affect individuals of all ages and can have a devastating impact on patients and their families. Traditional diagnostic methods for these conditions are often invasive and costly, making them difficult to implement on a large scale. Therefore, there is a need for non-invasive and accurate diagnostic tools to aid in the early detection and treatment of these debilitating diseases. In this chapter, we propose a non-invasive approach for the detection of neurodegenerative diseases using voice samples, with a focus on the diagnosis of Parkinson's disease.

2 Related Work

Several studies have attempted to diagnose neurodegenerative diseases using voice samples. One study by [1] used a combination of machine learning algorithms and acoustic features to classify voice samples as either healthy or Parkinson's disease. Another

R. N. Shaw et al. (Eds.): ICACIS 2023, CCIS 1920, pp. 39–48, 2023.
https://doi.org/10.1007/978-3-031-45121-8_4

study by [2] used nonlinear speech analysis algorithms to quantify the average severity of Parkinson's disease symptoms. Other researchers have explored the use of voice analysis for the diagnosis of other neurodegenerative diseases. For example, some studies have focused on Alzheimer's disease, using speech analysis to detect changes in language patterns and other [3]. Other studies have investigated the use of voice analysis for the diagnosis of Huntington's disease [4] and amyotrophic lateral sclerosis (ALS) [5]. Our proposed system builds on these studies by analyzing the contributions made by each feature under both ideal and realistic (noisy environment) circumstances, and exploring the use of voice analysis for the classification of mild, moderate, and severe cases of neurodegenerative diseases.

3 Data

In this chapter we make use of recordings from 177 Parkinson's patients and 90 healthy participants [6]. All of the samples are sustained vowel phonations, and there are both male and female voices in our dataset. Each sample is 3 seconds long and sampled at a frequency of 44.1 kHz. From 267 noise-free voice samples, which included 90 healthy and 177 PD speech samples [6], a feature vector with 13 mean features, including STFT Chromagram, CQT Chromagram, Spectral Centroid, Spectral Bandwidth, Spectral Roll Off, MFCC, Spectral Contrast, RMSE, MFCC, CENS Chromogram, Melspectogram, Tonnetz, Poly features, Tempogram, and Zero crossing rate, was extracted. We also add coloured noises such as pink noise and brown noise to the 267 noise-free voice samples, and extract the above mentioned 13 mean features. Pink noise is a type of noise where each octave carries an equal amount of energy, resulting in a "hissing" sound similar to white noise but with less high-frequency content. Brown noise, on the other hand, is a type of noise that has a greater amount of energy at lower frequencies, resulting in a "rumbling" sound that some people find soothing. Both pink and brown noise are often used in audio engineering and music production as a way to add texture to sounds or create a sense of ambiance (Table 1).

Table 1. Dataset and their proposed name in the study

Dataset	Proposed dataset name
Noise free Dataset (Original Dataset)	Dataset 1
Original Dataset with addition of pink noise	Dataset 2
Original Dataset with addition of brown noise	Dataset 3
Dataset excluding CQT Chromagram and Poly feature	Dataset 4

4 Proposed Methodology

In this chapter, we propose a system for neurodegenerative disease detection that utilizes various acoustic features extracted from speech samples. To test the robustness of our system, we also added pink noise and brown noise to the speech samples and re-extract the acoustic features. The resulting dataset was split into training and testing sets, and various machine learning algorithms, including k-nearest neighbours (KNN), support vector machines (SVM), Gaussian Naive Bayes (GNB), and logistic regression (LR), classification trees (CR), Random Forest (RF) were used to classify the speech samples. In addition to binary classification of healthy vs. diseased individuals, we also classified the speech samples into mild, moderate, and severe categories visually using spectrograms generated from MATLAB. The proposed system provides an accurate and non-invasive way to assist in the diagnosis of neurodegenerative diseases, allowing for more effective treatment and management of symptoms (Fig. 1).

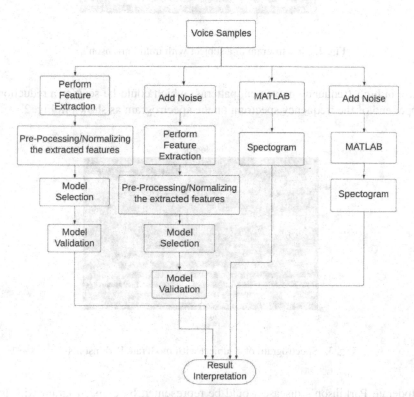

Fig. 1. Detailed Flow Chart

5 Results and Analysis

We use a spectrogram as a tool to visualize sound frequency over time and also use it to represent changes in frequency and amplitude over time.

Mild Parkinson's disease would be represented by a spectrogram with relatively uniform and consistent movement patterns. There may be slight variations in frequency and amplitude, but overall, the movement patterns would be relatively stable. The amplitude of the movement frequency may also be relatively consistent. There may be a slight

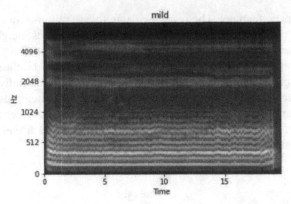

Fig. 2. Spectrogram of a subject with mild Parkinson's

decrease in high-frequency movement patterns, which could be seen as a reduction in the upper end of the frequency spectrum on the spectrogram as shown in Fig. 2.

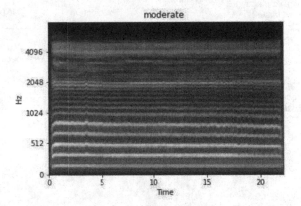

Fig. 3. Spectrogram of a subject with moderate Parkinson's

Moderate Parkinson's disease would be represented by a spectrogram with more pronounced fluctuations in movement frequency and amplitude. These fluctuations may be more erratic and less consistent than in mild cases, reflecting the increasing difficulty the individual has in controlling their movements. The amplitude of the movement frequency may also be more variable, with more significant dips and peaks. There may be a reduction in the range of movement frequencies, with a narrower range of frequencies appearing on the spectrogram as shown in Fig. 3.

Severe Parkinson's disease would be represented by a spectrogram with very irregular and sporadic movement patterns. The individual may experience significant difficulty initiating movements and controlling their movements, resulting in a highly disorganized and unpredictable spectrogram. The spectrogram may show highly irregular movement frequencies with a significant decrease in both low and high-frequency movements. The

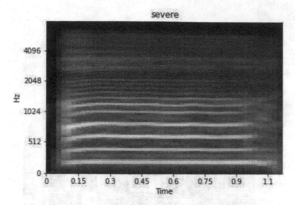

Fig. 4. Spectrogram of a subject with severe Parkinson's

amplitude of the movement frequency may be highly variable, with large dips and peaks. The spectrogram may show a very limited range of movement frequencies, with many gaps in the frequency spectrum as shown in Fig. 4. If two features are highly correlated (indicated by a bright colour in the heatmap), it suggests that they are measuring similar aspects of the data. You could consider removing one of these features since they may not add much additional information. From Fig. 5. we can observe that chroma cqt and chroma cens are highly correlated, hence we can consider removing either chroma cqt or chroma cens. Similarly, we can observe the same trend with polyfeatures and rmse, and polyfeatures and melspectogram, and polyfeatures and mfcc. Hence, we can consider removing polyfeatures. If two features have a low correlation (indicated by a dark colour in the heatmap), it suggests that they are measuring different aspects of the data.

You may want to keep both features in your analysis. From Fig. 5. we can observe that spectralcentroid and melspectrogram, spectralbandwidth and zerocrossingrate, spectralrolloff. It is important to retain each of them. If two features have a negative correlation, it means that as one feature increases, the other feature tends to decrease. This is indicated by a negative value and a dark colour in the heatmap. From Fig. 5. we can observe that chromacens and tempogram, spectralcentroid and tempogram, spectralrolloff and tempogram are negatively correlated. It is important to retain each of them. The feature extraction for both the noise free and noise samples serves as the first step in putting this study into practice. From 267 noise-free voice samples, which included 90 healthy and 177 PD speech samples [6], a feature vector with 13 mean features, including STFT Chromagram, CQT Chromagram, Spectral Centroid, Spectral Bandwidth, Spectral Roll Off, MFCC, Spectral Contrast, RMSE, MFCC, CENS Chromogram, Melspectogram, Tonnetz, Poly features, Tempogram, and Zero crossing rate, was extracted. Pink noise and brown noise have been added to the aforementioned dataset and the above mentioned 13 mean features was extracted for this dataset as well. The six proposed classification techniques—KNN Classifier, Gaussian Naive Bayes Classifier, Classification trees, Random Forest classifier, Logistic Regression, and SVM classifier—were then used to classify the data. Model validation is done after classification. Python has been used for

Content

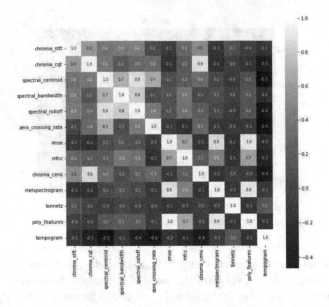

Fig. 5. Correlation heat map of 13 features

feature extraction, categorization, and validation. Both clean and noisy databases have undergone all of the aforementioned procedures (Tables 2 and 3).

Table 2. Train Accuracy in (%) for the 6 classifiers

Dataset	KNN	GNB	SVM	LR	RT	CT
Dataset 1	95	78	95.3	93	100	100
Dataset 2	93	76.5	88.2	87.3	100	100
Dataset 3	91	75	89	87	100	100
Dataset 4	95.3	79	95	92	100	100

Table 3. Test Accuracy in (%) for the 6 classifiers

Dataset	KNN	GNB	SVM	LR	RF	CT
Dataset 1	88	70	84	80	86	90
Dataset 2	81.4	68.5	80	78	78	80
Dataset 3	79	65	79	78	74	74
Dataset 4	86	70	82	78	88	90

The train and test accuracy of the model for the original dataset is shown in Fig. 6. From the train accuracies, we can observe that the Random Forest (RT) and Classification

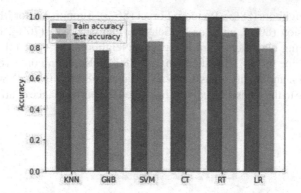

Fig. 6. Representation of train and test accuracy of Dataset 1

Tree (CT) classifiers performed the best, achieving perfect accuracy (100%), followed closely by the Support Vector Machine (SVM) and k-Nearest Neighbor (KNN) classifiers with accuracy above 90%. However, when evaluating the classifiers on the test set, we can observe that the Random Forest and Classification Tree classifiers still perform well with 90% accuracy, but the k-Nearest Neighbor and Support Vector Machine classifiers experience a drop in accuracy to 88% and 84%, respectively. The Gaussian Naive Bayes (GNB) and Logistic Regression (LR) classifiers, which had lower accuracy on the training set, also performed relatively poorly on the test set, with accuracies of 70% and 80%, respectively. In conclusion, while some classifiers may perform well on the training set, it is important to evaluate their performance on a separate test set to assess their generalization ability. Based on the test accuracies, the Random Forest and Classification Tree classifiers appear to be the best choices for this dataset.

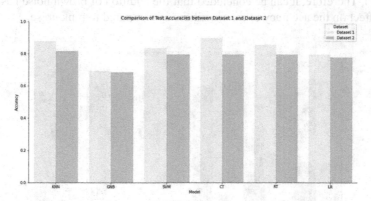

Fig. 7. Representation of comparison between test accuracy of Dataset 1 and Dataset 2

The test accuracy of the model for Dataset 1 and Dataset 2 is shown in Fig. 7. We observe that the test accuracies for all six classifiers are lower for Dataset 2 (the dataset with pink noise added to it) compared to Dataset 1 (the original dataset). For Dataset 1, the classifiers that performed the best were Classification Tree (90%), followed closely by K-Nearest Neighbors (88%), Random Forest (86%), Support Vector Machine (84%), Logistic Regression (80%), and finally Gaussian Naive Bayes (70%). For Dataset 2, the best performing classifiers were K-Nearest Neighbors (81.4%), followed by Support Vector Machine (80%), Classification Tree (80%), Random Forest (80%), Logistic Regression (78%), and finally Gaussian Naive Bayes (68.5%). Overall, we can see that adding pink noise to the dataset negatively impacted the performance of all six classifiers.

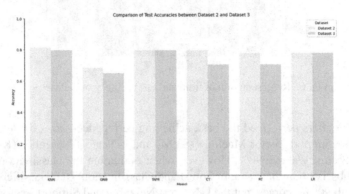

Fig. 8. Representation of comparison between test accuracy of Dataset 2 and Dataset 3

The test accuracy of the model for Dataset 2 and Dataset 3 is shown in Fig. 8. We can observe that the addition of brown noise to the dataset (Dataset 3) has negatively impacted the performance of the classifiers as compared to Dataset 2. The test accuracies of all the classifiers but Support Vector Machine (SVM) and Logistic Regression (LR) have decreased for Dataset 3, with the largest drop being observed for the Classification Trees (CT). Therefore, it can be concluded that the addition of brown noise has a more adverse effect on the accuracy of the classifiers as compared to pink noise.

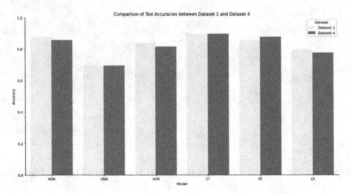

Fig. 9. Representation of comparison between test accuracy of Dataset 1 and Dataset 4

The test accuracy of the model for Dataset 1 and Dataset 4 is shown in Fig. 9. We can observe that the test accuracies of the six classifiers for dataset 4 are very similar to those of dataset 1. The only difference is that dataset 4 has 11 features, while dataset 1 has 13 features. This indicates that the two removed features, CQT chromogram and Poly, are highly correlated with the other features in the dataset, and are therefore redundant which can be observed in Fig. 5. In conclusion, we can say that even in the absence of CQT chromogram and Poly features from the original dataset, there is no significant loss in the performance of the classifiers, and the resulting dataset (dataset 4) is almost as good as the original dataset (dataset 1). This suggests that the two removed features do not provide any additional information for classification, and can be discarded.

6 Conclusion

In conclusion, our study analyzed the performance of six classifiers on four different datasets, each with its own unique characteristics. The results show that the Random Forest and Classification Tree classifiers consistently perform the best on both training and test sets, followed by the K-Nearest Neighbors and Support Vector Machine classifiers. The Gaussian Naive Bayes and Logistic Regression classifiers also show relatively good performance, although with lower accuracy scores. The addition of noise negatively impacts the performance of all classifiers, with brown noise having a more adverse effect compared to pink noise. Finally, we found that removing two highly correlated features from the original dataset does not significantly affect the performance of the classifiers, indicating that these features can be safely discarded without losing valuable information.

Our findings have important implications for the selection and evaluation of classifiers for similar classification tasks, and highlight the importance of carefully considering the characteristics of the dataset when choosing a suitable classifier.

References

1. Tsanas, A., Little, M., McSharry, P., Ramig, L.: Accurate telemonitoring of Parkinson's disease progression by noninvasivespeech tests. IEEE Trans. Bio-Med. Eng. (2009)
2. Tsanas, A., Little, M., Mcsharry, P.E., Ramig, L.: Robust parsimonious selection of dysphonia measures for telemonitoring of Parkinson's disease symptom severity. In: Seventh International Workshop on Models and Analysis of Vocal Emissions for Biomedical Applications MAVEBA (2011)
3. MohamedShreif, H.O., Lawgali, A.: Speech recognition for early detecting Alzheimer's disease by using machine learning algorithms. In: International Conference on Engineering and MIS (ICEMIS), pp. 1-6 (2022)
4. Fraser, K.C., Meltzer, J.A., Rudzicz, F.: Linguistic features identify alzheimer's disease in narrative speech. J. Alzheimer's Dis. **49**(2), 407–422 (2015)
5. UCI Machine Learning Repository. Parkinson's Disease Classification Dataset. https://archive.ics.uci.edu/ml/datasets/Parkinson%27s+Disease+Classification https://drive.google.com/drive/folders/1E-Bde8y_7nqU30TqHNSW17r5EY1CP8P9
6. Tsanas, A.: Acoustic analysis toolkit for biomedical speech signal processing: concepts and algorithms. Models Anal. Vocal Emissions Biomed. Appl. **2**, 37–40 (2013)
7. Cai, Z.N., Gu, J., Chen, H.: A new hybrid intelligent framework for predicting Parkinson's Disease. IEEE Access (2017)

8. Paul, S., Verma, J.K., Datta, A., Shaw, R.N., Saikia, A.: Deep learning and its importance for early signature of neuronal disorders. In: 2018 4th International Conference on Computing Communication and Automation (ICCCA) 2018, pp. 1–5. Greater Noida, India (2018). https://doi.org/10.1109/CCAA.2018.8777527

9. Benba, A., Jilbab, A., Hammouch, A.: Discriminating between patients with Parkinson's and neurological diseases using cepstral analysis. IEEE Trans. Neural Syst. Rehabil. Eng. **24**(10), 1100–1108 (2016)

10. Parisi, L., RaviChandran, N., Manaog, M.L.: Feature-driven machine learning to improve early diagnosis of Parkinson's disease. Expert Syst. Appl. **110**, 182–190 (2018)

11. Sakar, B., et al.: Collection and analysis of a Parkinson speech dataset with multiple types of sound recordings. IEEE J. Biomed. Health Inform. **17**(4), 828–834 2013

12. Mridha, K., et.al.: Deep learning algorithms are used to automatically detection invasive ducal carcinoma in whole slide images. In: 2021 IEEE 6th International Conference on Computing, Communication and Automation (ICCCA), pp. 123–129. Arad, Romania (2021). https://doi.org/10.1109/ICCCA52192.2021.9666302

13. Alhussein, M.: Monitoring Parkinson's disease in smart cities. IEEE Access **5**, 19835–19841 (2017)

14. Tsanas, A., Little, M.A., McSharry, P.E., Spielman, J., Ramig, L.O.: Novel speech signal processing algorithms for high-accuracy classification of Parkinson's disease. IEEE Trans. Biomed. Eng. **59**(5), 1264–1271 (2012)

15. Jiao, Y., Berisha, V., Liss, J., Hsu, S.C., Levy, E., McAuliffe, M.: Articulation entropy: an unsupervised measure of articulatory precision. IEEE Sign. Process. Lett. **24**(4), 485–489 (2016)

16. Orozco-Arroyave, J.R., et al.: Characterization methods for the detection of multiple voice disorders: neurological, functional, and laryngeal diseases. IEEE J. Biomed. Health Inform. **19**(6), 1820–1828 (2015)

Real-Time Drowsiness Detection System Using Machine Learning

Arnav Kotiyal[1], D. K. Santhosh Kumar[2], M. S. Guru Prasad[1]([✉]), S. R. Manjunath[3], S. Chandrappa[4], and B. P. Aniruddha Prabhu[5]

[1] Department of Computer Science and Engineering, Graphic Era (Deemed to be University), Dehradun, India
guru0927@gmail.com
[2] Department of Computer Science and Engineering, St Joseph Engineering College, Mangaluru, Karnataka, India
[3] School of Computing and Information Technology, Reva University, Bengaluru, India
manjunathsr.sr@reva.edu.in
[4] Department of Computer Science and Engineering, Jain (Deemed-to-be University), Bengaluru, India
[5] Department of Computer Science and Engineering, Graphic Era Hill University, Dehradun, India

Abstract. Road transport is an essential component of human endeavors and activities. On the highway, there are an uncountable number of drivers at all hours of the day and night. Lack of sleep is a problem for people who drive long distances, such as taxi drivers, bus drivers, truck drivers, and anyone who travels long distances by car. The driver's lack of alertness is to blame for a significant portion of the automobile collisions that take place every day. The experience of sleepiness lowers a driver's level of alertness, which heightens the risk of being involved in an accident and makes driving more difficult. In this context, the utilization of new technologies in the design and construction of systems that are able to monitor drivers and to assess the amount of concentration that they are giving to the task of driving during the entirety of the driving process is essential. Therefore, in order to stop these incidents from happening, we are going to design a system with Python, OpenCV, and Keras that will notify the driver if he begins to feel tired. The proposed work goal is to develop a sleepiness detection system that can identify when a person's eyelids are closed for a few seconds at a time. When it determines that the driver is becoming sleepy, this system will sound an alarm. During the course of this work, we will be making use of OpenCV to collect the pictures that are captured by the camera. These images will then be fed into a Deep Learning model, which will determine if the person's eyes are "open" or "closed."

Keywords: Drowsiness Detection System · Machine Learning · Deep Learning · OpenCV · Keras · Convolution Neural Network

R. N. Shaw et al. (Eds.): ICACIS 2023, CCIS 1920, pp. 49–58, 2023.
https://doi.org/10.1007/978-3-031-45121-8_5

1 Introduction

Non-invasive techniques include monitoring the driver's steering wheel motions, accelerator and brake patterns, and physiological feature–based approaches, which are more intrusive in nature, can be used to identify sleepiness, weariness, and exhaustion in the driver [1]. The non-intrusive nature of visual feature-based techniques has made them increasingly popular in recent years. While driving, the eye patterns of the vehicle's occupants can be used to identify drivers who are drowsy [2]. The goal of this machine learning research is to develop a sleepiness detection system that can detect when someone's eyes are closed for a few seconds. When sleepiness is detected, this system will sound an alarm for the driver [3].

Our work suggests a model that is both more accurate and quicker than the models that have been used in the past. Python possesses a highly powerful module for deep learning called TensorFlow [4]. This module is responsible for running deep learning neural convolutional networks for digit (which are handwritten) classification, picture pre-processing and recognition, and sequential models for translation [5]. This model makes use of a package called OpenCV in order to do image processing in real time [6]. Loading, displaying, and analyzing the data has also been accomplished with the assistance of a wide variety of additional libraries, such as NumPy and Pandas [7]. Keras is one of the libraries that is utilised in the coding of deep learning models, and this model makes use of it as well [8]. TensorFlow is used at the application's back end. The CNN classifier may be utilised to make an accurate prediction regarding the state of the eye or to compute the region of closure [9]. While we are providing the model with our pictures, we will need to conduct certain operations on the images since the model requires them to be in a particular dimension before it can begin [10]. After that, we compute a score value that will be used to determine the length of time that the individual has been keeping his eyes closed [11]. The score value is set to a high number if both eyes are closed for multiple consecutive frames, while the score value is set to a low number if both eyes are open for multiple consecutive frames. If the score's value is higher than the threshold, an alarm will be given to the driver [12].

A lot of the things that are needed for a full diagnosis of the eye condition are in the work that is being proposed [13]. This project draws its inspiration from aspects of people's day-to-day lives that are typically seen as having the least significance. Drowsy driving is responsible for approximately 40% of all traffic accidents [14]. Road accidents result in significant losses, not only to human life but also to the economy of the nation [15]. One of the factors that might contribute to drowsiness in a driver when they are travelling by car is not getting enough rest while travelling for an extended period of time. When you're tired while driving, you might not be able to drive as well, you might take longer to react, and you might be more likely to get into an accident [16].

Real-time processing of an incoming video stream is conducted in order to infer the amount of weariness that the driver is experiencing [17]. This processing is based on the capture of footage from the camera that is in front of the driver [18]. An alarm is triggered to inform the driver whenever the eye state is recognized as being closed for longer than a predetermined amount of time [19]. This is a new and creative idea in the car business that makes it possible for drivers to be careful when they are on the road.

2 Literature Survey

Alshaqaqi B, et al. [1] illustrated that an Advanced Driver Assistance System (ADAS) is a technology that uses visual information and artificial intelligence to identify when a driver is becoming drowsy, with the goal of reducing accidents caused by fatigued drivers. PerCLOS, a scientifically accepted measure of tiredness linked with sluggish eye closure, has been presented as an algorithm to find, monitor, and evaluate the face and eyes of the driver. Using a little camera, this device can assess the current mental state of the driver during the course of a typical day. Skin colour information is used to identify a person's face, and eyes are detected by looking for symmetry. Using the Hough Transform for Circles, one may identify the condition of the eye.

Deng W et al. [2] suggested a system called DriCare, which uses video pictures to identify the tiredness condition of drivers, such as yawning, blinking, and the length of eye closure. DriCare uses a tiredness signal by integrating the characteristics of the eyes and lips. DriCare's accuracy was tested and found to be about 92%. According to DriCare, blinking frequency, eye closure length, and yawning are all indicators of driver tiredness. DriCare will notify the driver of sleepiness if the readings exceed the threshold. The video feed from the car's camera takes the driver's portrait while the vehicle is in motion and immediately uploads it to the cloud server. After that, the video is analysed by the cloud server to determine the level of fatigue of the driver. Face tracking, facial key area identification, and driver weariness are all examined in this phase. We employ the MC-KCF algorithm to track the driver's face and identify facial key areas based on key-point detection in order to fulfil the system's real-time performance requirements. Next, the cloud server calculates the driver's current condition based on changes in the driver's eyes and lips. The driver's tiredness level is measured by DriCare using a non-contact approach. Multiple Convolutional Neural Networks (CNN)-KCF (MC-KCF) is a novel face-tracking method that improves on KCF.Lin C. Y et al. [3] explained that machine learning and gradient statistics are used to identify driver sleepiness. Modes for detecting whether or not the driver is wearing spectacles are included in the proposed eye detection algorithm for eye location. The technology will sound an alarm to alert the driver if it detects the motorist shutting his eyes or nodding for an extended period of time. The camera captures the pictures that are being sent into the system. The method relies on black-and-white photographs devoid of any colour data. Before any further processing, the picture is initially down-scaled to a 1/4 image scale. Next is filtering on both horizontal and vertical axes. A Haar-Adaboost-based face detection algorithm uses an integral picture calculated at this point to speed up the next step of face identification. The suggested system utilises the Haar-Adaboost facial detection method. As long as the glasses aren't being detected, either the procedure without glasses or one that is being used while wearing glasses is operational.

Sathasivam S et al. [4] using the Eye Aspect Ratio (EAR) approach, an image detection drowsiness system was presented to identify the condition of the automobile driver. The system's job is to determine the EAR value by identifying the location of the eyes in photos. This approach assigns six (x, y) coordinates to each eye in the landmarks supplied by the Dlib predictor function for labelling purposes. Beginning at the left-most corner of the focus, the labelling proceeds in a clockwise direction around the remainder of the area. When it comes to certain coordinates, there is a correlation between their distance. Therefore, the attention ratio, also referred to by its acronym, Eye Aspect Ratio, is derived (EAR). The experiment was a success, with an accuracy rate of 90%. Drivers' awareness of their surroundings might skyrocket in an instance like this. But there is still a lot of room for improvement in performance. The next round of research will concentrate on identifying driver distractions, such as yawning. Other than that, sensors, such as a liquor sensor and a pulse sensor, can be used to identify the driver's alcohol level and heartbeat rate.

Park S et al. [5] presented a new technology for detecting sleepiness in drivers and alerting them through an alarm. Eye and lip movements are used to construct a major DDS in the proposed system. The system's ratio algorithm is straightforward and easy to understand. We utilise a camera in order to extract the eye-lip area and calculate the eye-lip aspect ratio. A simple dialogue with the driver may be had using the included ChatBot. An SMS is sent to the driver's family members or a phone number specified by the driver after three successive detections. When a motorist becomes drowsy, the system's performance is swift enough to catch it right away. Only a camera is used to monitor the system, which does not employ any dangerous radiation sensors. Because the camera can project in a wide angle, the video functions of the system don't require the driver to stay in one place for as long.

Shah, D. et al. [3] implemented SVM, Decision Tree, Nave Bayes, and Random Forest algoritms in their work. These include deep neural networks and artificial intelligence (AI). The Weka Data Mining Tool is used to create this model. Clustering, classification, regression, visualisation, and feature selection are among the usual data mining activities that may be performed using the programme. It makes it simple to import data in the form of files, URLs, or databases. Computer-Structured Query Language (CSV). In the confusion matrix, true positive, accuracy, recall, and false negative are all analysed and shown in an easy-to-understand fashion. Each model has been analysed for its performance in terms of precision, recall, ROC (Receiver Operating Characteristic), and percent accuracy. Table IV displays the models' correctness in terms of performance. A ROC value of less than 0.80 is typically regarded as "GOOD," whereas a ROC value of less than 0.77 is seen as "FAIR." The model with the ROC value closest to 1 is regarded to be the most accurate.

Gavhane A et al. [4] proposed the decision tree and Ada-Boost algorithm model. Examples, diverse algorithms, and techniques for evaluation are some of the elements employed in a given piece of work. Using this strategy, you'll be taught by a teacher. For illness datasets and medical characteristics, the Kaggle warehouse is used. A person's risk of developing heart disease may be estimated using this collection of data. Training and testing sets are further subdivided. Attributes of the dataset utilised in this proposed research are 14. If "target," an independent variable, is correctly predicted, then a person is healthy or has heart disease.

3   Materials and Methods

This section is related to the materials and methods that were utilized in this research to accomplish the gesture recognition that this article is intended for. The materials can be broken down into two categories: raw data and processed data [20]. The dataset as well as any and all information pertinent to the subject matter is discussed in Sect. 3.1. In Sect. 3.2, we talk about how we approached the problem and the methods and strategies we used.

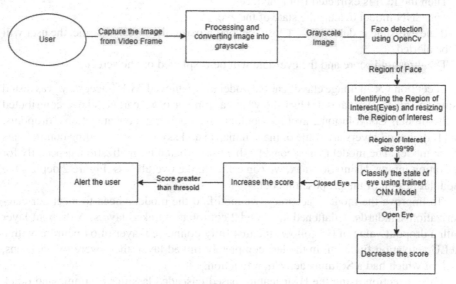

Fig. 1. Proposed Model

3.1 Datasets

We used data from the MRL, which included eye scans from 37 different people. These grayscale datasets were of varied sizes. Open-and closed-eye datasets were further subdivided. The images in these two groups totaled about 40 thousand. The test datasets represented 2% of the total datasets. Validation and training datasets were created from the remaining datasets. After all was said and done, the average image size was found to be 99 * 99. Data sets were replicated using ImageDataGenerator but the angle of rotation and sheering sizes were recalculated. The model was given a batch size of six in order to prevent it from crashing.

3.2 Proposed Model

The proposed model is as shown in Fig. 1. Firstly, the image is captured from the video. From the captured image, the face is detected before detecting the Region of Interest (ROI) from the image. We then extract the ROI from the image using CNN and classify the state of the eye. If the user's "eye" is closed for longer than the threshold time, the user will be notified.

The user will have to enter the required values, which will be taken as input. The data from the input is then retrieved which will be used for classification of the result.

The workflow of the proposed model is as follows:

- The System captures the image from the video feed.
- The face is detected from the captured image.
- Then the ROI is extracted from the face.
- The CNN model detects the state of the eye.
- If the eye-state is detected as 'Close' beyond a particular threshold time, the user will be alerted.
- The threshold score and the eye state will be displayed on the screen.

Inception v3, an image classification model that achieved 78.1% accuracy, was tested using an Image-Net dataset. Over the years, a number of researchers have contributed to the model. Convolutions, average pooling, max pooling, concatenations, dropouts, and fully linked layers are some of the symmetric and asymmetric building components of the model. The model makes considerable use of batch normalization, especially for activation inputs. Using Softmax, we can estimate the overall loss. Figure 2 depicts the modular design of the proposed model.

To improve the model's accuracy, we modified the model's head to meet our categorization standards. 1 flattened layer and 2 completely linked layers. A dropout layer with a dropout value of 0.3 follows the first fully connected layer of 64 neurons with a ReLU activation function. In the last completely linked layer, there were two neurons, each of which had a Softmax activation function.

Face detection using the Haar feature-based cascade classifier is simple and quick with good results. To train the cascade function, a large number of positive and negative images are used. Face detection may then be applied to other photos. They resemble our convolutional kernel in every way possible. It's possible to get a single value for each feature by dividing by the number of pixels beneath a white rectangle. Non-face regions occupy the majority of an image. A straightforward way of determining whether or not a window is part of the face region would be preferable. If it's not, toss it out and don't bother processing it any further. As an alternative, concentrate on areas where a face can be found.

4   Results and Discussion

Figure 3 shows the page the user will be redirected to once he clicks on the URL of the product. Here he can purchase the product by clicking on the 'Subscribe Now' button, which will redirect him to the payment gateway API. Once the payment is completed, the product will be downloaded onto his system in executable format. Figure 4 depicts the categorization of eye states; for example, when the model detects the eye to be in an open state, it will indicate this with a green box around the ROI (eye), but when it detects the eye to be in a closed condition, it will indicate this with a red box around the ROI (eye). If the eye is identified as being closed for longer than a predetermined amount of time, an alarm will sound to warn the driver.

The following are the results obtained using machine learning algorithms like SVM, Random Forest, KNN, and Deep Learning Algorithms like CNN. The proposed model predicts the accuracy as well as gives the graphical representation of the algorithms

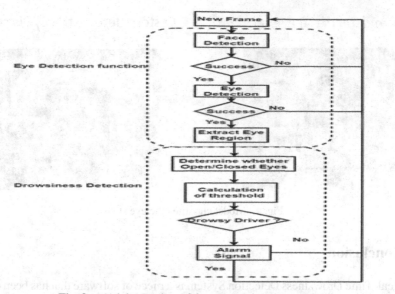

Fig. 2. Modular Design of the proposed system work

Fig. 3. Home page of the proposed system

for a given ratio of test and training data so that comparison can be done and the best algorithm can be obtained for the heart disease dataset.

System detects the Eye is Open   **System detects the Eye is closed**

Fig. 4. Model classifies the eye state

5 Conclusion

The Real-Time Drowsiness Detection System is a piece of software that has been created with the intention of contributing to the betterment of society. The construction of this system will be done primarily with the goal of enhancing the movement of automobiles via roadways because this sector plays a significant part in the overall growth of our nation. In the process of building the architecture and the use case for this product, one of the primary considerations was to develop a real-time detection model that can determine whether or not the driver is experiencing drowsiness while they are travelling on the road. Due to the fact that they offer drivers an extra source of assistance in maintaining a risk-free commute, cameras have evolved into an essential component of today's automobiles in the modern day. In light of this information, we have adopted a straightforward strategy for determining the level of exhaustion experienced by the driver throughout the course of a road trip.Our goal in developing this project was to make long-distance driving a pleasure for both the driver and the passengers, as stated in the summary. An eye model that distinguishes the open and closed states of the eye has been built for this purpose. By providing an Enterprise edition, the programme may be further scaled up and deployed as a large-scale commercial solution. To train and categorise the models, a lot of computational power is needed. If the user's system is weak, this can be mitigated by maintaining the model in the backend. For offline use, the user can select models that have been particularly optimised for this purpose. There are some eye movements that are difficult for the model to record and identify, thus it is preferable if the model can deliver a high level of accuracy with fewer photos.

There are plans to add further functionality, such as detecting the yawning of the driver, if extra resources and funds are available. The driver's sleepiness may be accurately measured using exterior elements such as steering wheel motions, tyre movements, and the vehicle's traction control.

References

1. Alshaqaqi, B., Baquhaizel, A.S., Ouis, M.E.A., Boumehed, M., Ouamri, A., Keche, M.: Vision based system for driver drowsiness detection. In: 2013 11th International Symposium on Programming and Systems (ISPS), pp. 103–108. IEEE (2013)
2. Deng, W., Wu, R.: Real-time driver-drowsiness detection system using facial features. IEEE Access **7**, 118727–118738 (2019)
3. Lin, C.Y., Chang, P., Wang, A., Fan, C.P.: Machine learning and gradient statistics based real-time driver drowsiness detection. In: 2018 IEEE International Conference on Consumer Electronics-Taiwan (ICCE-TW), pp. 1–2. IEEE (2018)
4. Sathasivam, S., Saon, S., Sidek, A., Som, M. M., Ameen, H.A.: Drowsiness detection system using eye aspect ratio technique. In: 2020 IEEE Student Conference on Research and Development (SCOReD), pp. 448–452. IEEE (2020)
5. Park, S., Pan, F., Kang, S., Yoo, C.D.: Driver drowsiness detection system based on feature representation learning using various deep networks. In: Chen, C.-S., Lu, J., Ma, K.-K. (eds.) ACCV 2016. LNCS, vol. 10118, pp. 154–164. Springer, Cham (2017). https://doi.org/10.1007/978-3-319-54526-4_12
6. Praveen Gujjar, J., Prasanna Kumar, H.R., Guru Prasad, M.S.: Advanced NLP frame-work for text processing. In: 2023 6th International Conference on Information Systems and Computer Networks (ISCON), pp. 1–3. Mathura, India (2023). https://doi.org/10.1109/ISCON57294.2023.10112058
7. Guru, P.M.S., Praveen, G.J., Dodmane, R., Sardar, T.H., Ashwitha, A., Yeole, A.N.: Brain tumor identification and classification using a novel extraction method based on adapted alexnet architecture. In: 2023 6th International Conference on Information Systems and Computer Networks (ISCON), pp. 1–5. Mathura, India (2023). https://doi.org/10.1109/ISCON5 7294.2023.10112075
8. Kumar, M.A., Pai, A.H., Agarwal, J., Christa, S., Prasad, G.M.S., Saifi, S.: Deep Learning model to defend against covert channel attacks in the SDN networks. In: 2023 Advanced Computing and Communication Technologies for High Performance Applications (ACC-THPA), Ernakulam, India, pp. 1–5 (2023). https://doi.org/10.1109/ACCTHPA57160.2023.10083336
9. Kirubasri, G., Sankar, S., Guru Prasad, M.S., et al.: LQETA-RP: link quality based energy and trust aware routing protocol for wireless multimedia sensor networks. Int. J. Syst. Assur. Eng. Manag. (2023). https://doi.org/10.1007/s13198-023-01873-9
10. Guru Prasad, M.S., Naveen Kumar, H.N., Raju, K., et al.: Glaucoma detection using clustering and segmentation of the optic disc region from retinal fundus images. SN Comput. Sci. **4**, 192 (2023). https://doi.org/10.1007/s42979-022-01592-1
11. Kumar, H.N.N., Kumar, S.A., Prasad, G.M.S., Shah, M.A.: Automatic facial expression recognition combining texture and shape features from prominent facial regions. IET Image Process. **17**, 1111–1125 (2023). https://doi.org/10.1049/ipr2.12700
12. Guru Prasad, M.S., Agarwal, J., Christa, S., Aditya Pai, H., Kumar, M.A., Kukreti, A.: An Improved Water Body Segmentation from Satellite Images using MSAA-Net. In: 2023 International Conference on Machine Intelligence for GeoAnalytics and Remote Sensing (MIGARS), pp. 1–4. Hyderabad, India (2023). https://doi.org/10.1109/MIGARS57353.2023.10064508
13. Chandrappa, S., Guruprasad, M.S., Kumar, H.N.N., et al.: An IOT-based automotive and intelligent toll gate using RFID. SN Comput. Sci. **4**, 154 (2023). https://doi.org/10.1007/s42979-022-01569-0

14. Gautam, J., Atrey, M., Malsa, N., Balyan, A., Shaw, R.N., Ghosh, A.: Twitter data senti-ment analysis using naive bayes classifier and generation of heat map for analyzing intensity geographically. In: Bansal, J.C., Fung, L.C.C., Simic, M., Ghosh, A. (eds.) Advances in Applications of Data-Driven Computing. AISC, vol. 1319, pp. 129–139. Springer, Singapore (2021). https://doi.org/10.1007/978-981-33-6919-1_10

15. Kumar, M.A., Abirami, N., Prasad, M.G., Mohankumar, M.: Stroke disease prediction based on ECG signals using deep learning techniques. In: 2022 International Conference on Com-putational Intelligence and Sustainable Engineering Solutions (CISES), pp. 453–458. Greater Noida, India (2022). https://doi.org/10.1109/CISES54857.2022.9844403

16. Mandal, S., et.al.: Lyft 3D object detection for autonomous vehicles. In: Artificial Intelligence for Future Generation Robotics, pp. 119–136. Elsevier (2021). ISBN 9780323854986, https://doi.org/10.1016/B978-0-323-85498-6.00003-4

17. Prasad, M.S.G., Pratap, M.S., Jain, P., Gujjar, J.P., Kumar, M.A., Kukreti, A.: RDI-SD: an efficient rice disease identification based on apache spark and deep learning technique. In: 2022 International Conference on Artificial Intelligence and Data Engineering (AIDE), pp. 277–282. Karkala, India (2022). https://doi.org/10.1109/AIDE57180.2022.10060157

18. Pai, A., Anandkumar, M., Prasad, G., Agarwal, J., Christa, S.: Designing a secure audio/text based captcha using neural network. In: 2023 13th International Conference on Cloud Com-puting, Data Science & Engineering (Confluence), pp. 510–514. Noida, India (2023). https://doi.org/10.1109/Confluence56041.2023.10048791

19. Agarwal, J., Christa, S., Pai, A., Kumar, M.A., Prasad, G.: Machine learning application for news text classification. In: 2023 13th International Conference on Cloud Computing, Data Science & Engineering (Confluence), pp. 463–466. Noida, India (2023). https://doi.org/10.1109/Confluence56041.2023.10048856

20. Patel, V., Guru Prasad, M.S., Aditya Pai, H., Kumar, A.S., Praveen Gujjar, J., Naveen Kumar, H.N.: Real-time face mask detector. In: 2023 IEEE 3rd International Conference on Technol-ogy, Engineering, Management for Societal impact using Marketing, Entrepreneurship and Talent (TEMSMET), pp. 1–5. Mysuru, India (2023). https://doi.org/10.1109/TEMSMET56 707.2023.10150182

Hate Speech Detection in Multi-social Media Using Deep Learning

Ashwini Kumar(✉) [ID] and Santosh Kumar

Graphic Era Deemed to be University, Dehradun, Uttarakhand, India
ashwinipaul@gmail.com

Abstract. In recent days lots of advancements on the Internet and various social media such as Facebook, Twitter, Gab, Reddit, YouTube, Stromfornt, etc., many people continue to use multiple online social media platforms to express their views or comments and sometimes post Hate Speech or Offensive Language. It is challenging to detect hate speech manually, especially from social media data. A robust mechanism is essential to handle this issue, which will automatically detect hate speech on social networks. Many researchers have addressed this issue through many means. However, most methods are not accurate enough in detecting hate speech because of the massive volume of data, data dependencies, excessive parameters, and the use of only homogeneous social media data. To resolve this issue, we have Investigated a cross-platform hate speech recognition mechanism for Social Media Interactions and developed a Deep Neural Network (DNN) approach to tackle heterogeneous multi-social media data as a generic platform. This paper proposes a model for hate speech detection based on Deep Learning architecture. This model comprises multiple Deep neural networks combining Bidirectional-Long Short-Term Memory (LSTM) and Convolutional Neural Networks (CNN) to produce the best performance on numerous social media datasets of 0.2 million (202377) annotated Tweets or comments. And also, the performance of the BiLSTM-CNN model has been analyzed, measured, and compared with existing classical machine learning methods. Our model is trained using ten epochs to split the dataset, 80% for training and 20% as validation data. Our proposed model's performance is evaluated using the precision, recall, and accuracy parameters. Finally, we compared the performance of our model with many machine learning methods such as Decision Trees, Support Vector Machine (SVM) Linear, Logistic Regression, and Naive Bayes methods. It is evident from the result that our proposed model achieved an accuracy of 92.5%, and the F1-score value is 92.1% in the detection of hate speech. Overall, the proposed model outperforms other state-of-art methods.

Keywords: Hate Speech · CNN · LSTM · Deep Learning · social media

1 Introduction

The number of Internet users and various social media's increasing very fast. People are sharing their views or comments through these mediums. Hate speech used by people in their opinions is very challenging to handle by these media or other agencies. This

R. N. Shaw et al. (Eds.): ICACIS 2023, CCIS 1920, pp. 59–70, 2023.
https://doi.org/10.1007/978-3-031-45121-8_6

utterance consists of abusive speech or comments in text, oral, or both. The term used "abusive", "hate speech", or "harmful speech" is called uncontrolled messages that target individuals or a particular society based on several characteristics such as religion, gender, country, color, organization, etc. Social media like YouTube, Twitter, Facebook, Instagram, Gab, Reddit, Stormfront, etc., continuously monitor and develop several methodologies to tackle this issue [11]. To do this, billions of dollars these organizations spent every year on its solution, including manpower. However, they manually identify and delete the online content of offensive materials. This process is time-consuming, manpower, and non-sustainable. In the last few years, emerging areas like Machine learning (ML) and Natural Language Processing (NLP) communities have been doing lots of research to identify an automated way to detect hate speech. In [12, 20], research has been done using NLP and ML with Deep Learning (DL) methods to detect online hate speech.

Recent work explored logistic regression and Support Vector Machine on character n-grams or words [7, 9] to perform better results against other baseline methods. The authors of [6] train datasets with an SVMLINEAR classifier as hate speech or offensive, and the feature of the character n-grams model does not achieve the best performance. However, the skip grams capture long-distance dependencies. In all the research papers we have read so far, mostly only one or two data sets of social media have been taken, and, on their basis, they design the model and measure its performance. When we check the performance of their model on any other social media, good results are not found there because the model which has been designed is done with the help of a homogenous dataset.

In the present paper, we focus on the problems associated with detecting hate speech classifying it as English Tweets annotated with two categories: 1). Hate Speech, 2). Neither. Most of the earlier work has been used as a supervised document classification task relies on manual feature extraction or any learning methods are compared several classifiers similar to Support Vector Machine (SVM), Naive Bayes (NB), Logistic Regression with L2 regularization, and Decision Trees, etc. [15, 20, 28]. However, the direction of learning methods is changing with deep learning models used to train classifiers and feature extraction. These new models involve deep learning architectures such as Long Short-Term Memory Networks (LSTM), Convolutional Neural Networks, Gated Recurrent Unit Networks, FastText, and Recurrent Neural Networks (RNN), etc., to give better performance in hate speech detection [13, 17]. However, one primary reason is the need for publicly labelled heterogeneous datasets or the ineffectiveness of improving generalized attributes.

Our proposed methodology is a BiLSTM-CNN model by adding pooling and dropout layers to enhance the performance of classifying hate speech. Our novel approach uses a BiLSTM Deep Neural Network suitable for capturing long-range dependencies in modelling sequence-based data such as sentiment analysis, textual data, etc. Along with a more effective Convolutional Neural Network to extract features from a combination of words or characters. This BiLSTM Deep Neural Network is more efficient, in which a sequence of words can read in Bi-directional mode, i.e., the given tweets or sequences of data can read in forward and backward mode. Therefore, the BiLSTM neural network will perform better in our proposed model. At last, we also have compared the better performance of our proposed model against classic machine learning methods.

The following significant contributions made by us in the paper to detect hate speech on multi-social media are as follows:

1. We Investigate cross-platform hate speech recognition for Social Media Interactions and develop a DNN approach to tackle heterogeneous multi-social media data as a generic platform.
2. We investigate BiLSTM-CNN neural network architecture for this task, in which BiLSTM used their gate signals to process a sequence of words from Bi-directional mode, i.e., Forward and Backward LSTM, to apprehend long dependencies in texts to make better performance.
3. We explore a novel Deep Learning (DL) neural network approach for detecting Hate Speech.
4. Our model has outperformed results against the classic baseline methods on benchmark heterogeneous multi-social media datasets in terms of recall, precision, and F1 score values.

In Sect. 1, we have discussed the introduction; the rest of the paper is organized as In Sect. 2 relevant work on the detection of hate speech; Sect. 3 describes our benchmark heterogeneous dataset and methodology used in our work; Sect. 4 introduces the BiLSTM-CNN model; Sect. 5 discuss our experiment results along with all comparative models; finally, Sect. 6 include the conclusion of this paper.

2   Related Work

We have included works focused on detecting hate speech using classic and deep learning approaches. In addition, several works have been published on hate speech detection on social networking platforms in the past few years.

In [11], authors discussed tasks based on Supervised Learning methods and generic features for hate speech detection. There are many works focused on the detection of the involvement of people in sharing hate speech and their bullying roles. The author also discussed supervised learning approaches for hate speech detection. As a classification method, mostly support vector machine is used. Some researchers also used relatively contemporary techniques like Deep Learning with Neural networks. The author discussed the challenging task of data and annotation. Any experiment performed on hate speech detection requires a labelled corpus. Although many authors usually collect their data. No one has a standard corpus for hate speech. The authors of [21] applied sentiment analysis, which was performed to detect bullying and to identify teasing posts using Latent Dirichlet Allocation [2] topic models. The authors of [3–5] have applied a binary classifier to classify tweets as hate speech vs neither, along with word embeddings. Most researchers have used different algorithms for classification purposes, including Support Vector Machine [6], Logistic Regression with L2 regularization [7, 9], etc.

The authors of [7] collected 25K tweets and labelled each tweet as hate speech, offensive, or neither by using manually coded by Crowd Flower workers and extracted features such as bigrams, unigrams, and trigrams. To capture syntactic structure using

NLTK [8], construct some tweet-level meta-information, including part-of-speech (POS) labelling, retweets, URLs, and counts of hashtags. They applied logistic regression with L1 and L2 regularization, performed well at this task, and performed all modelling using the machine learning toolkit sci-kit-learn. The authors of [6] proposed a system that used a linear Support Vector Machine classifier with two categories of feature extraction (Character n-grams and Surface n-grams) and obtained, as a result, by character 4-g feature to achieve 78% accuracy. They focused on the character n-grams to discriminate hate speech from generic profanity on social network platforms. In other attempts in Deep Learning models, the authors of [10] proposed a combining CNN+LSTM neural network model by adding dropout and global max pooling layers to extract word embeddings and trained binary classifier via SoftMax to discriminate between hate and non-hate on the Davidson dataset [7]. To improve accuracy, they used bi-directional LSTM as a one-layer with a 100-dimensional Glove model.

In the context of related work, the authors have proposed several methods. Still, most of the proposed methods are not accurate enough because of the use of only homogeneous social media. We will collect data from multi-social media platforms. We will Investigate cross-platform hate speech recognition for Social Media Interactions and develop a DNN approach to tackle heterogeneous multi-social media data as a generic platform. To learn the representation of deep learning features from input samples and pass them into stack layers to classify hate speech. In classic methods, encoding input components is only sometimes used for classification [4, 12, and 21]. For better representation of feature extraction to improve performance from learning, deep learning approaches shift their attention from manually designed features to automatically extracted features in given input samples.

3   Methodology

This section discusses the dataset and procedure of pre-processing used for our analysis and experiment works. The introduction of the background of LSTM Neural Networks is discussed in Sect. 3.1. The annotated dataset provided by authors from multi-social media platforms (e.g., Twitter, Facebook, YouTube, Gab, and Reddit) and used in our model are shown in Table 1. The dataset contains approximately 0.2 million tweets. Each annotated tweet is categorized into two different classes shown in Table 2.

Now, pre-processing in our given annotated tweets to convert them into Standard format as follows:

- Replace Twitter Users like "@John" to identifier " <Twitter user>".
- Remove characters such as |,; & ! ? \
- We convert hashtags into normal words, so #norefugees to no refugees.
- Convert all tweets to lowercase and lemmatization.
- Remove URLs, numbers, and emotions.

3.1   Long Short-Term Memory Neural Network Architecture

The background of the LSTM Neural Network is discussed. This model plays a vital role in the detection of hate speech. This feed-forward RNN was initially introduced by Hochreiter & Schmidhuber [1].

Table 1. Available Multi Social Media Hate Speech corpora

Social Media	Dataset	#Tweets
Twitter	Davidson et al. [7]	24783
	Thomas et al. [23]	7005
	Zampieri et al. [19]	13240
	Ousidhoum et al. [23]	5647
	Golbeck et al. [24]	20360
	Founta et al. [12]	45407
Facebook/YouTube	Chung et al. [25]	20186
	Salminen et al. [17]	3222
Gab	Kennedy et al. [26]	22527
Reddit	Kurrek et al. [27]	40000
Total Tweets from Multi Social Media		**202377**

Table 2. Statistics of Hate Speech dataset

Class	Tweets
Hate	113651
Neither	88726
Total	**202377**

This is capable of learning-wise range dependencies in textual data or Tweets explicitly. This LSTM Network is applicable in various sequence-based operations such as Image Caption, speech recognition, handwriting recognition, sentiment analysis, machine translation, and anomaly detection in network traffic.

A standard LSTM unit takes any specified set of inputs, the current word $x^{<t>}$ in our input, the previous word of activation is $a^{<t-1>}$, and the old cell state $c^{<t-1>}$ is the earlier time step. The cell state stores the current information in the memory after the earlier time step $c^{<t-1>}$. The LSTM network is depicted in Fig. 1 and the Notation and symbols used in LSTM architecture are listed in Table 3.

The LSTM has three gate signals to conserve and manage the cell state. The initial step is determining what information we pass from the cell state as relevant for the input sample. This decision is made by $f^{<t>}$ in Eq. 1.

$$f^{<t>} = \sigma(w_f[a^{<t-1>}, x^{<t>}] + b_f) \tag{1}$$

After that, to decide which LSTM unit processes new information items to store in the cell state. Initially, we have to update gate signals $u^{<t>}$ in Eq. 2, decide which value will update and create present candidate $c^{\sim<t>}$ value that could be incorporated into the

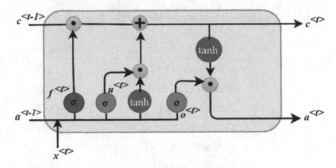

Fig. 1. Architecture of LSTM Neural Networks [1]

Table 3. Notation used in the LSTM architecture.

Notation	Meaning
f <t>	Forget Gate
u <t>	Update Gate
o <t>	Output Gate
w	Weights
b	Bias
tanh	Activation function $[-1, +1]$
σ	Sigmoid activation function $[0, 1]$

state using the tanh activation function in Eq. 3.

$$u^{<t>} = \sigma(w_u[a^{<t-1>}, x^{<t>}] + b_u) \tag{2}$$

$$c^{\sim<t>} = tanh(w_c[a^{<t-1>}, x^{<t>}] + b_c) \tag{3}$$

Now, update the information of the previous cell state $c^{<t-1>}$ over a newly added cell state $c^{<t>}$. The candidate $c^{<t>}$ in Eq. 4.

$$c^{<t>} = f^{<t>} * c^{<t-1>} + u^{<t>} * c^{\sim<t>} \tag{4}$$

Finally, we must decide on the output of the LSTM units based on our cell state $c^{<t>}$. The output gate signals $o^{<t>}$ is computed in Eq. 5.

$$o^{<t>} = \sigma(w_o[a^{<t-1>}, x^{<t>}] + b_o) \tag{5}$$

An output activation $a^{<t>}$ is computed for the current word in Eq. 6.

$$a^{<t>} = o^{<t>} * tanh(c^{<t>}) \tag{6}$$

We have used Bi-directional LSTM to utilize the feature of three gated signals $(f^{<t>}, u^{<t>}, o^{<t>})$ in the proposed abusive language detection method.

4 Experimental Evaluation

4.1 BiLSTM-CNN Model Architecture

The BiLSTM-CNN neural network is depicted in Fig. 2. We used Glove 6B 200D word embeddings [16] as a matrix in the first layer of our detection model. This matrix is a sequence of 200-dimensional embedding vectors. One drop-out layer was added after the embedding layer with the value of 0.2, the role of which is to drop rows of the matrix or avoid overfitting. The output feds into a Bidirectional LSTM layer of size 128 to capture long-range dependencies from both sides. Again, the output vector is fed with a 1-Dimensional Convolutional layer over 64 output filters, and the window size is 4. The output vector is the same as the input vector with the activation function *Rectified Linear Unit* [14]. This convolutional layer is fed by a 1-Dimensional Global Max Pooling layer that emerges to "flatten" in the form of a 1-Dimensional Array, producing 1×64 output vectors further fed into a dense layer of dimension 1×24.

Finally, the last dense Layer with two sigmoid units is to predict probability depending on the task. We have used an optimizer called Adam with 0.001 as a learning rate. The loss function is cross entropy to train our model using ten epochs. This architecture is compelling to squeeze the best performance in our benchmark dataset. In Table 4, we also show each Layer having output shape and parameter details of the BiLSTM-CNN model.

Table 4. Details of BiLSTM-CNN Model

Layer (type)	Output Shape	Param#
Embedding (Embedding) 200 D	(None, 120, 200)	21280800
dropout (Dropout)	(None, 120, 200)	0
Bidirectional (Bidirectional LSTM)	(None, 120, 128)	135680
conv1d (Conv1D)	(None, 117, 128)	65664
global_max_pooling1d(Global)	(None, 128)	0
dense (Dense)	(None, 24)	3096
dense_1 (Dense)	(None, 1)	25

Total params: 21,485,265
Trainable params: 21,485,265
Non-trainable params: 0

We evaluate our method with the heterogeneous social media dataset. The annotated tweets classification is shown in Table 5. We train our model using 10 epochs to split the benchmark dataset, 80% for training data to update parameter tuning and 20% as validation data to measure performance after training.

We evaluated performance using our proposed model's precision, recall, and accuracy and compared the performance of our Deep Learning Neural Network model against classical machine learning baseline methods [18]. In addition, we have performed with

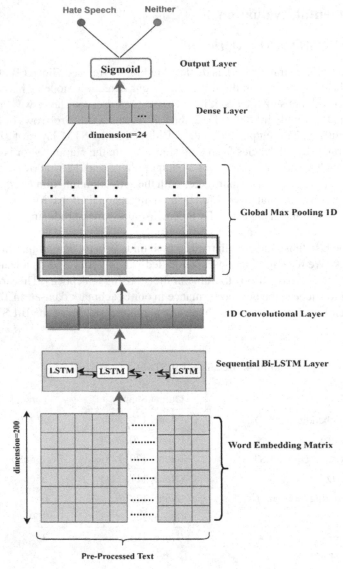

Fig. 2. Structure of Proposed BiLSTM-CNN Neural model architecture

Table 5. Distribution of multi social media dataset

Class	Train	Validation	Total
Hate	90921	22730	113651
Neither	70981	17745	88626

multiple classifiers such as Decision Trees, SVM Linear, Logistic Regression, and Naive Bayes methods [19, 22].

5 Results

We have trained our model using the Keras framework with Tensorflow 2.6.0 as a backend, text tokenizer, Pre-trained Glove embeddings 6B 200D, and machine learning toolkit Scikit-learn. After training, the proposed model performed well on hate speech and offensive language detection with existing classic baseline methods. The classifier's performance in our novel approach is compared based on various matrices shown in Table 6.

Table 6. Performance Metrics of our model

Performance Metrics	Formula
Accuracy	$\frac{tp+tn}{tp+fn+tn+fp}$
Precision	$\frac{tp}{tp+fp}$
Recall	$\frac{tp}{tp+fn}$
F1-Score	$2 \times \frac{Precision*Recall}{Precision+Recall}$

tp = True Positive, tn = True Negative, fp = False Positive, fn = False Negative.

The results of various techniques for classical machine learning baseline methods and deep learning neural networks are listed in Table 7.

Table 7. Comparison of our proposed model with machine learning baseline methods

Models	Precision	Recall	F1 Score	Accuracy
SVM Linear [6]	–	–	–	78.00
Naïve Bayes	46.00	54.00	64.00	61.00
Decision Tree	78.00	78.00	78.00	78.00
Logistic Regression [7]	86.60	86.40	86.50	91.00
CNN LSTM [10]	90.70	90.40	90.50	90.82
Proposed BiLSTM-CNN	**92.10**	**92.10**	**92.10**	**92.50**

Next, we use Deep BiLSTM-CNN-based Neural Networks to detect hate speech. Our proposed network architecture achieves an accuracy **of 92.5%**, and the F1-score value is **92.1%** in detecting hate speech. We established them to our model significantly improved performance than the machine learning baseline methods and deep learning models. We have analyzed how accuracy and loss change between numbers of epochs. The training and validation set used is shown in Figs. 3 and 4.

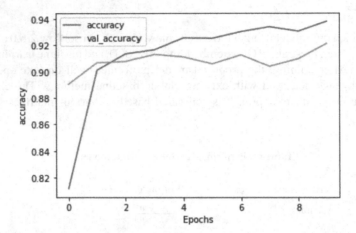

Fig. 3. Training with Validation performance

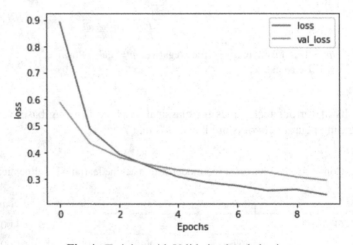

Fig. 4. Training with Validation loss behavior

A learning curve for training and validation yielded towards best performance with the continuation of epochs. Furthermore, we observe that the accuracy of our proposed model increased continuously as the number of epoch instances increased. This suggests that even higher accuracy will likely provide more training data.

The cost of incorrect prediction is relatively low, but the percentage of detection of hate speech accuracy is very high. In our heterogeneous multi-social media dataset, some tweets or comments have been misclassified by annotators who tended to annotate some samples containing hate words. However, those samples are only hated with an assumption about the language used in their daily communications. We also observed that hate samples are more frequently confused based on geographic location, social context, and specific social group.

6 Conclusion and Future Work

The centric views of hate speech have increased significantly in the last few years. A novel process for automatically identifying hate speech using deep neural network architecture combined with BiLSTM and CNN stacked layers with the best accuracy values is discussed in the paper. Our proposed model outperformed classic methods on the heterogeneous multi-social media datasets regarding accuracy, precision, recall, and F1 score. Their results often need to improve in traditional methods that depend on sophisticated engineering features, but automatic feature selection methods based on deep neural networks produce better results. In the experiment reported here, LSTM recurrent neural network architecture is beneficial to resolve Natural Language Processing problems. In future work, we plan to explore more publicly available corpus on hate speech detection and further fine-tune our different ensembling neural networks can be more beneficial.

References

1. Hochreiter, S., Schmidhuber, J.: LSTM can solve hard long time lag problems. In: Advances in Neural Information Processing Systems (1996)
2. Blei, D., et al.: Latent dirichlet allocation. In: Advances in Neural Information Processing Systems (2001)
3. Burnap, P., et al.: Cyber hate speech on twitter: an application of machine classification and statistical modeling for policy and decision making. Policy Internet, 223–242 (2015)
4. Djuric, N., et al.: Hate speech detection with comment embeddings. In: WWW 2015 Companion Proceedings of the 24th International Conference on World Wide Web, pp. 29–30. Association for Computing Machinery, Inc. (2015)
5. Nobata, C., et al.: Abusive language detection in online user content. In: 25th International World Wide Web Conference, WWW 2016, pp. 145–153. International World Wide Web Conferences Steering Committee (2016)
6. Malmasi, S., et al.: Detecting hate speech in social media. In: International Conference Recent Advances in Natural Language Processing, RANLP, pp. 467–472. Association for Computational Linguistics (ACL) (2017)
7. Davidson, T., et al.: Automated hate speech detection and the problem of offensive language. In: Proceedings of the 11th International Conference on Web and social media, ICWSM 2017, pp. 512–515. AAAI Press (2017)
8. Bird, S., et al.: Natural Language Processing with Python: (Analyzing Text with the Natural Language Toolkit), 1st edn. O'Reilly, Sebastopol (2009)
9. Waseem, Z., Hovy, D.: Hateful symbols or hateful people? Predictive features for hate speech detection on Twitter, pp. 88–93. Association for Computational Linguistics (ACL) (2016)
10. Zhang, Z., et al.: Hate speech detection using a convolution-LSTM based deep neural network. In: Eurpoean Semantic Web Conference, pp. 745–760 (2018)
11. Schmidt, A., et al.: A survey on hate speech detection using natural language processing, pp. 1–10. Association for Computational Linguistics (ACL) (2017)

12. Founta, P., et al.: Large scale crowdsourcing and characterization of twitter abusive behavior. In: Proceedings of the International AAAI Conference on Web and Social Media, vol. 12. no. 1 (2018)
13. MacAvaney, S., et al.: Hate speech detection: challenges and solutions. PLoS ONE (2019)
14. Devlin, J., et al.: BERT: pre-training of deep bidirectional transformers for language understanding. In: NAACL HLT 2019 – 2019 Conference of the North American Chapter of the Association for Computational Linguistics: Human Language Technologies - Proceedings of the Conference, pp. 4171–4186. Association for Computation al Linguistics (ACL) (2019)
15. Houlsby, N., et al.: Parameter-efficient transfer learning for NLP. In: 36th International Conference on Machine Learning, ICML 2019, pp. 4944–4953. International Machine Learning Society (IMLS) (2019)
16. Pennington, J., et al.: GloVe: global vectors for word representation. In: EMNLP 2014 – 2014 Conference on Empirical Methods in Natural Language Processing, Proceedings of the Conference, pp. 1532–1543. Association for Computational Linguistics (ACL) (2014)
17. Salminen, J., et al.: Developing an online hate classifier for multiple social media platforms. Hum. Centric Comput. Inf. Sci. (2020)
18. Gambäck, B., et al.: Using convolutional neural networks to classify hate –speech, pp. 85–90. Association for Computational Linguistics (ACL) (2017)
19. Zampieri, M., et al.: Predicting the type and target of offensive posts in social media. In: NAACL HLT 2019 - 2019 Conference of the North American Chapter of the Association for Computational Linguistics: Human Language Technologies – Proceedings of the Conference, pp. 1415–1420. Association for Computational Linguistics (ACL) (2019)
20. Watanabe, H., et al.: Hate speech on Twitter: a pragmatic approach to collect hateful and offensive expressions and perform hate speech detection. IEEE Access 6, 13825–13835 (2018)
21. Xu, J.M., et al.: Learning from bullying traces in social media. In: NAACLHLT 2012 – 2012 Conference of the North American Chapter of the Association for Computational Linguistics: Human Language Technologies, Proceedings of the Conference, pp. 656–666. Association for Computational Linguistics (ACL) (2012)
22. Kurrek, J., et al.: Towards a comprehensive taxonomy and large-scale annotated corpus for online slur usage. In: Proceedings of the Fourth Workshop on Online Abuse and Harms, pp. 138–149 (2020)
23. Mandl, T., et al.: Overview of the hasoc track at fire 2019: hate speech and offensive content identification in indo-european languages. In: Proceedings of the 11th Forum for Information Retrieval Evaluation, pp. 14–17 (2019)
24. Golbeck, J., et al.: A large, labeled corpus for online harassment research. In: Proceedings of the 2017 ACM on Web Science Conference, pp. 229–233 (2017)
25. Chung, Y.L., et al.: CONAN-counter narratives through nichesourcing: a multilingual dataset of responses to fight online hate speech. arXiv preprint arXiv:1910.03270 (2019)
26. Kennedy, B., et al.: Introducing the Gab Hate Corpus: defining and applying hate-based rhetoric to social media posts at scale. Lang. Resour. Eval. 56(1), 79–108 (2022)
27. Kurrek, J., Saleem, H.M., Ruths, D.: Towards a comprehensive taxonomy and large-scale annotated corpus for online slur usage. In: Proceedings of the Fourth Workshop on Online Abuse and Harms, pp. 138–149 (2020)
28. Diwakar, M., et al.: Directive clustering contrast-based multi-modality medical image fusion for smart healthcare system. Netw. Model. Anal. Health Inform. Bioinform. 11(1), 1–12 (2022)

Breast Cancer Detection by Using Decision Tree

Apurva Vashist[✉], Anil Kumar Sagar, and Anjali Goyal

Department of Computer Science and Engineering, Sharda University, Greater Noida, UP, India
apurva.vashist@gmail.com, {anil.sagar,anjali1}@sharda.ac.in

Abstract. A machine learning's (ML) objective, the goal of this field of artificial intelligence technology is to improve the precision and effectiveness of medical work. Once skin the type of cancer that most frequently affects women is breast cancer. Unchecked breast cell proliferation is the root cause of breast cancer. The national cancer institute estimates that 287,850 new cases of cancer, or 15% of all new cases, will be diagnosed in 2022. Estimated death toll in the USA year 2022 will be 43,250. 15% of all newly diagnosed cancer cases in the United States are in women with breast cancer. 1, 62,468 new instances of breast cancer were discovered in 2018 in India, and there were 87,090 cases of the disease-related death. In order to determine which Machine Learning algorithms are optimal for breast cancer detection made possible by the use of machine learning, this study will examine the various phases of breast cancer, examine datasets, and assess supervised Machine Learning algorithms. The outcome demonstrates that the decision tree's accuracy is superior to the K-nearest neighbor.

Keywords: Machine learning · decision tree · breast cancer · supervised algorithms · KNN

1 Introduction

A woman in India receives a breast cancer (BC) diagnosis every four minutes, according to some reports [1]. In India, BC is becoming more common in both urban and rural areas. More than half of Indian women who are diagnosed with cancer have stage 3 or stage 4 BC, which has a worse prognosis for survival than earlier stages of the disease. Comparatively, it was discovered that 80% of American women with BC live after the cancer is gone, compared to only 60% of Indian women [2]. In the United States, BC is currently more prevalent than cervical cancer. Between 25 and 32% of all female cancer diagnoses in major cities like Mumbai, Delhi, Bengaluru, Bhopal, Kolkata, Chennai, and Ahmedabad are due to breast cancer. This accounts for more than 25% of all cancer diagnoses in women [3].

Additionally, this behavior is more likely to be seen in younger age groups. People between the ages of 25 and 50 make up little under half of all cases. Additionally, more than 70% of patients in the advanced stage had poor survival rates and high mortality rates [4].

According to data and records kept by the World Health Organization (WHO), BC is one of the illnesses that affects women the most frequently. As a result, a cell's genes

R. N. Shaw et al. (Eds.): ICACIS 2023, CCIS 1920, pp. 71–79, 2023.
https://doi.org/10.1007/978-3-031-45121-8_7

start to mutate, and the cell grows swiftly and uncontrollably. The two primary types of cancerous tumors are benign and malignant. However, utilizing diagnostic pictures (mammograms or MRI), there is currently no technology in use to automatically identify early BC and estimate risk. In this work, machine learning, image processing, and computer vision technologies are used to investigate automated breast cancer detection, breast density recognition, risk prediction, and solution suggestion. Using MRI (Magnetic Resonance Imaging) images, it is possible to forecast the presence of breast cancer, which is a significant application for pattern recognition in the medical sector. The detailed images of breast tissue generated by MRI enable the diagnosis and characterization of alarming abnormalities. Pattern recognition (PR) algorithms can examine MRI images and identify certain patterns and features linked to the disease in order to detect and diagnose breast cancer.

After being trained on a big dataset of MRI scans, the model demonstrated excellent accuracy in identifying benign and malignant breast tumors. By detecting patterns of atypical tissue augmentation, shape abnormalities, roughness, radius, and other factors, the programmer was able to successfully detect the presence of breast cancer in MRI scans.

Figure 1 shows the different types of BC.

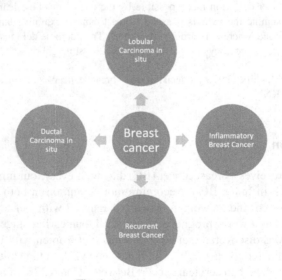

Fig. 1. Breast cancer types

2   Literature Review

In 2022 Sandhu et al. explore datasets, analyze supervised and unsupervised machine learning algorithms, and comprehend the many stages of breast cancer. Machine Learning (ML) algorithms to determine which ones are most effective for predicting early breast cancer through the use of machine learning or deep learning.

The categorization method used by the machine learning model for cancer prediction was highlighted in Kumari et al.'s (2018) study. Support vector machines, linear regression, and KNN can find good accuracy using the Wisconsin breast cancer dataset. Applied classification approach, feature selection and training, feature comprehension and preparation, and data source.

A classification model was developed by Caleb et al. (2021) to identify cancer. One of its features is the processes used to analyses the raw data, which included a data dictionary, dataset summary statistics, exploratory data analysis, and model building and evaluation.

The authors of this article present two distinct classifiers for identifying breast cancer, test the efficacy of each of the two novel approaches, and provide a comparison between them. Cross-validation is used to examine the two novel approaches' relative performance. The statistics show that the K-Nearest Neighbor (KNN) classifier has a higher accuracy rate (87.51%) and a lower error rate (86.19%) than the Naive Bayes (NB) classifier in 2018 by M. Amrane.

Chiu et al. (2020) used transfer learning, multilayer perceptron, support vector machine, and principal component analysis to predict BC. The experimental portion also covers data preprocessing, data description, and k-fold cross-validation. There are fewer algorithms employed in this research document gap. They may be used more widely, resulting in high accuracy and simple diagnosis detection.

Kumar et al. applied a few classifier models for identification in 2019. Algorithms employed included KNN, SVM, Naive Bayes and others. The procedure made use of unprocessed datasets, data statistics, data preparation, classification methods, and performance calculation.

The majority of new cancer diagnoses and cancer deaths worldwide, according to statistics, are due to breast cancer. This makes breast cancer a major public health issue in our society today. Breast cancer is one of the most prevalent types of cancer in women worldwide in 2016 by V. S. Reddy.

3   Dataset

3.1   Wisconsin Breast Cancer Diagnosis Dataset

Dr. William H. Wolberg18 of the University of Wisconsin Hospitals developed the Wisconsin Breast Cancer Dataset (WBCD), which was published online in 1992. It is composed of information gathered from patient breasts during FNAC biopsy tests on nuclear properties. The data set consists of 699 patients, 241 (34.5%) of whom had malignant BC tumors, and 248 (65.5%) of whom had benign BC tumors. Clump thickness, homogeneity of cell size and shape, marginal adhesion, single epithelial cell size, naked nuclei, bland chromatin, normal nucleoli, and mitoses are among the nine independent features. Each of the nine attributes has a value between 1 and 10, with 1 being a normal state.

3.2   Breast Cancer Dataset

The characteristics in this dataset were generated from a breast tumor image that was digitally captured by a fine needle aspiration (FNA). The target feature keeps track of the prognosis (malignant or benign). The dataset consists of 286 occurrences with 10 attributes, 85 of which are recurrent events and 201 of which are not. The property (node-caps) status was empty in 8 items of the Breast Cancer dataset.

4 Machine Learning Methods and Algorithms in BC Prediction

In the field of machine learning (ML), computers are taught to automatically learn from and adapt to new situations utilizing the available data. A range of events can be predicted using the trained model, which is created by using these statistical correlations from any dataset [5]. In addition to improving object product yield, strain upgrading, flux prediction, route design and optimization, and gene circuit design, machine learning (ML) has emerged as a powerful approach for metabolic engineering. This is because data on microbial metabolism in diverse cellular and physiological states is readily available. The effects of several ML approaches, such as supervised learning and unsupervised learning on BC prediction are briefly reviewed in this article.

4.1 Supervised Learning

In conjunction with a set of inputs, supervised ML algorithms can calculate a response. Numbers or categories are used to indicate both the output values and the input attributes. With the use of this machine learning technique, a function might be inferred from labelled training data made up of several sets of case studies. As a result, the qualified examples are pairs of matching input features and output responses. Over the past few years, supervised ML methods have been used the most in the BC prediction when compared to other ML techniques.

4.2 Unsupervised Learning

Unsupervised learning infers the order of the data without the aid of labels, it is more difficult than supervised learning. The objective of cluster analysis is to determine whether the observations can be divided into significantly different sets. Classifying or predicting phenotypes from omics information has become easier because to unsupervised learning methods [6].

4.3 Methodology

The authors used the kaggle dataset as the basis for their analogy because of this study. The authors then processed the data using the Jupyter notebook tools, the Python programming language, and associated libraries. To better understand the data, the writers had conducted data statistics. To determine malignancy with the highest degree of precision, the classifier approach was applied. Figure 2 displays the cancer methodology. In this figure, DT stands for Decision Tree and KNN for K-nearest neighbor.

Fig. 2. Workflow for designing the detection of BC

5   Result and Conclusion

After training, a machine learning (ML) model is evaluated using a "test set," or an unexplored region of a dataset. The Confusion Matrix (CM) table is used to evaluate the performance of this model. When using the Confusion Matrix, decision trees commonly use the following metrics to assess model performance: accuracy, precision, recall or sensitivity, specificity, F1 score, and accuracy are just a few.

$$Accuracy = \frac{TP + TN}{TP + TN + FP + FN} \tag{i}$$

$$Precision = \frac{TP}{TP + FP} \tag{ii}$$

$$Recall\ or\ Sensitivity = \frac{TP}{TP + FN} \tag{iii}$$

$$Specificity = \frac{TN}{TN + FP} \tag{iV}$$

$$F1\ score = \frac{2 \times (Precision \times Recall)}{Precision + Recall} \tag{V}$$

In conclusion, the usage of ML algorithm (Decision tree) enables effective BC detection and diagnosis.

Dataset

	id	Radius_mean	Texture_mean	perimeter_mean	area_mean
count	5.690000e+02	569.000000	569.000000	569.000000	569.000000
mean	3.037183e+07	14.127292	19.296678	91.969033	654.889104
std	1.250206e+08	3.524049	4.301816	24.298981	351.914129
min	8.670000e+03	6.981000	9.710000	43.790000	143.500000
25%	8.692180e+05	11.700000	16.170000	75.170000	420.300000
50%	9.060240e+05	13.370000	18.870000	86.240000	551.100000
75%	8.813129e+06	15.780000	21.800000	104.100000	782.700000
max	9.113205e+08	28.110000	39.280000	188.500000	2501.000000

By using KNN

	precision	recall	f1-score	support
0	0.83	0.90	0.86	117
1	0.81	0.70	0.75	71
accuracy			0.82	188
macro avg	0.82	0.80	0.81	188
weighted avg	0.82	0.82	0.82	188

Confusion Matrix

$$[[105 \quad 12]$$
$$[\ 21 \quad 50]]$$

By using Decision tree
Data Visualization

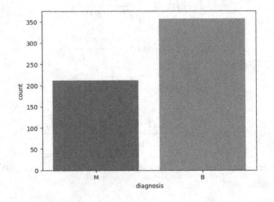

Pairplot

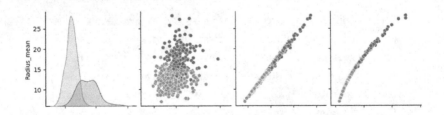

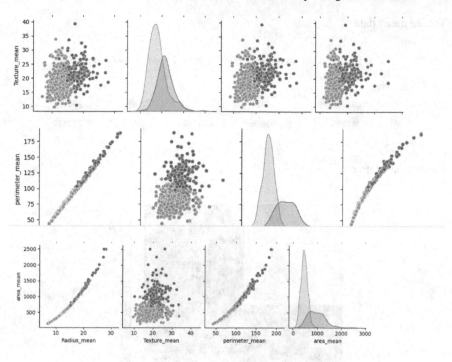

diagnosis
- M
- B

Normal distribution curve

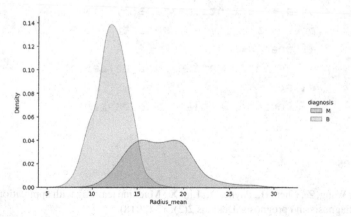

Decision Tree Classifier
classifier.score (X_test, y_test)
Accuracy 0.9210526315789473

Whole mean data

diagnosis	id	Radius_mean	Texture_mean	perimeter_mean	area_mean
B	2.654382e+07	12.146524	17.914762	78.075406	462.790196
M	3.681805e+07	17.462830	21.623774	115.365377	978.376415

2 rows × 31 columns

Confusion Matrix

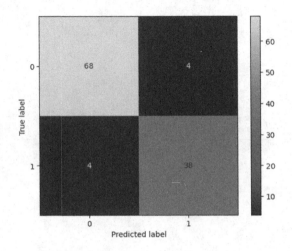

```
pred = patient1.reshape(1,-1)
pred = classifier.predict(pred)
if pred == 0:
    print ('Patient has no cancer')
else:
    print ('Patient has cancer')
```

References

1. Yue, W., Wang, Z., Chen, H., Payne, A., Liu, X.: Machine learning with applications in breast cancer diagnosis and prognosis. Designs 2(2), 13 (2018)
2. Li, Y., Chen, Z.: Performance evaluation of machine learning methods for breast cancer prediction. Appl. Comput. Math. 7(4), 212–216 (2018). https://doi.org/10.11648/j.acm.201 80704.15

3. Bazazeh, D., Shubair, R.: Comparative study of machine learning algorithms for breast cancer detection and diagnosis. In: 2016 5th International Conference on Electronic Devices, Systems and Applications (ICEDSA), pp. 1–4 (2016). https://doi.org/10.1109/ICEDSA.2016.7818560

4. Uddin, S., Khan, A., Hossain, M.E., Moni, M.A.: Comparing different supervised machine learning algorithms for disease prediction. BMC Med. Inform. Decis. Mak. **19**(1), 1–16 (2019)

5. Camacho, D.M., Collins, K.M., Powers, R.K., Costello, J.C., Collins, J.J.: Nextgeneration machine learning for biological networks. Cell (2018). https://doi.org/10.1016/j.cell.2018.05.015

6. Ernst, J., Kellis, M.: ChromHMM: automating chromatin-state discovery and characterization. Nat. Methods (2012). https://doi.org/10.1038/nmeth.1906

7. Treloar, N.J., Fedorec, A.J.H., Ingalls, B., Barnes, C.P.: Deep reinforcement learning for the control of microbial co-cultures in bioreactors. PLoS Comput. Biol. **16** (2020). https://doi.org/10.1371/journal.pcbi.1007783

8. .Mellor, J., Grigoras, I., Carbonell, P., Faulon, J.L.: Semisupervised gaussian process for automated enzyme search. ACS Synth. Biol. **5**, 518–528 (2016). https://doi.org/10.1021/acssynbio.5b00294

9. DeSantis, C.E., Ma, J., Goding Sauer, A., et al.: Breast cancer statistics, 2017, racial disparity in mortality by state. CA **67**(6), 439–448 (2017)

10. Rawat, R., Mahor, V., Chirgaiya, S., Shaw, R.N., Ghosh, A.: Sentiment analysis at online social network for cyber-malicious post reviews using machine learning techniques. In: Bansal, J.C., Paprzycki, M., Bianchini, M., Das, S. (eds.) Computationally Intelligent Systems and their Applications. SCI, vol. 950, pp. 113–130. Springer, Singapore (2021). https://doi.org/10.1007/978-981-16-0407-2_9

11. Amrane, M., Oukid, S., Gagaoua, I., Ensari̇, T.: Breast cancer classification using machine learning. In: 2018 Electric Electronics, Computer Science, Biomedical Engineerings' Meeting (EBBT), pp. 1–4 (2018). https://doi.org/10.1109/EBBT.2018.8391453

12. Suryachandra, P., Reddy, P.V.S.: Comparison of machine learning algorithms for breast cancer. In: 2016 International Conference on Inventive Computation Technologies (ICICT), pp. 1–6 (2016). https://doi.org/10.1109/INVENTIVE.2016.7830090

13. Sandhu, J.K., Kaur, A., Kaushal, C.: Analysis of breast cancer in early stage by UsingMachine LearningAlgorithms: a review. In: 2022 IEEE International Conference on Current Development in Engineering and Technology (CCET), Current Development in Engineering and Technology (CCET), [s. l], pp. 1–7 (2022)

Sugarcane Leaf Disease Classification Using Deep Learning

Rahul Maurya$^{(\boxtimes)}$, Arun Kumar, and Jagrati Singh

Centre for Advanced Studies, Dr. A.P.J. Abdul Kalam Technical University Lucknow,
Lucknow 226031, UP, India
`rahulcs0105@gmail.com, {drarun,jagrati}@cas.res.in`

Abstract. The most significant industry that affects a nation's economic development is agriculture, which is strongly tied to the four pillars of society. Among various agricultural resources that India possess, the most promising crop is sugarcane. But there are also many challenges that a farmer has to face while growing these crops, like diseases in crops, leaf's, etc. Deep learning is an intriguing technology that can be used to resolve these issues. This research work aims to integrate deep learning model to identify and detect sugarcane leaf diseases with the maximum level of accuracy possible. A customized dataset has been used for this purpose which consists of four classes. The proposed customized VGG16 model achieved a maximum accuracy of 94.47% using Adam optimizer, the model is trained on NVIDIA DGX server. This research work has the capability to become a pioneer in enabling the farmers to successfully integrate artificial intelligence with their excellent skillset to produce a healthier and rich crops without having to worry about these challenges.

Keywords: Sugarcane · Deep Learning · Vgg16 · Leaf Disease · Classification · Computer Vision · Artificial Intelligence

1 Introduction

Sugarcane is a significant cash crop that is vital to world economy because of its byproducts that is of sugar and ethanol. Millions of farmers in worldwide depends on it for their livelihoods. However, a number of diseases that can adversely affect sugarcane plants' growth, yield, and general productivity exist. Early disease detection is essential for putting effective control measures in place and reducing crop losses.

In breeding process, it is important to estimate the severeness of diseases of plants in order to create the widest range of disease-resistant sugarcane. The spots diseases in sugarcane, which is present in 15% of the leaves, has significantly reduced sugarcane production. To reduce these infections and illness of sugarcane crop, the disease must be identified and treated sooner rather than later [1].

Leaf infections are one of the main ailments affecting sugarcane. These illnesses primarily show up on the leaves as visible symptoms like discoloration, lesions, patches, or wilting. Bacterial blight, rust, red-rot, brown stripe, leaf scald are a few examples of

R. N. Shaw et al. (Eds.): ICACIS 2023, CCIS 1920, pp. 80–89, 2023.
https://doi.org/10.1007/978-3-031-45121-8_8

common diseases that affect sugarcane leaves. Due to the similarity of their outward appearances, it is impossible to identify many disorders manually and assessment with naked eyes [2], precision evaluation with computational vision is a possible way for minimizing the risk of human mistake on identify illnesses because using pesticides to treat these plant diseases raises the possibility of hazardous residues on agricultural goods and surface water contaminations, and when this isn't handled carefully then the cost of production increases [3].

Technology breakthroughs, notably in the fields of image recognition and artificial intelligence (AI), have opened up new possibilities for automating the detection and diagnosis of sugarcane leaf diseases. These tools analyze leaf images of sugarcane and categorize them based on the presence of disease using different methods of image processing and trained algorithms.

The main deep learning method used in this study was convolutional neural networks. CNN, which uses a lot of data to do pattern recognition tasks, well-known ways to show advanced approaches. The study is only one example of the way CNN can recognize a plant just by looking at pictures of its leaves. Artificial intelligence is a technique for programming machines to think like people. Instead of just giving computers a set of instructions like traditional programming does, artificial intelligence (AI) is based on a distinct way of interacting with computers that allows it to find patterns in data [4].

Main Contributions

The main contributions are as follows:

1. The dataset is customized images of sugarcane leaf disease, the gathered data is of different class like bacterial blight, rust, red-rot and healthy. Jupyter Notebook and Python are used to perform the task.
2. Raw data is pre-processed and data augmentation is done to make the training of model with efficient number of dataset.

2 Related Work

A neural network is used by (Naik et al. 2016) [5] in their research on identifying plant diseases. When the system discovers a contaminated leaf, additional processing is carried out to identify the type of diseases. (Surbhi et al. 2017) [6] the discrimination algorithm undergoes training using the generator after being transformed into some multi-class classifiers. In this chapter transfer learning for neural networks based on the Inception-V3 model was employed for content-based image recommendation.

To extract complex qualities, (Hinton et al. 2017) [7] and other researchers introduce deep neural architectures. Their approach proved successful in extracting highly abstract characteristics that may retain the most information from raw data, allowing complex relationships to be reduced to a smaller number of components. In some areas, the ConvNet is more advanced than humans.

(Evy Kamilah, et al. 2014) [8] a model is put out for judging the severity of particular spot illnesses, which show up as segmented patches on leaves. The division of the spot is created by thresholding the a* component of the L*a*b* colour space. The classifier support vector machines (SVM) uses the L*a*b* colour space for colour attributes and the

Grey Level Co-Occurrence Matrix (GLCM) for textural characteristics. The suggested model has an accuracy of 80% with a mean error intensity prediction of 5.73, which allows it to identify the various forms of spot disorders.

(Militante, et al. 2019) [9] the goal of this study is to combine different DL models of CNN architectures to identify and detect sugarcane illnesses. The models achieved a accuracy of 95.40% after training, utilizing the sugarcane leaves disease of 14,725 images of healthy and infected. In order to conduct this investigation, StridedNet, LeNet, and VGGNet, three CNN architectures, were used with accuracy of 90.10%, 93.65%, 95.40% respectively.

(Dionis A., et al. 2019) [10] uses Support Vector Machine to develop a system that, through image analysis technique, can identify the yellow spotted infection in sugarcane leaf. The dataset uses have yellow spot and healthy leaves of sugarcane in which classification of the leaves was made possible with assistance from an SRA-LAREC Science Research Expert in sugarcane Pests and Diseases.

(Srivastava, Sakshi, et al. 2020) [11] explores a unique approach of deep learning to classify the infected leaves of sugarcane by examining the stem, color, leaves, etc. InceptionV3, VGG16 and VGG19 models are used with different classifiers such as SVM, SGD, naive Bayes, KNN. The highest accuracy of 90.2% was achieved using SVM as classifier with VGG16.

(Kumar, Prince, et al. 2021) [12] executes CNN operations on pictures of 2940 leaves of sugarcane comprising 6 distinct categories that were collected from the state Uttarakhand and Bihar with cameras. The proposed model results the accuracy of 93.20% by using the YOLO and Faster-RCNN algorithms.

(Tamilvizhi, T., et al. 2022) [13] this study offers a highly accurate model for classification and detection of sugarcane leaf disease based on quantum behaved particle swarm optimization (QBPSO-DTL). The model deep stacked autoencoder used for the classification and identify the damaged regions in the leaf images, and as the feature extractor the squeezenet model is used.

(Li, Xuechen, et al. 2022) [14] suggests of a hybrid network called the SLViT, where the transformer encoder is converted to an adaptable plugin (LViT) after which it is incorporated into multiple locations of a CNN architecture (SHDC). SLViT begins its training on the openly accessible Plant Village illness datasets before moving to the customized SLD10k dataset, which includes 10,309 photos of sugarcane diseased leaves and comprises seven categories.

(Sujithra, J., et al. 2022) [15] presents the CRUN method for leaf disease segmentation from augmented dataset of leaves. The model is most effective for early identification and avoidance of leaf disease on real-time pictures of leaf disease of banana such as black sigatoka and on sugarcane leaf disease (Table 1).

Table 1. A Review of Related Work.

S. no	References	Dataset	Technique
1	(Evy Kamilah, et al. 2014) [8]	Real-time sugarcane images dataset is collected from Mojokerto, Indonesia	SVM classifier
2	(Militante, et al. 2019) [9]	7 classes of sugarcane images (6- types of diseases and one to the healthy class)	LeNet model
3	(Dionis A., et al. 2019) [10]	photos of sugarcane leaves with 84 ring, 99 yellow marks, and 81 healthy leaves	SVM classifier
4	(Srivastava, Sakshi, et al. 2020) [11]	120 diseased and 120 healthy sugarcane leaves	VGG-16 with SVM
5	(Kumar, Prince, et al. 2021) [12]	2940 images of different diseases sugarcane leave	Quicker R-CNN
6	(Tamilvizhi, T., et al. 2022) [13]	Customized dataset of diseased and non- diseases images of sugarcane leaf	QBPSO-DTL
7	(Li, Xuechen, et al. 2022) [14]	2095 self-collected images of sugarcane leaf disease (SLD10k) which has 7classes	SLViT hybrid Network
8	(Sujithra, J., et al. 2022) [15]	3126 images of red-rot, bacterial blight and healthy class	CRUN-MP

3 Materials and Methods

3.1 Dataset Description

In this research, a customized dataset of sugarcane leaf disease has been used. It has four classes as Healthy, Bacterial blight, Red-rot, Rust disease (Table 2).

Table 2. Dataset detail descriptions.

Class of Leaf	Symptoms	Favourable conditions	No. Images before Augmentation	No. Images after Augmentation
Healthy	Normal, green and rough surface	Temperature 20–30 °C, humidity >70–80%	100	1600

(*continued*)

Table 2. (*continued*)

Class of Leaf	Symptoms	Favourable conditions	No. Images before Augmentation	No. Images after Augmentation
Bacterial Blight	Reddish stripes extend over the entire leaf, with watery green stipes in the midrib and base	Spread through diseased seed material and cutting knife	100	1600
Red Rot	Stalks become smudged and hollow. Rotten grains, discolored and sour odor	Cool, wet weather, high soil moisture	100	1600
Rust	The earliest signs are small, yellowish spots. Reddish brown	High humidity, warm temperature	80	1585
Total			380	6385

3.2 Proposed Model

The proposed model creates a method to categories diverse sugarcane leaf diseases into different groups using the idea of transfer learning. In Fig. 1 the essential system graph is shown.

To improve the overall accuracy of ML models, transfer learning, a mechanism of storing and transferring knowledge, was developed (Zhuang, et al. 2020) [16]. Weights and biases are changed during training to get the model as accurate as possible, and the weights are then stored to be used for making predictions (Qureshi, et al. 2017) [17]. The weights of previously trained CNN models are assigned to a new model during transfer learning. Even if using the transferred models alone is an option, the model will not acquire anything new, hence doing so will lead to mediocre results. As a result, training requires the introduction of consecutive layers.

After performing the augmentation on the dataset using Keras ImageDataGenerator class with shifting of height and width by 0.2, shear of 0.2, zoom range of 0.2, rotation clockwise and anti-clockwise of 40°, rescale of 1. /255, and scaling (half and double) of images, the dataset of 380 images increased to 6385 images. Starting with the previously trained VGG16 model, training is then completed with the addition of a Flattening layer, the Dense layer having 2048 unit parameters, and the Rectified Linear Unit (ReLU) activating function. The classification dense layer that was activated by Soft-Max is then coupled to the model.

Tensorflow and Keras are machine learning and AI open source software libraries used to create deep learning models directly or wrapping the libraries and implementing

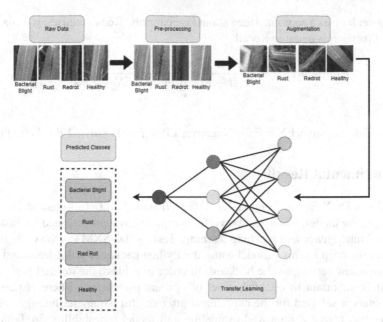

Fig. 1. Proposed Model for sugarcane leaf disease classification.

neural networks, respectively. Following the creation of the model, the datasets were split into three groups for training, validation, and testing, with a ratio of around 7:2:1. Test images are separated first and augmentation is done on remaining images and used for validation and training of model. The model's performance is on training and validation dataset, and the final assessment is made using distinct test images.

3.3 Evaluation Metrics

- **Accuracy:** It provides the percentage of all predictions that were accurate.

$$\text{Accuracy} = \frac{TN + \text{TP}}{TN + TP + FN + FP} \tag{1}$$

- **Precision:** It explains the proportion of accurately anticipated cases that really materialized as positive cases.

$$\text{Precision} = \frac{TP}{FP + TP} \tag{2}$$

- **Recall:** Recall illustrates the number of the actual positive outcomes our model was able to accurately predict.

$$\text{Recall} = \frac{TP}{FN + TP} \tag{3}$$

- **F1-score:** It gives a combined idea about Precision and Recall metrics. It is maximum when Precision is equal to Recall.

$$\mathbf{F1-score} = \frac{2 * Recall * Precision}{Recall + Precision} = \frac{2 * TP}{FN + FP + 2 * TP} \qquad (4)$$

where,

TN = True Negative, **FN** = False Negative, **TP** = True Positive, **FP** = False Positive.

4   Experimental Results

The NVIDIA DGX Server Version 4.7.0 (GNU/Linux 4.15.0-130-generic x86_64) is used to train the model, which is a powerful computing system designed for tasks such as artificial intelligence and machine learning. Tesla V100-SXM3 is the GPU helps to implement the deep learning model using the Python packages scikit-learn and Keras, with Tensor-flow serving as the backend. In order to achieve the desired performance results, it is important to establish a set of optimal parameters. There, a perfect set of parameters is selected for the experiment after careful parameter tuning. The same parameter was used for improved evaluation and model repeatability. In Table 3 the model's input parameters are shown.

Table 3. Hyper-Parameter Values

Hyper-parameters	Values
Batch Size	32
Early Stopping Criteria	Validation Accuracy
Activation Function	ReLU, Softmax
Optimization Algorithm	Adam
Number of Epochs	100
Learning Rate	0.001
Loss	Categorical Cross Entropy

First, we have decided to go with inception v3 because of its deep neural network ability to give promising result then v1 and v2 model but the accuracy received was only 90%. To achieve greater and better result VGG16 is chosen with customized layers according to the dataset, the average output was 94.47% which is better than previously applied inception model.

During model training, the training data is divided into 32 batches, trained with different number of epochs as 20, 50, 100, 150, 200, 250 with Adam optimizer. Accuracy has been optimized as the metric, and a binary cross-entropy loss has been experienced. At the end of the training data with 100 epochs, the accuracy was 99.00%, and the loss was 24.11%. The model's accuracy on test data is 94.47%, as shown in Fig. 2. Information

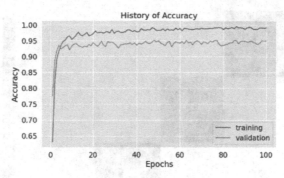

Fig. 2. Accuracy Curve of Training and Validation.

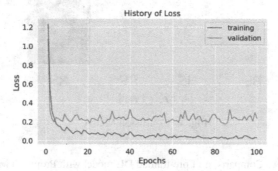

Fig. 3. Loss Curve Training and Validation.

on the model's performance is provided by validation accuracy and training loss. Our model is not in the learning phase if validation loss rises while validation accuracy falls. Our model is overfitting if validation loss and accuracy are increasing. Validation loss must decrease and validation accuracy must increase for model learning and operation to be successful. Figures 2 and 3 show improvements in validation accuracy and a decrease in validation loss, respectively.

The suggested model learning is effective and has attained the highest accuracy when compared to other classification techniques. In Fig. 4 The model confusion matrix is shown, and it was created using the ground truth actual labels and the predicted labels produced by the trained model on a specific dataset. The suggested model's accuracy and robustness in differentiating across classes are shown by greater values in the confusion matrix's diagonal elements.

5 Experimental Conclusion and Future work

An automated, lightweight, rapid, reliable, and cost-effective technique to identify sugarcane leaf disease is presented in a study. Initially, a deep-learning model was developed using a dataset of sugarcane leaf disease. The output of many pre-trained networks has been compared are shown in Table 4 using the transfer learning technique. Top accuracy for the customized VGG16 was 94.47%.

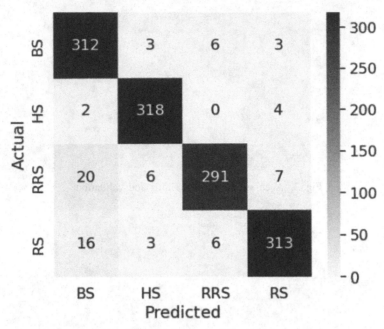

Fig. 4. Confusion Matrix.

Table 4. Comparison of pre-trained DL model with Proposed Model

Model	Precision	Recall	F1-score	Accuracy
VGG-16	87.00%	82.00%	86.20%	88.00%
VGG-19	91.00%	92.00%	91.50%	92.05%
Inception V3	89.00%	91.00%	89.98%	90.00%
Proposed Model	**92.11%**	**95.65%**	**93.85%**	**94.47%**

The suggested approach can examine enormous volumes of data, spot trends, and generate precise forecasts. The models discussed above may be used in future work with more datasets to validate them and more learning rates and optimizers. Includes experimenting with newer and alternative architectures to improve the model's performance on the training set. As a result, farmers can utilize this study as a decision-making tool to help and familiarize them with the sugarcane illnesses that can be detected in the study.

References

1. Datta, A., Dey, A., Dey, K.N.: Automatic multiclass classification of foliar leaf diseases using statistical and color feature extraction and support vector machine. In: Mandal, J., Mukhopadhyay, S., Dutta, P., Dasgupta, K. (eds.) CICBA 2018, Part I. CCIS, vol. 1030, pp. 3–15. Springer, Singapore (2019). https://doi.org/10.1007/978-981-13-8578-0_1

2. Vibhute, A., Bodhe, S.K.: Applications of image processing in agriculture: a survey. Int. J. Comput. Appl. **52**(2), 34–40 (2012)
3. Rathod, A.N., Tanawal, B., Shah, V.: Image processing techniques for detection of leaf disease. Int. J. Adv. Res. Comput. Sci. Softw. Eng. **3**(11) (2013)
4. Ciresan, D.C., et al.: Flexible, high performance convolutional neural networks for image classification. In: Twenty Second International Joint Conference on Artificial Intelligence (2011)
5. Naik, M.R., Sivappagari, C.M.R.: Plant leaf and disease detection by using HSV features and SVM classifier. Int. J. Eng. Sci. **3794**(260) (2016)
6. Jain, S., Dhar, J.: Image based search engine using deep learning. In: 2017 Tenth International Conference on Contemporary Computing (IC3). IEEE (2017)
7. Krizhevsky, A., Sutskever, I., Hinton, G.E.: ImageNet classification with deep convolutional neural networks. Commun. ACM **60**(6), 84–90 (2017)
8. Ratnasari, E.K., et al.: Sugarcane leaf disease detection and severity estimation based on segmented spots image. In: Proceedings of International Conference on Information, Communication Technology and System (ICTS) 2014. IEEE (2014)
9. Militante, S.V., Gerardo, B.D.: Detecting sugarcane diseases through adaptive deep learning models of convolutional neural network. In: 2019 IEEE 6th International Conference on Engineering Technologies and Applied Sciences (ICETAS). IEEE (2019)
10. Padilla, D.A., et al.: Portable yellow spot disease identifier on sugarcane leaf via image processing using support vector machine. In: 2019 5th International Conference on Control, Automation and Robotics (ICCAR). IEEE (2019)
11. Srivastava, S., et al.: A novel deep learning framework approach for sugarcane disease detection. SN Comput. Sci. **1**, 1–7 (2020)
12. Mandal, S., Balas, V.E., Shaw, R.N., Ghosh, A.: Prediction analysis of idiopathic pulmonary fibrosis progression from OSIC dataset. In: 2020 IEEE International Conference on Computing, Power and Communication Technologies (GUCON), Greater Noida, India, pp. 861–865 (2020). https://doi.org/10.1109/GUCON48875.2020.9231239
13. Mridha, K., et al.: Deep learning algorithms are used to automatically detection invasive ducal carcinoma in whole slide images. In: 2021 IEEE 6th International Conference on Computing, Communication and Automation (ICCCA), Arad, Romania, pp. 123–129 (2021). https://doi.org/10.1109/ICCCA52192.2021.9666302
14. Li, X., et al.: SLViT: shuffle-convolution-based lightweight vision transformer for effective diagnosis of sugarcane leaf diseases. J. King Saud Univ. Comput. Inf. Sci. (2022)
15. Sujithra, J., Ferni Ukrit, M.: CRUN-based leaf disease segmentation and morphological-based stage identification. Math. Probl. Eng. **2022** (2022)
16. Zhuang, F., et al.: A comprehensive survey on transfer learning. arXiv 2020. arXiv preprint arXiv:1911.02685 (2020)
17. Qureshi, F.F., et al.: Integration of OMNI channels and machine learning with smart technologies. J. Ambient Intell. Humaniz. Comput., 1–17 (2017)

A Comprehensive Review of the Latest Advancements in Large Generative AI Models

Satyam Kumar(✉), Dayima Musharaf, Seerat Musharaf, and Anil Kumar Sagar

School of Engineering and Technology, Sharda University, Greater Noida, India
{2020540155.satyam,2020442645.dayima,
2020442638.seerat}@ug.sharda.ac.in, Anil.sagar@sharda.ac.in

Abstract. There has been an increase in big generative models like ChatGPT and Stable Diffusion over the last two years. These models are capable of a wide range of activities, including providing general answers and producing creative representations. They have a significant impact on a variety of businesses and society since they have the ability to transform established work roles. Generative AI may, for instance, convert text into images using the DALLE-2 model, 3D images using the Dreamfusion model, photos into text using the Flamingo model, and even text into video using the Phenaki model. While ChatGPT can translate text into other texts, the AudioLM model can translate text into audio. Text is converted into code by the Codex model and scientific texts using the Galactica model. Algorithms like AlphaTensor can also be developed through generative AI. This research seeks to present a thorough overview of the most important generative models that have recently been released and their impact on various industries. It also makes an effort to taxonomize these models in order to better comprehend their functions and applications.

Keywords: AI generative models · Text-to-image · Text-to-voice · Text-to-video · Text-to-code · Text-to-3D · Text-to-text · Text-to-Science · Image-to-text

1 Introduction

A specific type of artificial intelligence identified as "generative AI" is capable of producing new material as opposed to only analysing or processing data, as was the case with conventional expert systems. Knowledge bases and an inference engine that produced content using an if-else rule database made comprised expert systems.

But discriminator and generator now make up the two main parts of contemporary generative AI, which has greatly advanced in recent years. The discriminator can translate input data into a high-dimensional latent space after being trained on a corpus or dataset [1]. The generator, on the other hand, responds to a prompt by producing stochastic behaviour and unique material, even if the prompt is repeated. Depending on the methods employed, the learning process might be unsupervised, semi-supervised, or supervised.

It's critical to understand how generative AI models vary from systems that use predictive machine learning. Systems that use predictive machine learning only carry

R. N. Shaw et al. (Eds.): ICACIS 2023, CCIS 1920, pp. 90–103, 2023.
https://doi.org/10.1007/978-3-031-45121-8_9

out discrimination tasks to address classification or regression issues. On the other hand, generative AI models have the capacity to both recognise information and produce new information from the altered input data or prompt.

It's critical to understand how generative AI models vary from systems that use predictive machine learning. Systems that use predictive machine learning only carry out discrimination tasks to address classification or regression issues [2]. On the other hand, generative AI models have the capacity to both recognise information and produce new information from the altered input data or prompt.

Generative models' scale and ability to process enormous amounts of data are key features. It is now possible to feed generative models a vast amount of data, including the entirety of Wikipedia, Github, social networks, Google pictures, and more, because to breakthroughs in computing technology. Deep neural networks, transformers, and other models like variational autoencoders and generative adversarial networks have all emerged recently, making it possible to describe the complexity of this data without worrying about underfitting.

The high-dimensional probability distribution of words or images in a particular or generic domain can be modelled using these models. It is feasible to convert input data between different formats when combined with generative models that map the latent high-dimensional semantic space of language or images to a multimedia representation like text, audio, or video [3]. This opens up a wide range of application possibilities because a model may be taught to produce multimodal outputs in diverse formats, such as text, audio, or video, from different input formats.

In this paper, we intend to give a thorough review of the most widely used generative AI models and their effects on numerous sectors, including the arts and education. These sectors must change and adopt these methods because they can produce original artistic content and lengthy texts, continuing to add value. These models inspire artists and raise the standard of the content produced by instructors, not taking the place of human labour. The organisation of the paper is as follows: The primary generative models now in use are presented in a taxonomy first. We then examine the applications of each taxonomy category in depth. We wrap up by summarising the results and making recommendations for additional research. Note that we are not interested in the technical intricacies of these models' operation, but rather the applications of these models and the material they provide. We suggest using other references to gain a deeper understanding of deep learning and generative models.

2 Classification of Generative Artificial Intelligence Models

In this study, we have made an effort to taxonomize the present generative artificial models based on the primary mapping between input and output categories for multimedia. Figure 1 shows our results and emphasises 9 categories of models. Each of the models shown in Fig. 1 will have a detailed discussion in the section that follows. The emphasis of this manuscript is on the most recent developments in generative AI models, and all models mentioned have just recently been published, it is crucial to emphasise.

The deployment of these concepts has only involved six organisations. This is due to the fact that estimating the parameters of such models calls for a lot of processing power and a highly skilled team of data scientists and engineers. Therefore, only businesses that worked in tandem with acquired startups and academic institutions were able to successfully implement generative AI models. After examining and presenting the most recent generative artificial intelligence models, we will go into further detail about each category in the taxonomy shown in Fig. 1 in the following section.

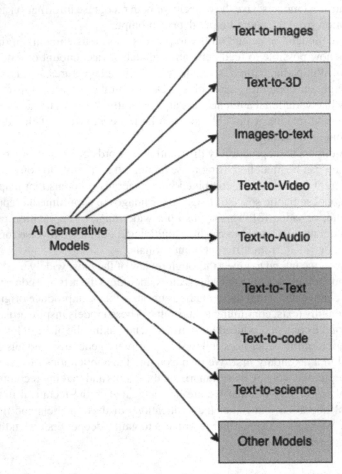

Fig. 1. A taxonomy depicting the classification of popular generative AI models based on their input and the format of the output they generate.

3   Categories of Generative AI Models

The nine categories depicted in Fig. 1 from the previous part will be further discussed in this section.

3.1 Text-to-Image Models

We'll look at models that accept a text prompt as input and produce an image to begin the analysis.

DALL·E 2. In response to a written prompt, DALLE 2, a generative model created by OpenAI, can create real-world visuals and artwork. Fortunately, this model can be accessed using the OpenAI API. As a result of utilising the CLIP neural network, DALLE 2 is able to combine ideas, attributes, and styles. Various (image, text) pairs were used to train the neural network known as CLIP (Contrastive Language-Image Pre-Training). With the help of instructions in natural language, CLIP can choose the most pertinent text excerpt given an image and has lately become a successful representation learner for images [4]. The desirable characteristics of CLIP embeddings include their amazing zero-shot capabilities, robustness to picture distribution shift, and fine-tuning to produce cutting-edge results. The CLIP image embedding decoder module is paired with an earlier model that creates potential CLIP image embeddings from a given text caption in order to obtain a whole generative model of images. Figure 2 displays an illustration of an image produced in response to a prompt.

Fig. 2. Image generated from the prompt "passing by street in cold winter while snowing at night in london street, digital art".

IMAGEN. It is a model that does text-to-image synthesis using huge transformer language models. Large language models that have been trained on text-only data are particularly good at encoding text for picture synthesis, which is one of the model's key conclusions. This model was made by Google, and their website has information on its API. The model has a good level of realism and image-text alignment, per Google's tests [5]. Google developed Drawbench, a collection of 200 prompts that facilitate the evaluation and comparison of text-to-image models, to assess the model. In order to translate text to a series of word embeddings, IMAGEN use a pretrained text encoder like BERT. Then, these embeddings are mapped to images with progressively higher resolutions using a cascade of conditional diffusion models.

Stable Diffusion. Alternative generative AI models include Stable Diffusion, a latent-diffusion model created by the CompVis group at LMU Munich. The use of a latent diffusion model, which permits image alteration through operations in the model's latent space, distinguishes Stable Diffusion from other diffusion models. Stable Diffusion's website API can be used to access it. The model comprises of a text encoder and an age generator, the latter of which operates only in the latent space for faster diffusion than earlier models [6]. Figure 3 displays an illustration of an image produced using Stable Diffusion.

Fig. 3. Image generated from the prompt "frog jumping in rain, digital art".

Muse. The Muse model is a text-to-image converter that produces stunning images while being more effective than diffusion or autoregressive models. This is because it requires fewer sample iterations and uses discrete tokens [7]. Muse is more effective than an autoregressive model due to parallel decoding; it is 10 times faster at inference time than Imagen-3B or Parti-3B and 3 times faster than Stable Diffusion v1.4, despite the fact that both models operate in a VQGAN's latent space.

3.2   Text-to-3D Models

Models that turn text cues into 2D graphics were covered in the section before. However, some sectors, like the gaming industry, demand the creation of 3D images. We will provide a quick description of two text-to-3D models in this section: DreamFusion and Magic3D.

DreamFusion. It is a Google Research model that seeks to produce 3D graphics from text cues. To do this, the model distils a loss from a 2D diffusion model and substitutes the prior CLIP approaches with a pretrained 2D text-to-image diffusion model. This implies that samples are produced using the diffusion model as a loss in a general continuous optimisation problem. Creating 3D models that resemble decent photos when rendered from random angles is difficult because sampling in parameter space is substantially more difficult than sampling in pixel space [8]. It tackles this issue by using a differentiable generator rather than only focusing on sampling pixels. This enables the model to produce 3D models that from various perspectives resemble appealing photographs. It's important to note that the DreamFusion website allows you to view the entire animated image.

Magic3D. The Dreamfusion text-to-3D model's drawbacks of a protracted processing time and poor image quality have been addressed by NVIDIA Corporation's Magic3D text-to-3D model [20]. A sparse 3D hash grid structure is used to accelerate a low-resolution diffusion prior that Magic3D builds using a two-stage optimisation frame-work. A textured 3D mesh model is produced as a result of this procedure, which is further optimised using a quick differentiable render [9]. Magic3D outperforms Dream-Fusion in human evaluations, with 61.7% of respondents saying they prefer it. The quality of the generated 3D shapes is far superior than that of DreamFusion's, both in terms of geometry and texture.

3.3 Image-to-Text Models

The task of producing a textual description of a picture, which is the inverse mapping of the text-to-image synthesis models previously addressed, is the main topic of this section. This section examines Flamingo and VisualGPT, two models that carry out this duty in addition to others.

Flamingo. It is a Visual Language Model made by Deepmind that only requires a small amount of learning to carry out a variety of vision and language tasks when given a limited number of input/output samples. It is made up of visually conditioned autoregressive text generation models that accept as input a string of text tokens interspersed with images and/or videos and generate text as the result [10]. Flamingo produces a text response in response to a query that includes a photo or video. The model combines a huge language model that executes a fundamental form of reasoning with a vision model that analyses visual scenes. On a sizable corpus of textual data, the language model is trained.

VisualGPT. It is a model for image captioning created by OpenAI that makes use of the GPT-2 language model's expertise. To close the semantic gap between various modalities, the model includes a unique encoder-decoder attention mechanism with an unsaturated rectified gating function [11]. The fact that VisualGPT uses less data than other image-to-text algorithms is one of its main advantages. This may enable rapid data curation, descriptions of unusual objects, and applications in specialised fields. Additionally, this model's API is accessible on GitHub.

3.4 Text-to-Video Models

The capacity to create images from text has been proven in the previous subsections. Given this, it makes sense to produce videos, which are essentially a series of images, from text. We will talk about two models that are capable of doing this in this section: Phenaki and Soundify.

Phenaki. Phenaki is a video synthesis model created by Google Research that can produce lifelike films in response to textual cues. This model's API is more broadly accessible because it is accessible from GitHub. The ability of Phenaki to generate films from open domain time-variable cues makes it special. It was trained on both a sizable dataset of image-text pairs and a smaller dataset of video-text examples in order to overcome difficulties with data scarcity. Because text-video datasets are smaller and have fewer inputs than image-text datasets, this approach was able to generalise beyond the capabilities of video datasets. Due to computing capacity for videos of varied length, there are restrictions, nevertheless. The C-ViViT encoder, training transform, and video generator are the three parts of the model. Videos are compressed by the encoder, and the initial tokens are converted into embeddings before being passed via a spatial and temporal transformer [12]. The output of the spatial transformer is then activate-free, single-linear projected back to pixel space. This method creates different, temporally consistent films based on free domain prompts, even when the prompt is a novel concept assemblage. The model can produce videos up to several minutes in length, while being trained on 1.4 s videos.

Soundify. Runway created a method called Soundify to help professionals with video editing discover and match the right sounds. The system makes use of high-quality sound effect libraries and the zero-shot image classification capabilities of CLIP, a neural network. Specifically, classification, synchronisation, and mix make up its three main components. Sound effects are matched to videos in the classification phase by categorising the sound emitters present. [13] The video is divided based on absolute colour histogram distances, which helps to reduce the number of unique sound emitters. In the synchronisation phase, intervals are found by comparing the labels of the effects with each frame and spotting repeated matches above a predetermined threshold. Effects are divided into one-second segments in the mix section, which are subsequently combined using crossfades.

3.5 Text-to-Audio Models

We discovered in the previous subsection that non-structured data formats other than photos are also significant. In many instances, like movies and music, audio is also essential. So, in this subsection, we'll look at three models that accept text as input and output audio.

AudioLM. By converting the input audio into a series of discrete tokens and treating the synthesis of audio as a language modelling task in this representation space, Google has created the AudioLM model, which produces high-quality audio with long-term consistency. The model is able to provide realistic and coherent continuations when given brief instructions because it was trained on vast corpora of unprocessed audio waveforms. Despite not having been trained with any symbolic representation of music, the model can even be extended beyond speech to produce logical piano music continuations. This model's API is available on GitHub. It might be difficult to provide great audio quality while demonstrating consistency since audio signals contain several abstraction scales.

To overcome this difficulty, AudioLM combines recent developments in neural audio compression, self-supervised representation learning, and language modelling. Raters listened to a 10-s clip and identified whether it was human speech or a synthetic continuation to assess the performance of the model. Based on 1000 ratings, 51.2% of the ratings were correctly classified, which is not statistically significant when labels are chosen at random [14]. This shows that it is impossible for humans to tell the difference between artificial and actual audio samples produced by the model.

Jukebox. This article discusses an OpenAI model for making music that can produce songs with singing in the raw audio domain. On GitHub, you can access the model's API. The goal of this technique is to produce music directly as raw audio, in contrast to earlier text-to-music models that produced symbolic piano-roll representations. However, due to the high dimensionality of raw audio and its high long-range dependencies, learning the high-level semantics of music is challenging. The model uses a hierarchical VQ-VAE architecture to compress the audio into a discrete space while maintaining the most information possible with a unique loss function in order to address this. The model's VQ-VAE contains 5 billion parameters and was trained over three days on 9-s audio clips using a dataset of 1.2 million English songs from LyricWiki [15]. The model is able to produce music in a variety of genres, including jazz, rock, and hip-hop.

Whisper. An audio-to-text converter model that was created by OpenAI is capable of carrying out a number of tasks, including language identification, translation, and multilingual speech recognition. Its API is accessible on the GitHub website, similar to that of other models. The primary difficulty for a voice recognition system is to function well in a variety of settings without necessitating supervised decoder fine-tuning for each deployment distribution. However, the absence of a top-notch pre-trained decoder makes this difficult to accomplish. The model is trained using a sizable dataset of 680,000 h of labelled audio data, which is acquired from the internet to cover a wide distribution of audio from various contexts, recording setups, speakers, and languages in order to solve this. To avoid degrading the model, the model makes sure that the dataset only contains human voice and leaves out machine learning voice. The architecture used by the model, an encoder-decoder transformer, has been shown to scale consistently.

3.6 Text-to-Text Models

The models mentioned so far concentrate on transforming unstructured data into different formats. To execute duties like responding to common questions, it may occasionally be necessary to transform text into another text. The four models listed below are examples of this kind; they handle text inputs and produce text outputs in order to satisfy specific needs.

ChatGPT. OpenAI created ChatGPT, a sophisticated conversational AI model. It is a powerful model that can interact in a conversational manner with users, providing natural language answers to questions and to follow-up inquiries. Similar to earlier language models like GPT-2 and GPT-3, the model is based on a transformer architecture, allowing it to process enormous volumes of text and produce high-quality responses.

The capacity of ChatGPT to use reinforcement learning to learn from user comments is one of its distinctive features. Human instructors provided conversational scenarios where they took on the roles of both the user and the AI assistant during the training process. In order to assist the model, learn and develop, the human trainers would subsequently provide feedback on the model's responses to those conversations.

The training procedure for ChatGPT combines reinforcement learning with supervised fine-tuning. In the beginning, the model is trained using supervised fine-tuning, in which human trainers provide conversational examples, and the model learns to generate responses based on those examples [14]. The model is then improved further through reinforcement learning, where it receives comments from human trainers on its generated responses and learns to become more sociable.

ChatGPT is able to solve simple mathematical equations and generate code in addition to being able to carry on a conversation. This makes it a flexible tool for a variety of applications, such as chatbots, personal assistants, and customer support. Overall, ChatGPT is a promising tool for enhancing future human-AI interactions and represents a substantial leap in conversational AI (Figs. 4 and 5).

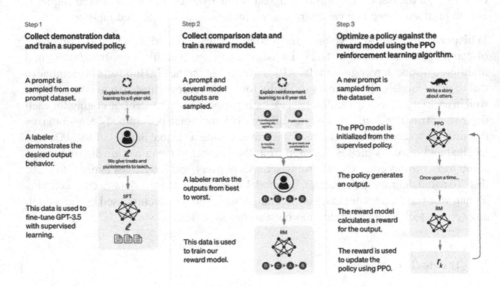

Fig. 4. Training steps of ChatGPT, combining supervised learning with reinforcement learning.

LaMDA. LaMDA is a specialised neural language model based on transformers that is intended for dialogue applications. It was particularly trained on dialogues, unlike other language models, and it has up to 137B parameters. One of the largest pre-trained language models, the model was pre-trained using 1.56T words of public dialogue data and web content. The model can be fine-tuned to increase its level of safety and factual

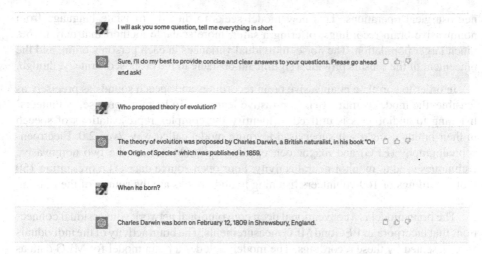

I will ask you some question, tell me everything in short

Sure, I'll do my best to provide concise and clear answers to your questions. Please go ahead and ask!

Who proposed theory of evolution?

The theory of evolution was proposed by Charles Darwin, a British naturalist, in his book "On the Origin of Species" which was published in 1859.

When he born?

Charles Darwin was born on February 12, 1809 in Shrewsbury, England.

Fig. 5. Example of a dialog made with ChatGPT.

correctness. LaMDA is well appropriate for model scaling since it makes use of the Transformers' capacity to handle long-term dependencies in text.

The model uses a single architecture to carry out a number of tasks: it creates a number of potential responses to a prompt, eliminates any that are hazardous or improper, and then bases the remaining responses on an outside knowledge source to assure their accuracy [16]. The highest-quality response for the particular question is then chosen by re-ranking the grounded responses. The model is a useful tool for a range of applications since it can manage complex dialogues with various responses.

PEER. The "Collaborative Writing Assistant," a collaborative language model created by Meta AI research, is intended to encompass the complete writing process. The four steps of the model are Plan, Edit, Explain, and Repeat. Until the text is in a satisfactory state and doesn't need any more updates, these steps are repeated.

The concept enables the division of the writing of a paper task into numerous simpler subtasks. The model also enables human interaction at any time and permits model steering in any direction.

The strategy is self-training, utilising models to fill in missing data and then training other models on this synthetic data. The model is mostly trained using Wikipedia edit histories. A retrieval method that occasionally fails to make up for the fact that comments are frequently loud and devoid of citations is one drawback.

To create a sequence of texts, the entire process of developing a plan, gathering information, editing it, and presenting it can be repeated several times. A DeepSpeed transformer is employed during the training of this model. The Collaborative Writing Assistant is a promising tool for group writing that could help authors at every stage of the writing process.

Meta AI Speech from Brain. To assist those who are unable to communicate normally through speech, typing, or gestures, Meta AI has created a model. Such individuals have in the past been forced to rely on invasive brain-recording methods that demand neurosurgical operations. This new model seeks to directly translate language from noninvasive brain recordings, offering a safer, more scalable method that may help a much larger population. The noise, individual variances in each person's brain, and the placement of the sensors provide a significant obstacle to the proposed strategy, though.

In order to correlate noninvasive brain recordings and speech sounds as precisely as feasible, the model is trained via contrastive learning. To be more precise, volunteers' listening to audiobooks is utilized to identify the complex representations of speech in their brains using a self-supervised learning model called wave2vec 2.0. Electroencephalography (EEG) and magnetoencephalography (MEG) are the two noninvasive techniques used to monitor neural activity. Four open-source datasets representing 150 h of recordings of 169 volunteers listening to audiobooks are the source of the training data.

The brain model is a conventional deep convolutional network with residual connections that incorporates EEG and MEG measurements. The brain activity of the individuals is represented by these recordings. The model includes a brain model for MEG data as well as a speech model for sound.

The study's findings suggest that a number of algorithmic elements were helpful to decoding performance, and an examination reveals that the algorithm gets better as the number of EEG and MEG recordings rises. The study shows that despite noise and data unpredictability, self-supervised trained AI can decipher perceived speech. Though the study primarily focuses on speech perception, expanding this research to include speech production is the ultimate objective. Despite this drawback, the research has positive implications for people who struggle to communicate in conventional ways.

3.7   Text-to-Code Models

While there are many models that can be used with text written in natural language, it's important to remember that not all text has the same syntax, particularly when it comes to programming code. Programming requires the translation of concepts into code, and tools like Codex and Alphacode can be helpful in accomplishing this process.

Codex. The AI system Codex, created by OpenAI, can translate language into code, making it a useful tool for programming chores. This all-purpose programming approach is intended to assist programmers in decomposing large issues into smaller, easier-to-manage ones, which can then be mapped to pre-existing code libraries, APIs, or functions. Coding's second phase is frequently the most time-consuming, and this is where Codex excels. It was trained on 179 GB of distinct Python files under 1MB that were gathered from GitHub's open-source software repositories in May 2020. GPT-3, which has strong natural language processing capabilities, provides the basis for Codex's fine-tuning [18]. On the website for OpenAI, one can access Codex's demo or API to use it.

Alphacode. Although some language models can produce code, they perform poorly when tested against challenging, uncharted problems. The language model Alphacode was created for code creation and can handle more complex reasoning. A combination of elements, including a sizable and effective transformer-based architecture, a large-scale model sampling strategy, and a huge dataset for training and evaluation, is the secret to its success.

Code from GitHub repositories totaling 715.1 GB makes up the dataset used by Alphacode for training, which is significantly greater than the dataset used by Codex for pre-training. A dataset from the Codeforces platform is also used to fine-tune the model. The coding competition platform Codeforces offers a useful data set for model validation and performance enhancement.

In contrast to decoder-only models frequently employed in other code generation systems, the architecture of Alphacode employs an encoder-decoder transformer paradigm, allowing for bidirectional description and enhanced flexibility [19]. The model makes use of both shallow and deep encoders to increase efficiency. Additionally, multi-query attention is used to lower sampling costs.

3.8 Text-to-Science Models

With the development of the Galactica and Minerva models, the application of generative AI is expanding to include scientific literature as well. Investigation of the earliest initiatives towards automating scientific text generation is crucial, despite the fact that there has been little development in this area.

Galactica. Galactica is a new huge AI model created by Papers with Code and Meta AI with the goal of autonomously organising scientific content. The model's capacity to train for numerous epochs without overfitting, enhancing upstream and downstream performance with repeated tokens, is one of its key advantages. All data is processed in a standard markdown format to combine knowledge from various sources, ensuring an effective strategy. The model uses a specific token to predict citations, and its accuracy rises with scale and improved citation distribution [20]. Additionally, the model is capable of multi-modal tasks like protein sequences and SMILES chemical formulas. Across all model sizes, Galactica uses a transformer architecture with GeLU activation that is only used in a decoder setup.

Minerva. A language model called Minerva was created primarily to answer mathematical and scientific problems using a sequential line of reasoning. The model may generate models at scale and use the finest inference approaches because the training data is carefully gathered to concentrate on quantitative reasoning issues. Without using external tools like calculators, Minerva generates solutions step-by-step using math and symbolic manipulation. This is a novel method of problem-solving.

3.9 Other Models

There are more models that are worthwhile taking into consideration in addition to the generative AI models already described. Deepmind's Alphatensor, which was created, is capable of finding new algorithms. For instance, it can produce more effective matrix multiplication algorithms, which is crucial for enhancing calculations in neural networks and scientific computing routines. The method makes advantage of deep reinforcement learning, and the AlphaTensor agent is trained to play a single-player game that entails locating tensor decompositions in a finite factor space. Synthetic training games are used by AlphaTensor to leverage symmetries using a specialised neural network architecture.

GATO, a single generalist agent that functions as a multi-modal, multi-task, and multi-embodiment generalist policy, is another Deepmind model. The same network may carry out many tasks including playing Atari, captioning photos, talking, stacking blocks, and more with the same weights. The requirement for manually creating policy models with their unique inductive biases is reduced when using a single neural sequence model for all tasks, while the quantity and variety of training data are also increased. This universal agent is effective at a variety of activities, and it can be modified with little additional data to be effective at an even greater variety of tasks.

As demonstrated by ChatBCG, other published generative AI models can similarly produce human motion or slides using ChatGPT as a stand-in model.

4 Conclusions and Further Work

The amazing capabilities of generative AI in tasks like text-to-image and text-to-audio, which demonstrate its inventiveness and personalisation, are highlighted in this research. Additionally, text-to-science and text-to-code tasks' accuracy shows the potential for generative AI to optimize both creative and non-creative tasks, which could have a significant positive impact on economies.

Although generative AI models have impressive capabilities, there are still a number of restrictions and difficulties that need to be resolved. The lack of datasets is one of the biggest problems, especially for difficult jobs like text-to-science or text-to-audio. Finding appropriate data takes time, and some models' massive dataset requirements make training them much more challenging. Another concern is that these models are limited in their capacity for innovation and adaptability since they struggle to handle issues that fall outside the purview of their training data.

The extensive computing required to run these models presents another difficulty. It can take several days or even weeks to train them because it demands sophisticated computational resources. Additionally, there is a chance that the training data will be biased, which could impact the models' precision and dependability. Although some models, like Galactica, make an effort to address this problem through bias reduction techniques, it is still a major obstacle for generative artificial intelligence.

The Minerva model, among other recent innovations, has demonstrated encouraging results in terms of comprehending and piecemealing equations. This represents a significant advance because one of the key drawbacks of these models is that they do not fully comprehend the tasks at hand. However, some models, like text-to-video, still struggle with accuracy because it's difficult to create accurate and realistic videos.

These models are also fraught with ethical issues, particularly in light of text-to-video technology's potential for producing deep fakes. As a result, it's important to limit the usage of these models and make sure their ethical implications are carefully taken into account.

Last but not least, we have only just begun to fully understand the potential and function of generative artificial intelligence. Given that each model has unique advantages and disadvantages, comparisons between them, such as that between Google and ChatGPT3, are not entirely accurate. It is crucial to be conscious of these restrictions and seek to enhance the models in the upcoming years.

References

1. Bhavya, B., Xiong, J., Zhai, C.: Analogy generation by prompting large language models: a case study of instructgpt. arXiv preprint arXiv:2210.04186 (2022)
2. Budzianowski, P., Vulic, I.: Hello, it's gpt-2–how can i help you? Towards the use of pretrained language models for task-oriented dialogue systems. arXiv preprint arXiv:1907.05774 (2019)
3. Chang, H., et al.: Muse: text-to-image generation via masked generative transformers. arXiv preprint arXiv:2301.00704 (2023)
4. Borsos, Z., et al.: AudioLM: a language modeling approach to audio generation. arXiv preprint arXiv:2209.03143 (2022)
5. Balaji, Y., et al.: Text-to-image diffusion models with an ensemble of expert denoisers. arXiv preprint arXiv:2211.01324 (2022)
6. Heusel, M., Ramsauer, H., Unterthiner, T., Nessler, B., Hochreiter, S.: GANs trained by a two time-scale update rule converge to a local nash equilibrium. In: Advances in Neural Information Processing Systems, vol. 30 (2017)
7. Kim, J.-H., Kim, Y., Lee, J., Yoo, K.M., Lee, S.-W.: Mutual information divergence: a unified metric for multimodal generative models. arXiv preprint arXiv:2205.13445 (2022)
8. Ramesh, A., Dhariwal, P., Nichol, A., Chu, C., Chen, M.: Hierarchical text-conditional image generation with clip latents. arXiv preprint arXiv:2204.06125 (2022)
9. Saharia, C., et al.: Photorealistic text-to-image diffusion models with deep language understanding. arXiv preprint arXiv:2205.11487 (2022)
10. Song, Y., Sohl-Dickstein, J., Kingma, D.P., Kumar, A., Ermon, S., Poole, B.: Score-based generative modeling through stochastic differential equations. arXiv preprint arXiv:2011.13456 (2020)
11. Chowdhery, A., et al.: Palm: Scaling language modeling with pathways. arXiv preprint arXiv:2204.02311 (2022)
12. Zhou, Q., et al.: A comprehensive survey on pretrained foundation models: a history from BERT to ChatGPT. arXiv preprint arXiv:2302.09419 (2023)
13. Papineni, K., Roukos, S., Ward, T., Zhu, W.-J.: BLEU: a method for automatic evaluation of machine translation. In: Proceedings of the 40th Annual Meeting of the Association for Computational Linguistics, pp. 311–318 (2002)
14. Lin, S., Hilton, J., Evans, O.: Truthfulqa: measuring how models mimic human falsehoods. arXiv preprint arXiv:2109.07958 (2021)
15. Rajawat, A.S., Bedi, P., Goyal, S.B., Shaw, R.N., Ghosh, A.: Reliability analysis in cyber-physical system using deep learning for smart cities industrial IoT network node. In: Piuri, V., Shaw, R.N., Ghosh, A., Islam, R. (eds.) AI and IoT for Smart City Applications. SCI, vol. 1002, pp. 157–169. Springer, Singapore (2022). https://doi.org/10.1007/978-981-16-7498-3_10
16. Thoppilan, R., et al.: Lamda: language models for dialog applications. arXiv preprint arXiv:2201.08239 (2022)
17. Pant, P., et al.: Study of AI and ML Based Technologies used in international space station. Glob. J. Innov. Emerg. Technol. 1(2) (2022). https://doi.org/10.58260/j.iet.2202.0102
18. Carlini, Liu, Y., Daume III, H., Erlingsson, U., Kohno, T., Song, D.: Extracting training data from large language models. In: 30th USENIX Security Symposium (USENIX Security 21) (2021)
19. Madaan, A., Zhou, S., Alon, U., Yang, Y., Neubig, G.: Language models of code are few-shot commonsense learners. arXiv preprint arXiv:2210.07128 (2022)
20. Taylor, R., et al.: Galactica: a large language model for science. arXiv preprint arXiv:2211.09085 (2022)

Cloud Computing Enabled Autonomous Forest Fire Surveillance System Using Internet-of-Things

Kaushal Mehta and Sachin Sharma$^{(\boxtimes)}$ (iD)

Department of Computer Science and Engineering, Graphic Era Deemed to be University,
Dehradun, India
`sachin.cse@geu.ac.in`

Abstract. Our planet's surface is one-third covered in forests. Despite being a great source of natural resources, the world has experienced numerous dangerous calamities, both natural and man-made, which have done a lot of damage to humanity. The forest fire is one such catastrophe. This paper shows a workaround system to detect forest fires as well as a monitoring station to simultaneously monitor the forest area in order to prevent the forest from suffering severe losses from fire. IoT is the technology in use. Here the sensors detect any changes in the environment, and with the integration of the Node MCU Microcontroller, the recorded fluctuation is sent to Cloud Storage which is "Google Firebase." The concerned officials can monitor the relevant system based on real-time updates in the monitoring station. This early detection of a forest fire would help to take necessary measures to control and prevent the fire which might spread throughout the forest.

Keywords: Fire Detection · Sensors · IoT · Node MCU · Monitoring Station · Google Firebase

1 Introduction

As per the report of Global Forest Resources Assessment it is found that area covered by forests is 4.06 billion hectares (10.0 billion acres; 40.6 million square kilometres; 15.7 million square miles), which is approximately 31% land of the world, as per 2020. It is the home of various species of flora and fauna. Even humans are dependent on forests for fresh oxygen and other resources. These are the most critical factors affecting the lives of every biotic or abiotic component of the environment. Forests also protect wildlife from floods, soil erosion, and pollution. It is also a source of employment to many tribes and cultures around the world. In India, many festivals are associated with the worship of forests and various events are organized for thanking the forests. Forest fires have caused more damage in recent times. The survey report from "National Interagency Centre" states that more than 58.985 wildlife has been affected in 2021. In 2020, the damage existed around 58,950 and about 10 million acres were blazed in the forest fire.

R. N. Shaw et al. (Eds.): ICACIS 2023, CCIS 1920, pp. 104–116, 2023.
https://doi.org/10.1007/978-3-031-45121-8_10

But awareness schemes and the latest innovations for forest fire detection have shown results in a reduction in damages which is less as compared to the year 2017 i.e., 71,499 fires. Figure 1 depicts the acres of land damaged due to forest fire through the world. Figure 2 illustrates the number of fires taken place in forest through the world. Thus, it has to be considered that earliest detection of fires in the forest and the induction of appropriate measures can prevent as well as minimize loss and casualties due to the forest fires.

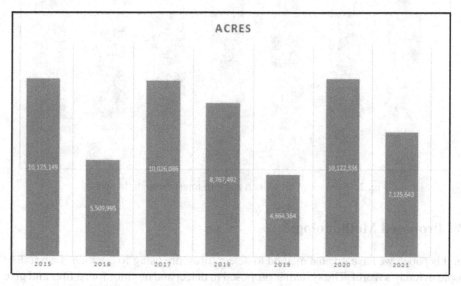

Fig. 1. Acres of land damaged due to forest fire through the world.

2 Literature Review

In [1], authors have made an IoT device that is using ESP32 module, GSM module, and GPS module. These are placed in certain areas of the forest and then detection is sent via SMS from the GSM module to the user's mobile phone. This is quite unique. But the drawback is we have to recharge the SIM Card to get the SMS on the mobile phone, which adds extra cost to the system. In [2], authors have discussed an emerging technology that is IoT with Image processing. The processing of data is done using MATLAB software. The alert is generated as well as the water pump is situated near every node which spread out water in case of fire. The cost of setting up this system is very high and installation is quite complex. There are many more researches have done a lot of work in these fields but we have thought outside of the box and provided a more efficient solution to forest fires which is mentioned in the proposed methodology of this paper.

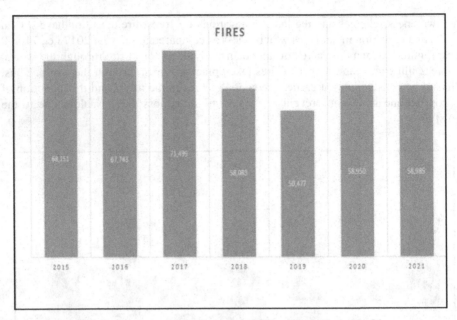

Fig. 2. Number of fires taken place in forest through the world.

3 Proposed Methodology

In this paper, we have given a method to detect forest fire using IoT, which is a trending topic in today's world. The system is proposed to detect and monitor forest fires and give real-time updates to the concerned officials. The system is based on sensors and a Wi-Fi-enabled microcontroller which needs internet connectivity to operate [3]. The sensors are "Flame Sensor" and "MQ2 Gas Sensor". The Wi-Fi-enabled microcontroller is used to send the data gathered from the sensors, and then it sends the data after processing the values to the cloud storage which is further transmitted to the monitoring station, that can be viewed anytime and from anywhere [4]. The sensors are placed throughout the forest according to the grid mapped on the vector image of the forest. The distance measured to map is in the ratio of 1:4. For example, within 1 km, only 5 sensors can be placed at an interval of 250 m end points inclusive. Following each node as a central point the pattern can be extended to horizontal as well as vertical line. Thus, creating a grid. The number of nodes required to place in the forest can be seen using grid mapping. The formula used is 1 km area is divided into four parts such that each node is placed at a distance of 250 m apart. The placement of sensors starts from the Centre of the map. Further Gas Sensors are placed first in the grid Holes. After placing Gas sensors, flame sensors are placed in between the gas sensors. The Ideology for this arrangement of sensors is to avoid false alerts and cover the forest at the requirement of minimum sensors and maximum coverage of the forest area. Furthermore, the mapping of the vector image of the forest is done, which shows the location of the sensors in the monitoring station [5].

IoT consists of hardware prototype used for our proposed system is explained below.

- *Flame Sensor:* It is used to detect the presence of fire, gives the upper hand over sensors like Temperature and IR sensors, as it detects actual Fire instead of Looking for Colour change and increase in temperature.
- *MQ2 Gas Sensor:* It is used to detect the emission of CO_2 gas from the environment.
- *NodeMCU Microcontroller:* It is used to connect all the Sensors to this Microcontroller and enable the transfer of data via the WIFI Module. Further, the code of the IoT is stored in this module, which is non-volatile until the life of the Module.
- *Jumper Wires:* It is used to make wired connections among the sensors.
- *Breadboard:* It is used as the base for holding the overall system and supports their inter-communication
- *Micro-USB Cable:* It is used to provide power supply to NodeMCU.

The setup is shown in Fig. 8. Monitoring station has made some specific modules to make the Monitoring station a working website, which is dynamic in nature and supports real time updates.

- *App.js:* The main component of the Monitoring Station, Providing Connectivity to Splash Screen and Header Component.
- *Firebase.js:* The component having all the keys required for firebase connectivity.
- *ForestSection.js:* This component fetches data from the firebase and does the mapping of the values to the corresponding nodes in form of icons, placed in the monitoring station. The mapping is done using an array where Id is used as a reference to the actual variables used to store values in Firebase real-time datatypes. Ternary Operator is used for mapping "Blue" and "Green" Components in the Map.
- *Header.js:* This component has feature of tab layout in the system which currently supports 2 tabs.

There are other modules too, which are created to run functionalities of the Monitoring Station. All these are manually coded and hence can be customized as per the user's demand. The "Flame Sensor" and the "Gas Sensor" are connected to the "NodeMCU Microcontroller", ESP8266 enabled Wi-Fi module, via connecting wires, the Power Supply is given through a "Micro-USB" cable connected to a 5 V power supply. After connecting the hardware setup, it is then programmed with a computer system and the codes are uploaded to the NodeMCU Module. And tested in the serial Monitor of the Arduino Software. After successful testing in the system, the hardware is ready to be used and just needs a power supply to work effectively. Now as the system starts to get power supply it sends the data to the cloud storage at an interval of 1000 ms which is 1 s. The data is processed through the Wi-Fi module ESP8266 and then collected in the real-time data of the Firebase Database which can be accessed through the firebase account. As data is stored in the firebase real-time database, now our monitoring station can get the data from there and we can make the working system live. Now the colour code used for the flame sensor is Blue and for the gas sensor is green. As we get any detection of fire or smoke through the embedded hardware in the forest area the respective location of the node in the monitoring system will turn red. All these updates can be seen live in the station through real-time mapping of data. Now as the changes get redder, detection of forest fire is confirmed and the concerned officials can take necessary actions against it.

This system also helps to distinguish between false alarms. Such as only the gas sensor is turned red and the flame sensors are still blue [6]. Then we can rest assured that fire has not occurred and someone is having a campfire or bonfire at the forest location.

Thus, the prototype model not only gives forest fire detection but also saves us from false alarms. The events in the system are only triggered at their specific threshold values, such as the flame sensor will only send data when there is a real flame nearby [7]. Similarly, the gas sensor will send the data continuously but the system will only turn red when the value of the gas sensor reaches more than or equal to 300 ppm. Below this it will not update the system, only data will be sent to the firebase.

Figure 3 illustrates the block diagram of the proposed model. For the internet, Wi-Fi connectivity is provided from the nearby Forest Department. The threshold set for the alert on detection of CO_2 gas is passed after which the value of nodes is placed in the sensor displayed on a web-page-based monitoring system [8].

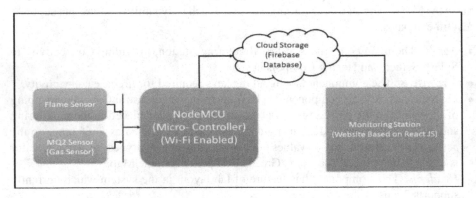

Fig. 3. Block diagram of proposed system.

The workflow explains the working of the setup which is used for detecting the forest fire in our proposed methodology (Fig. 4). Firstly, the flame sensor and the smoke sensor measure the status of the environment in terms of values that are driven by the changes nearby the sensors [9]. In case of any detection, the value is sent to the cloud database (Google's Firebase Database). If the threshold value is not exceeded the sensors will keep sensing. Thus, we get real-time updates from the hardware setup [10]. Once the value is reached to firebase it is mapped into the monitoring station and changes the value of the corresponding nodes where initially the status is Blue or Green in colour of the icon, then if a certain node has detected something it will turn its color to Red [11]. Also, we are able to get the exact location of the forest fire where it has taken place on the basis of real-time updates. After this, the forest officials can take necessary actions to tackle the forest fire [12].

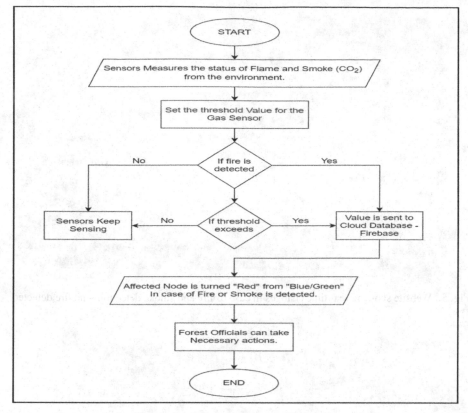

Fig. 4. Workflow of the proposed system.

4   Results Analysis and Discussion

We have developed the website to monitor the forest fire using React JS, JavaScript, HTML, and CSS. This website is live with the help of Google's Firebase database, where we have used the facilities of Hosting Fire store and Real-time database. The monitoring station is divided into two portions. First is the "Home" tab, where there are two Portions. The first section depicts the mapping of the forest with the grid map providing the location of the sensors and another depicts the usage of the icons for gas sensors as well as a flame sensor for clarity purposes.

Secondly, there is the developers' info, where we have discussed our role in the project, and adjacent to this a feedback form is given where users can give us feedback or can contact us, the data is saved in the fire store section of the Firebase database. The activity of the monitoring station can be seen Fig. 5 and Fig. 6. The update is visible, which is taken when we run this project for demonstration purposes. Further, the real-time updates can be monitored on the Firebase website within the "Real-time database" component. All the variables which are used for the real-time capturing of data are shown with their corresponding values, in Fig. 7. Figure 8 depicts the hardware setup of IoT devices

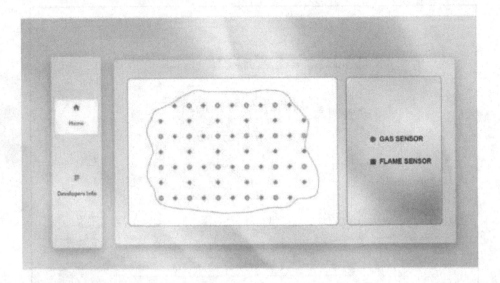

Fig. 5. Website showing real-time changes in case of fire and smoke detection – no fire detected.

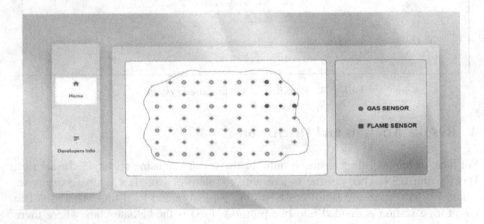

Fig. 6. Website showing real-time changes in case of fire and smoke detection – fire detected.

Fig. 7. Firebase real-time data updates

Fig. 8. Hardware setup of IoT devices.

5 Advantages

Cloud computing enabled autonomous forest fire surveillance systems using Internet of Things (IoT) offer several advantages compared to traditional forest fire surveillance methods. Some of these benefits include (Fig. 9):

- *Real-time monitoring:* IoT devices equipped with sensors can provide real-time data about the temperature, humidity, and smoke levels in the forest, allowing authorities to quickly detect and respond to a fire outbreak.

Fig. 9. Advantages.

- *Improved accuracy:* IoT devices provide more accurate and reliable data compared to manual monitoring methods, reducing the risk of false alarms and increasing the effectiveness of fire response efforts.
- *Scalability:* Cloud computing allows for easy scaling of the system, making it possible to add more devices as needed without having to invest in new infrastructure. *Cost effectiveness:* Cloud computing enables cost-effective storage and processing of large amounts of data, reducing the cost of monitoring and response efforts.
- *Easy access to data:* Storing data in the cloud makes it accessible from anywhere with an internet connection, allowing authorities to quickly access critical information and make informed decisions in real-time.
- *Predictive analytics:* Using advanced analytics tools, cloud based forest fire surveillance systems can analyse data from multiple sources to identify patterns and predict potential fire outbreaks, allowing for proactive fire prevention efforts.

6   Challenges

While cloud computing enabled autonomous forest fire surveillance systems using Internet of Things (IoT) offer several advantages, there are also several challenges that need to be addressed to ensure their effective implementation (Fig. 10):

- *Network connectivity:* IoT devices require a stable and reliable network connection to transmit data to the cloud, which can be a challenge in remote and rural areas where connectivity is limited.

Fig. 10. Challenges.

- *Data privacy and security:* Storing sensitive data in the cloud increases the risk of data breaches and cyberattacks, requiring strong security [13] measures to protect sensitive information.
- *Interoperability:* IoT devices from different manufacturers may not be compatible with each other, causing difficulties in integrating data from multiple sources and implementing a cohesive forest fire surveillance system.
- *Cost:* The cost of purchasing and deploying IoT devices, as well as the cost of storing and processing data in the cloud, can be a challenge for some organizations, especially in developing countries.
- *Maintenance and upgrades:* Maintaining and upgrading IoT devices and cloud infrastructure can be costly and time consuming, requiring ongoing investment and effort to ensure the system remains effective.
- *Technical expertise:* Implementing and maintaining a cloud computing enabled forest fire surveillance system using IoT requires technical expertise and specialized skills, which can be a challenge for some organizations to acquire.

7 Future Perspectives

The future of cloud computing enabled autonomous forest fire surveillance systems using Internet of Things (IoT) looks promising, as the technology continues to evolve and advance. Here are some of the trends and developments that are likely to shape the future of this field (Fig. 11):

- *Advancements in IoT devices:* IoT devices are becoming more compact, affordable, and sophisticated, making it possible to deploy more devices in more areas to provide more comprehensive coverage and real-time monitoring. *Improved data analytics:* Advances in artificial intelligence (AI) and machine learning (ML) will allow for

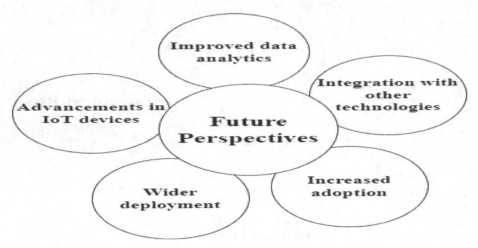

Fig. 11. Future perspectives.

more accurate and sophisticated data analysis, enabling more effective fire detection, prediction, and response.

- *Integration with other technologies:* Cloud computing enabled forest fire surveillance systems using IoT are likely to become more integrated with other technologies such as satellite imagery, drones, and unmanned aerial vehicles (UAVs), providing a more comprehensive and integrated approach to fire monitoring and response.
- *Increased adoption:* As the benefits of cloud computing enabled forest fire surveillance systems become more widely recognized, it is likely that more organizations will adopt this technology, leading to increased investment and development in this field.
- *Wider deployment:* The use of cloud computing enabled forest fire surveillance systems is likely to expand beyond just forest fire monitoring and into other areas, such as agriculture, wildlife conservation, and disaster response, providing a wider range of benefits to communities and the environment.

8   Conclusion

Modern technology is working round-the-clock to find solutions to challenging real-world issues. They must be effective in terms of cost and resource use in addition to being a way to make things go well. With our suggested system, we have helped this race. The majority of the problems can be solved by our system during testing, but it should also be used in real-world situations when there is a real risk of forest fires and other variables that could impact the hardware module. Additionally, we don't utilise any third party applications like ThingSpeak or Blynk app, so data is not shared with any other applications, and our monitoring station may be adjusted to the user's requirements. These factors together make our system a cost-efficient system. The use of cloud computing and Internet of Things (IoT) in forest fire surveillance can provide a real-time, efficient and effective solution for detecting and monitoring forest fires. In such a system, IoT devices, such as sensors and cameras, are deployed in the forest to gather data about temperature, humidity, and smoke levels. The data is then transmitted to the cloud for processing, analysis and storage. The cloud computing platform allows for the processing of large amounts of data and provides a centralized location for storing and accessing the data. This data can be used to create real-time maps and visualizations of the fire's spread, as well as provide early warnings to the authorities to help them respond quickly to the emergency. Furthermore, cloud computing enables collaboration between different stakeholders, such as government agencies, firefighting organizations, and researchers, to effectively manage and prevent forest fires. The system can also be integrated with other technology such as drones, which can be used to get a closer look at the fire and provide additional data to support decision making. The use of cloud computing and IoT in autonomous forest fire surveillance can greatly improve the speed, accuracy and effectiveness of forest fire detection and response. It provides a more comprehensive solution for managing the threat of forest fires and helps ensure the safety of people and the environment.

References

1. Divya, A., Kavithanjali, T., Dharshini, P.: IoT enabled forest fire detection and early warning system. In: 2019 IEEE International Conference on System, Computation, Automation and Networking (ICSCAN), pp. 1–5. IEEE (2019)
2. Pareek, S., Shrivastava, S., Jhala, S., Siddiqui, J.A., Patidar, S.: IoT and image processing based forest monitoring and counteracting system. In: 2020 4th International Conference on Trends in Electronics and Informatics (ICOEI) (48184), pp. 1024–1027. IEEE (2020)
3. Dubey, V., Kumar, P., Chauhan, N.: Forest fire detection system using IoT and artificial neural network. In: Bhattacharyya, S., Hassanien, A., Gupta, D., Khanna, A., Pan, I. (eds.) International Conference on Innovative Computing and Communications. LNNS, vol. 55, pp. 323–337. Springer, Singapore (2019). https://doi.org/10.1007/978-981-13-2324-9_33
4. Vega-Rodríguez, R., Sendra, S., Lloret, J., RomeroDíaz, P., Garcia-Navas, J.L.: Low cost LoRa based network for forest fire detection. In: 2019 Sixth International Conference on Internet of Things: Systems, Management and Security (IOTSMS), pp. 177–184. IEEE (2019)
5. Kalatzis, N., Avgeris, M., Dechouniotis, D., Papadakis-Vlachopapadopoulos, K., Roussaki, I., Papavassiliou, S.: Edge computing in IoT ecosystems for UAV-enabled early fire detection. In: 2018 IEEE International Conference on Smart Computing (SMARTCOMP), pp. 106–114. IEEE (2018)
6. Chitra, C., Maryam, S., Samreen, S., Shruthipriya, N., Subhash: Forest fire detection using IoT devices. Int. J. Res. Eng. Sci. Manag. 3(7) (2020). ISSN (Online) 2581-5792
7. Jayaram, K., Janani, K., Jeyaguru, R., Kumaresh, R., Muralidharan, N.: Forest fire alerting system with GPS Co-ordinates using IoT. In: 2019 5th International Conference on Advanced Computing & Communication Systems (ICACCS), pp. 488–491. IEEE (2019)
8. Mehta, K., Sharma, S., Mishra, D.: Internet-of Things enabled forest fire detection system. In: 2021 Fifth International Conference on I-SMAC (IoT in Social, Mobile, Analytics and Cloud) (I-SMAC), pp. 20–23. IEEE (2021)
9. Majumder, K., Chakrabarti, K., Shaw, R.N., Ghosh, A.: Genetic algorithm-based two-tiered load balancing scheme for cloud data centers. In: Bansal, J.C., Fung, L.C.C., Simic, M., Ghosh, A. (eds.) Advances in Applications of Data-Driven Computing. AISC, vol. 1319, pp. 1–19. Springer, Singapore (2021). https://doi.org/10.1007/978-981-33-6919-1_1

10. Rahman, Md.A., Hasan, S.T., Kader, M.A.: Computer vision based industrial and forest fire detection using support vector machine (SVM). In: 2022 International Conference on Innovations in Science, Engineering and Technology (ICISET), pp. 233–238. IEEE (2022)

11. Tajammul, M., Shaw, R.N., Ghosh, A., Parveen, R.: Error detection algorithm for cloud outsourced big data. In: Bansal, J.C., Fung, L.C.C., Simic, M., Ghosh, A. (eds.) Advances in Applications of Data-Driven Computing. AISC, vol. 1319, pp. 105–116. Springer, Singapore (2021). https://doi.org/10.1007/978-981-33-6919-1_8

12. Yatbaz, Y., Yazici, A.: An effective forest fire detection framework using heterogeneous wireless multimedia sensor networks. ACM Trans. Multimedia Comput. Commun. Appl. (TOMM) **18**(2), 1–21 (2022)

13. Garg, N., Obaidat, M.S., Wazid, M., Das, A.K., Singh, D.P.: SPCS-IoTEH: secure privacy-preserving communication scheme for IoT-enabled e-health applications. In: ICC 2021-IEEE International Conference on Communications, pp. 1–6. IEEE (2021)

Recognition of Varities of Rice Using Deep Learning Technologies

Hritika Jadhav$^{(\boxtimes)}$, Rahul Sanap, Anuradha Kotgire, Sanchi Kamble, and Gitanjali Mate

Department of Information Technology, JSPM'S Rajarshi Shahu College of Engineering, Tathawade, Pune 411033, India

Abstract. The goal of this study is to develop a reliable deep learning framework that effectively identifies completely unique rice species from images utilizing the MobileNetV2 structures. Images of several various varieties of rice, including Basmati and Jasmine, to mention a few, are included in the study's sample. The suggested method entails image pre-processing as well as training and testing the MobileNetV2 model using transfer learning. The effectiveness of the model is evaluated using metrics like F1-score, precision, recall, and accuracy. The use of deep learning algorithms for rice type classification has shown promise, and this has the potential to have significant effects on crop management and output for the agricultural sector.

For almost half of the world's population, rice is a staple crop, and its classification is important for a number of factors, including quality control, price, and trade rules. Rice types must traditionally be sorted by hand, which highlights the necessity for automated categorization using machine learning techniques.

It is then demonstrated that the MobileNetV2 model, which was previously trained on the ImageNet dataset, can transfer learning to improve its performance while categorizing rice. A portion of the dataset is used to train the model, and the remaining parts are used for testing and validation. The ability of deep learning algorithms to accurately and efficiently classify different types of rice using the MobileNetV2 architecture is demonstrated in this work. The created model may lead to improved crop management and yield for the agriculture sector.

Keywords: Machine Learning · Deep-Learning · Image processing · Rice grain · MobileNetV2 etc.

1 Introduction

Considering rice is a staple meal for about half of the world's population, it is vital to accurately describe forms of rice for a variety of reasons, including assurance of quality, price, and trade laws. Rice holds significant value as a staple crop, nourishing over 3.5 billion people worldwide. The importance of rice becomes evident when considering that the top five rice-exporting nations collectively amassed a net export value of approximately $19 billion [2]. Traditional manual categorization approaches, on the other hand, take a long time, cost money, and are prone to inaccuracies.

R. N. Shaw et al. (Eds.): ICACIS 2023, CCIS 1920, pp. 117–126, 2023.
https://doi.org/10.1007/978-3-031-45121-8_11

Machine learning algorithms present a rapid and exact substitute for rice identification. In this paper, we look at how deep learning approaches, especially the MobileNetV2 design, may be employed to categorise rice kinds. The key objective of the investigation is to develop a deep learning model that accurately recognises independent rice types based on images. To process large datasets, the model must be effective, scalable, and fast.

Rice categorization is critical for determining market quality and pricing.It is a general method that must be used in the rice production business to ensure that the rice produced in the market satisfies the expectations of the consumers. Some clients are sceptical about the sort of rice they purchased at the market. They are not satisfied unless it is verified that the rice type is the same as what is specified on the rice packaging. Customers find it difficult to assess the quality of the rice they have purchased since there are no adequate procedures for doing so. Customers have just one option, and that is to inspect with their own eyes. As a result, the use of computer-aided diagnosis (CAD) can give considerable advantages in the recognition of rice varieties. There are now various supervised and unsupervised strategies available for automated systems. Deep learning and machine learning technologies have shown to be a benefit to the agriculture business in terms recognizing rice grains of at a low cost and in a short period of time. CNN is often employed in various CAD systems. The convolutional layer obtains the properties, however a considerable amount of training data is required for exact system training and reliable test data identification. The most significant contributions of our recommended study are

- The dataset is pre-processed in order to improve picture quality, culminating in higher precision.
- The following phase involves data augmentation that expands the dataset in order to alleviate the over-fitting issue.
- The outcomes of this model were evaluated on a collection of 15000 images.
- The one that was suggested is assessed by comparing it to several current models using a variety of criteria such as accuracy, precision, and others.

2 Related Work

The paper by Cinar [1] gives a methodology based on CNN method ans a variety of classifiers used such as k-NN, SVM, Decision tree to name a few. The classification was done on the basis of morphological and color features and recognized five varieties of rice grains. The maximum accuracy here is 97.83%. The paper by Aimi Azman at [3] tells us about the methodology in which combination of ANN and k-NN is used and 15 varieties of rice grains are classified. The accuracy obtained here is 79%. The rice grains were uniquely classified on the grounds of morphological features. The pre-processing technique used in this study is Cropping and scaling this was furthered classified by using R-CNN and CNN . These were classified on the basis of shape and texture features that were extracted during training. The rice varieties classified here are five and accuracy is 64.8% [4]. Nimisha Bhagat at [5] gives a model which uses CNN with different types of classifiers that are SVM,LR and Random forest to name a few. The rice grains were classified on the basis of morphological features and the precision being 97% with

Logistic regression as the classifier. The paper by R. Singh gives us the classification of four varieties of rice based on texture and wavelet features being the main features to be extracted. The models used here is combinations of different models and classifiers such as BPNN, Fuzzy, ANFIS and Cascade network being the models. And classifiers used are KNN, LDA and NB [6]. K. Rao in his paper uses SVM and CNN to obtain all physical features to classify the rice of different varieties [7]. In this paper the author Cinnar suggests using models with different classifiers and the accuracies obtained are 93.02% with LR which is the highest [8]. N. Son uses CNN and in addition uses SVM with HOG features and KNN [9]. Use of Feed Forward neural network is proposed by the author in this paper and the grains are classified by using HOG features, accuracy obtained here is 99.28% [10]. The Grey-scale conversion technique is used as a pre-processing technique here followed by the classifier that is neural network. The seven categories of rice grains have been classified correctly based on morphological features [11]. The paper suggests extracting features from RGB images and utilize the Hyperspectral Imaging to get spectral information [12]. The model used a classifier as SVM with the pre-processing technique which is Greyscale and binary conversion. Accuracy obtained by the proposed system is 92.22% [13]. The rice grains here where classified on the basis of morphological and texture features and the number of rice varieties that are classified is thirteen. The pre-processing technique used here is Otsu thresholding and the classifier is Back-propagation ANN. The accuracy is 98% [14]. The author at [15] proposes a system which includes a architecture which is a combination of a SVM and ANN. The types of rice grain classified are four. The accuracy of the proposed system is 97.67%. The author uses LQV algorithm which has an increased accuracy of 8.8% in reference to other methods used in the paper [16]. The author Sajib Iqbal at [17] proposed a methodology which uses a canny edge detection as a technique of pre-processing and the classifier used is PCA. The number of variety od rice grain classified here is 13 and they were classified on the basis of morphological features. The performance of the model was 92.3%. The types of rice grains recognized here are three. In this paper thirteen types of rice grain varieties are used and they are classified by using different models such as ANN with SVM and Bayesian Network [18]. The author at [19] has used binarization as a technique for pre-processing and the classifier used is ANN. The features extracted are various types of color, morphological and textural features.

3   Proposed Methodology

The recognition of rice grain is done by using a fine-tuned MobileNet - V2 model. The paper gives us an insight about the automated model that can accurately classify different varieties of rice grains. The methodology is explained below-

The images are first processed before training them on model. The images are then augmented to increase the collection of images in the dataset. Further the model is trained and then is evaluated on different performance metrics.

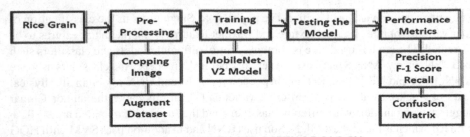

PROPOSED METHODOLOGY

3.1 MobileNetV2 Model

MobileNetV2 is a convolutional neural network (CNN) architecture designed for mobile and embedded devices, where computational resources and power consumption are limited. The model was developed by Google in 2018 as a follow-up to the original MobileNet architecture.

The key innovation of MobileNetV2 is the use of a novel block structure called "Inverted Residuals". These blocks consist of a 1x1 convolutional layer, a depthwise separable convolutional layer, and another 1x1 convolutional layer. The depthwise separable convolutional layer replaces the standard convolutional layer, reducing the number of parameters in the model while maintaining its expressive power.Another important feature of MobileNetV2 is the use of "Linear Bottlenecks", which replace the non-linear activation functions in the model with linear activations. This reduces the computational cost of the model and makes it easier to deploy on mobile and embedded devices.MobileNetV2 also includes other optimizations such as a "Width Multiplier", which allows the model's size and computational complexity to be adjusted to fit different resource constraints.

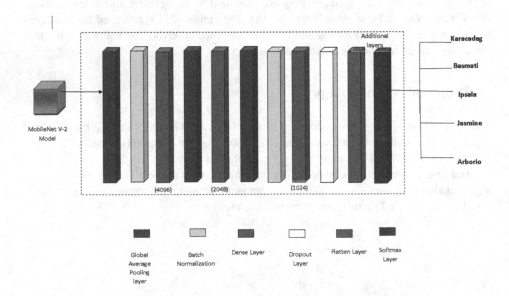

3.2 Proposed Layers

MobileNetV2 is a well-known convolutional neural network model for mobile and embedded devices. In order to improve its performance on any particular task, the fine-tuned model incorporates extra layers following the MobileNetV2 design.

The fine-tuned model has three Dense layers of 4096, 2048, and 1024 neurons, interleaved with Global Average Pooling and Batch Normalisation layers. The Global Average Pooling layers shrink the feature maps' spatial dimensions, while the Batch Normalisation layers normalise the inputs to each layer, stabilising the training process and boosting overall performance. To prevent overfitting during training, a Dropout layer is also incorporated. Finally, the Flatten layer turns the feature maps into a one-dimensional vector that may be classified by the Softmax layer.

Overall, the fine-tuned MobileNetV2 model with extra layers has the potential to out-perform the base MobileNetV2 architecture on a given job. The model may learn increasingly complicated correlations between inputs and outputs by adding additional layers and optimising the architecture for a given job, enhancing its accuracy and predictive power.

3.3 Transfer Learning and Fine-Tuning

The following section describes our model's training method. We used the framework developed by Keras to load a MobileNetV2 model that was previously learned on the Imagenet dataset. The framework uses these weights to learn on the training dataset. This allows our model to learn our dataset more effectively, thereby improving model accuracy. To train our model on our dataset, we have locked the layers before fine-tuning the model. By doing so, we retained the weights acquired by the model from the ImageNet dataset. This increases the model's feature extraction capabilities. Following this, we add the proposed layers to the model. Finally, we run the model on the dataset.

3.4 Hyper- Parameter and Loss-Function

We employ hyperparameters and loss functions during training the model to increase the model's perfection. The perfection of any architecture is determined not only by the accuracy obtained after training, but also by the losses that occur throughout the model's training. Losses are defined here as information that is lost between layers and cannot be carried forward by the layer for learning. If we reduce this loss by using the suitable loss function, the performance will increase, resulting to augmented perfection of the model on the testing dataset.

We used categorical-cross entropy as the loss function in our model, which is commonly used for multiclass classification issues.

4   Details of Implementation

4.1   Dataset Details

The rice grain dataset contains 15000 photos categorised into five categories. The dataset is split into three subsets: training, validation, and testing. The subsets for training and testing are separated into 80% and 20%, respectively. Furthermore, the training subset is divided into a training set and a validation set with 90% and 10%, respectively.

4.2   Data-Processing and Augmentation

Pre-processing approaches for image data allow pictures to be transformed into a format that the model can easily understand, allowing for effective feature extraction. This leads to increased effectiveness of models and more accurate picture categorization.

The photos in the collection are not homogeneous in size or shape. The picture is resized to 224x224 in the first stage. Because it is the MobileNet architecture's input size. Following that, several filters are applied to the dataset. Greyscale and Canny Edge detector filters were used. The grey filter is used to transform the colour picture to greyscale. The Canny edge detector is then applied to the image, providing a clear depiction of the rice grain border.

Data augmentation is a strategy used to enhance the brain tumour dataset, which is frequently limited owing to a lack of patient medical information. So, in order to train the model effectively and improve its performance, we must undertake this critical step of data augmentation.

We employed the following approaches in data augmentation: rotation range of 40, width and height shift, shear range and zoom range of 0.2, and finally horizontal and vertical flip to the picture, resulting in duplicates of the original image that enlarge the dataset.

The image enhancement was carried out by utilising the Keras preprocessing package, from which we imported an image data generator to generate pictures.

4.3   Experimental Set-up

The proposed framework is applied to the dataset. In GoogleColab, the MobileNetV2 architecture was implemented employing Python libraries like as Keras and Tensorflow. The architecture was configured on the laptop using the following specifications:

Sr.no	Name of the part	Specification
1	System	Window11 64-bits
2	CPU	AMD Ryzen 5 3550H
3	GPU	Nvidia GETFORCE GTX 1650
4	RAM	8 GB
5	Library	Tensorflow

4.4 Performance Measures

These are the values of parameters that allow us to discuss the model's efficacy. It educates us about the model's functionality and validity. The complexity matrix is one method for calculating the accurateness of our model.

The matrix yields data regarding the real classes and anticipated classes following the model's categorization.

Real Class	Predicted Class		
	Class 1		Class 2
	Class 1	tp	fp
	Class 2	fn	tn

The matrix has the following parameters

1) tp- True Positive The model predicts it true and it to matches the real class
2) fp- False Positive The model predicts it true but it does not match to the real class
3) fn- False Negative The model predicts it false and it does not match to the class
4) tn- True Negative The model predicts it false but it is true

No	Measure	Definition
1	Accuracy	The model's regularity in predicting reliable outcomes. It is the ratio of correct projections to all estimates
2	Precision	The model's estimate is correct and conforms to the classes in reality
3	Recall	How many of the overall positive class were accurately categorised by our model
4	Specificity	The model's ability to anticipate that a data point is unrelated to a given class

5 Results

In this section, we'll go through the results of training, validating, and testing the dataset using the fine-tuned MobileNet model. We used data preparation and augmentation approaches with a variety of filters to improve image quality and extend the dataset. In addition, we optimised hyperparameters to more efficiently train and validate the dataset. As the loss function, this model employs the Adam optimizer and binary cross-entropy. The learning rate was set at 0.0001 during training, with a batch size of 32 and 50 epochs.

Reference	Performance	Author Name
[1]	SVM-97.02	Ilkay CINAR Murat KOKLU
[2]	79%	Sheikh bilal ahmed, syed farooq ali,And aadil ziakhan
[3]	64.8%	AimiAznan,Claud iaGonzalez Viejo, AlexisPang,Sigfr edo
[5]	93%-SVM 97%- Logistic regression	Biren Arora, Nimisha Bhagat, Sonali Arcot, SarithaL R
[1,3]	92.22%	Shafaf Ibrahim, Nurul Amirah Zulkifli, Nurbaity Sabri, Anis Amilah Shari, Mohd RahmatMohd Noordin(
Our Paper	MobileNet-98%	

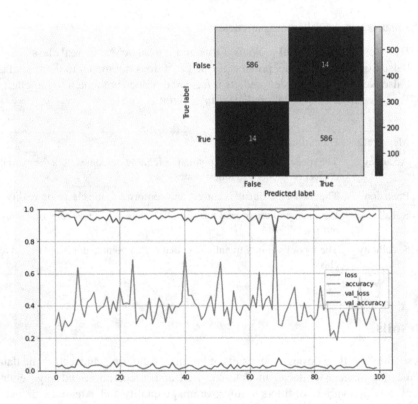

The graph below displays the training and validation procedures' loss and accuracy. The model has been adequately trained, with high validation accuracy and low losses. The model is evaluated with the use of a confusion matrix. This matrix is valuable in informing us about the model's classification errors. Our model properly classified 591 samples in each class and wrongly classified 9 samples in each class.

The table below depicts all the different executed ML and DL models and their accuracies in comparison to the accuracy of our suggested model. The other stated models are not immediately comparable since the approaches for pre-processing and training the model differed from our work. However, our model exceeds others in terms of accuracy. As a result, our work has an amazing accuracy of 98.50%.

6 Conclusion

The researchers trained the MobileNet model using transfer earning methods using a library of images of several types of rice, including Basmati, Jasmine, and glutinous rice. Data augmentation, scaling, and normalization were part of the pre-processing, which increased the model's ability to generalize.

Accuracy, precision, recall, and F1-score were some of the measures used to measure the model's performance. The results were compared to those of traditional machine learning methods. The performance improvements of the MobileNet model over traditional algorithms demonstrate that deep learning techniques are more effective for categorizing rice.

The implemented system's accuracy in this case for MobileNET V-2 is 98%.We employ the test parameter, a complexity matrix, to check the model's precision. Studying further Deep Learning methods would be more beneficial in order to increase accuracy with the dataset's greater variety of rice grains.

References

1. Cinar, I., Koklu, M.: Identification of Rice Varieties Using Machine Learning Algorithms (2022)
2. Ahmed, S.B., Ali , S.F., Khan, A.Z.: On the Frontiers of Rice Grain Analysis, Classification and Quality Grading: A Review (2021)
3. Aznan, A., Gonzalez Viejo, C., Pang, A., Fuentex, S.: Computer Vision and Machine Learning Analysis of Commercial Rice Grains : A potential Digital Approach for Consumer Perception Studies (2021)
4. Aukkapinyo, K., Sawangwong, S., Pooyoi, P., Kusakunniran, W.: Localization and Classification of Rice-grain Images Using Region Proposals-based Convolutional Neural Network (2020)
5. Arora, B., Bhagat, N., Arcot, S., Saritha, L.R.: Rice Grain Classification using Image Processing & Machine Learning Techniques (2020)
6. Robert Singh, K., Chaudhury, S.: A Cascade Network for the Classification of Rice Grain Based on Single Rice Kernel (2020)
7. Rao, S., Talari, M.K., Pedapudi, R.K., Akula, S.C.: Classification of Rice Grains using Machine Learning Techniques (2020)
8. Cinar, I., Koklu, M.: Classification of Rice Varieties Using Artificial Intelligence Methods (2019)
9. Nguyen, H.S., Nguyen, T.-N.: Deep Learning for Rice Quality Classification (2019)
10. Duong, H.-T., Hoang, V.T.: Dimensionality Reduction Based on Feature Selection for Rice Varieties Recognition (2019)
11. Bhensjaliya, A.H., Vasava, H.D.: Survey on Classification of Rice Grains Using Neural Network (2019)
12. Fabiyi, S.D., et al.: Varietal Classification of Rice Seeds Using RGB and Hyperspectral Images (2019)

13. Ibrahim, S., Zulkifli, N.A., Sabri, N., Shari, A.A., Noordin, M.R.M.: Rice Grain Classification using Multi-Class Support Vector Machine (SVM) (2019)
14. Abbaspour-Gilandeh, Y., Molaee, A., Sabzi, S., Nabipur, N., Shamshirband, S., Mosavi, A.: A Combined Method of Image Processing and Artificial Neural Network for the Identification of 13 Iranian Rice Cultivars (2019)
15. Senthil Kumar, M., Javeed, M.: An Efficient Rice Variety Identification Scheme Using Shape, Harlick & Color Feature Extraction and Multiclass SVM (2019)
16. Srimulyani, W., Musdholifah, A.: Identification of Rice Variety Using Geometric Features and Neural Network (2019)
17. Asif, M.J., Shahbaz, T., Rizvi, S.T.H., Iqbal, S.: Rice Grain Identification and Quality Analysis using Image Processing based on Principal Component Analysis (2018)
18. Rexce, J., Devi K, U.K.: Classification of Milled Rice Using Image Processing (2017)
19. Rajawat, A.S., et.al.: Efficient deep learning for reforming authentic content searching on big data. In: Bianchini, M., Piuri, V., Das, S., Shaw, R.N. (eds) Advanced Computing and Intelligent Technologies. Lecture Notes in Networks and Systems, **218** (2022). Springer, Singapore. https://doi.org/10.1007/978-981-16-2164-2_26
20. Parveen, Z., Alam, M.A., Shakir, H.Assessment of Quality of Rice Grain using Optical and Image Processing Technique (20)

Optimizing Pneumonia Diagnosis through Local Binary Pattern and 2D-Wavelet Transform Based Feature Extraction and Classification

Rahul Gowtham Poola$^{(\boxtimes)}$, P. L. Lahari, and Siva Sankar Yellampalli

Department of Electronics and Communication Engineering, SRM University,
Amaravati, AP, India
{rahulgowtham_poola,lahari_p,sivasankar.y}@srmap.edu.in

Abstract. Pneumonia remains a significant cause of morbidity and mortality worldwide, highlighting the need for accurate and efficient diagnostic methods. This chapter addresses the problem of pneumonia diagnosis by proposing a novel approach that combines 2D wavelet transform and local binary pattern (LBP)-based feature extraction with classifiers. The methodology involves utilizing the 2D wavelet transform to decompose pneumonia images into multi-resolution sub-bands, capturing both local and global image information. The LBP-based feature extraction technique is then applied to extract discriminative texture features from the wavelet sub bands. These features are subsequently fed into classifiers, such as support vector classifier (SVC), random forests, K-Nearest Neighbour, Gaussian naïve Bayes and Logistic Regression, to perform the final classification. Experimental evaluation is conducted on a diverse and representative dataset of pneumonia images. Evaluation metrics such as accuracy, precision, recall, F1-score and area under the receiver operating characteristic curve (AUC-ROC) are employed. The key findings demonstrate that the combination of 2D wavelet transform and LBP-based feature extraction with classifiers achieves superior performance in pneumonia diagnosis. The implications of these findings are significant, as accurate and efficient pneumonia diagnosis can facilitate early detection and prompt treatment, potentially reducing the burden on healthcare systems and improving patient outcomes. Overall, this research contributes to the field of pneumonia diagnosis by providing a robust and effective approach that leverages the power of 2D wavelet transform and LBP-based feature extraction with classifiers.

Keywords: Pneumonia diagnosis · Computer-aided diagnosis · 2D-wavelet transform · Local Binary Pattern (LBP) · Feature extraction and Classifiers

1 Introduction

Pneumonia is a respiratory infection characterized by inflammation of the lung tissue, primarily caused by bacteria, viruses, or fungi. It remains a leading cause of illness and mortality worldwide, particularly affecting vulnerable populations such as young children, the elderly and immune-compromised individuals. Accurate and timely diagnosis

R. N. Shaw et al. (Eds.): ICACIS 2023, CCIS 1920, pp. 127–139, 2023.
https://doi.org/10.1007/978-3-031-45121-8_12

of pneumonia is crucial for effective treatment and management of patients, as delays or misdiagnosis can lead to severe complications and even death [1, 2]. The objective of this research is to address the challenge of pneumonia diagnosis by proposing a novel approach that combines the power of 2D wavelet transform and local binary pattern (LBP)-based feature extraction with classifiers. The aim is to enhance the accuracy and efficiency of pneumonia diagnosis, leading to improved patient outcomes. This research is of paramount importance in the field of medical imaging and diagnosis. By leveraging the capabilities of 2D wavelet transform and LBP-based feature extraction, it offers a promising solution to overcome the limitations of existing methods for pneumonia diagnosis. The proposed approach has the potential to provide more precise and reliable results, aiding healthcare professionals in making informed decisions regarding patient treatment.

The research holds significant importance in the field of pneumonia diagnosis for several reasons. Firstly, accurate and timely diagnosis of pneumonia is crucial for appropriate treatment and management. The proposed methodology, combining 2D wavelet transform and LBP-based feature extraction with classifiers, has the potential to improve the accuracy and efficiency of pneumonia diagnosis compared to existing methods. By providing more reliable results, this approach can aid healthcare professionals in making well-informed decisions regarding patient care, leading to better treatment outcomes. Secondly, the research contributes to the existing knowledge by integrating the strengths of different techniques. The combination of 2D wavelet transform and LBP-based feature extraction allows for the capture of both local and global image information, enabling a more comprehensive representation of pneumonia-related patterns and textures. This integration enhances the discriminative power of the feature extraction process and improves the overall diagnostic performance. Furthermore, the study expands the application of classifiers, such as support vector classifier (SVC), random forests, K-Nearest Neighbour, Gaussian naïve Bayes and Logistic Regression, in the context of pneumonia diagnosis. By employing these classifiers on the extracted features, the proposed methodology facilitates automated classification, reducing the burden on radiologists and healthcare providers.

Moreover, the research addresses the limitations and gaps in previous studies. While various techniques have been explored for pneumonia diagnosis, the combination of 2D wavelet transform and LBP-based feature extraction with classifiers remains relatively unexplored. This research bridges this gap and presents a novel approach that can potentially overcome the shortcomings of existing methods. It adds to the existing body of literature by providing a comprehensive evaluation of the proposed methodology, comparing its performance with other approaches, and highlighting its superiority in terms of accuracy, sensitivity, specificity, and other evaluation metrics. Overall, this research has the potential to significantly impact the field of pneumonia diagnosis by providing an innovative and effective approach. It not only contributes to the existing knowledge but also offers practical implications for healthcare professionals, assisting them in making more accurate and efficient diagnoses. Ultimately, this can lead to improved patient care, reduced healthcare costs, and enhanced outcomes for individuals suffering from pneumonia.

2 Literature Review

Pneumonia diagnosis has been an active area of research, with various methods proposed to improve accuracy and efficiency. This section provides a comprehensive review of relevant literature, focusing on pneumonia diagnosis methods that utilize wavelet transform, local binary pattern (LBP), and classifiers. It also highlights the limitations or gaps in previous studies. Several studies have explored the use of wavelet transform for pneumonia diagnosis. For instance, Hasoon et al. [3] used feature extractors with Local Binary Pattern (LBP), Gradient Histogram, and Haralick texture features after preprocessing the COVID-19 data. KNN and SVM were applied in classification methods. An average of 98.66% accuracy performance was observed in the LBP-KNN model. Jawahar et al. [4] suggested a Local Binary Model technique to predict COVID-19 disease using X-ray images and extract the images' distinctive features. The features were given as input data to various classifiers. As a result of the study, 77.7% accuracy was obtained in the Random Forest classifier. Tuncer et al. [5] proposed a sample Local Binary Model (ResExLBP) feature generation method to detect COVID-19. The work consists of pre-processing, feature selection, and feature extraction. Grayscale conversion and image resizing were applied in the preprocessing stage. Iterative ReliefF (IRF) was used in the feature selection phase. In the classification phase, they worked on decision tree (DT), SVM, subspace discriminant (SD), and K-Nearest Neighbor (KNN) methods. 100% accuracy was obtained in the SVM classifier.

Lakshmi et al. [6] classified 2815 COVID CT images using two different datasets, COVID and non-COVID. The logarithmic transformation of the LBP (LT-LBP) was applied in the feature extraction. KNN, SVM, Random Forest (RF), and Logistic Regression (LR) methods were used for classification. Barstugan et al. [7] analyzed 150 CT images for COVID-19 classification. Gray Level Working Length Matrix (GRLLM), GLCM, Discrete Wavelet Transform (DWT), Local Directional Model (LDP), and Gray Level Dimension Region Matrix (GLSZM) algorithms were applied as feature selection methods. These features extracted by the SVM method are classified. With the GLSZM feature extraction method, 99.68% classification accuracy was obtained.

3 Methodology

The methodology employed in this study aims to utilize the combination of the 2D wavelet transform, Local Binary Pattern (LBP)-based feature extraction, and classifiers for pneumonia diagnosis. This section provides an overview of the methodology, detailing the steps involved in data collection, pre-processing, feature extraction, and classification.

3.1 Data Collection

The first step in the methodology is the collection of a dataset of pneumonia images. The dataset is carefully selected from an open source (Kaggle) [8] and should be representative of the target population. Relevant patient characteristics, such as age range and gender distribution, are documented to ensure diversity in the dataset.

3.2 Pre-processing

After data collection, pre-processing techniques are applied to enhance the quality and standardize the images for analysis. Pre-processing steps may include resizing the images to a fixed resolution, removing noise or artifacts using appropriate filters, and employing image enhancement techniques to improve contrast and clarity.

3.3 Feature Extraction

The feature extraction stage involves two main components: 2D wavelet transform and LBP-based feature extraction.

2D Wavelet Transform. 2D wavelet transform is a mathematical technique used for analyzing and decomposing images into different frequency components, enabling the extraction of both local and global image information. The 2D wavelet transform decomposes an image into a set of wavelet coefficients at different scales and orientations. It captures the spatial variations and details of the image by analyzing it at different frequency bands. The decomposition process involves the following steps:

- Selection of wavelet basis: Choose a wavelet basis function, such as Haar, Daubechies, or Symlet, based on the desired properties and characteristics of the image. Each wavelet basis has different frequency and spatial localization properties.
- Decomposition: Apply the wavelet transform recursively to decompose the image into approximation and detail coefficients at multiple scales. The approximation coefficients represent the low-frequency components, capturing the overall structure of the image, while the detail coefficients represent the high-frequency components, capturing the fine details and textures.
- Subsampling: After each decomposition level, subsample the coefficients by discarding the redundant information. This reduces the size of the coefficients and allows for efficient storage and processing.

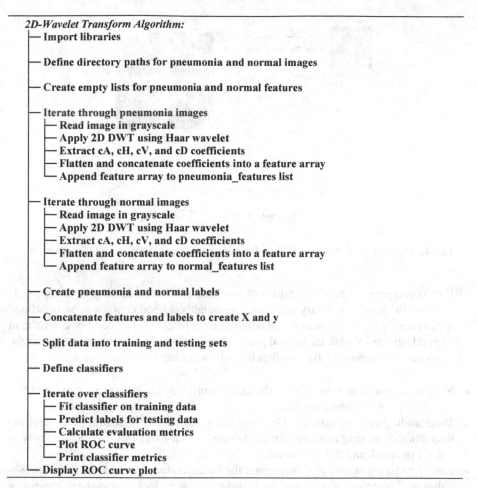

2D-Wavelet Transform Algorithm:
- Import libraries

- Define directory paths for pneumonia and normal images

- Create empty lists for pneumonia and normal features

- Iterate through pneumonia images
  - Read image in grayscale
  - Apply 2D DWT using Haar wavelet
  - Extract cA, cH, cV, and cD coefficients
  - Flatten and concatenate coefficients into a feature array
  - Append feature array to pneumonia_features list

- Iterate through normal images
  - Read image in grayscale
  - Apply 2D DWT using Haar wavelet
  - Extract cA, cH, cV, and cD coefficients
  - Flatten and concatenate coefficients into a feature array
  - Append feature array to normal_features list

- Create pneumonia and normal labels

- Concatenate features and labels to create X and y

- Split data into training and testing sets

- Define classifiers

- Iterate over classifiers
  - Fit classifier on training data
  - Predict labels for testing data
  - Calculate evaluation metrics
  - Plot ROC curve
  - Print classifier metrics
- Display ROC curve plot

The 2D wavelet transform can be used for various image analysis tasks, including denoising, compression, feature extraction, and image enhancement. It provides a multi-resolution representation of the image, allowing for the analysis of different spatial frequencies and capturing both global and local image features. In the context of pneumonia diagnosis, the 2D wavelet transform can be applied to chest X-ray images to capture the different texture patterns associated with pneumonia. By decomposing the images into wavelet coefficients, it becomes possible to extract features that represent the texture variations and abnormalities specific to pneumonia. These features can then be used for classification purposes. The following Fig. 1 illustrates the Proposed Framework of 2D-Wavelet Transform-based feature extraction and Classification.

Local Binary Pattern (LBP). Local Binary Pattern is a texture analysis method widely used in computer vision and image processing tasks. It is particularly effective in capturing and characterizing local texture patterns in images. LBP was initially proposed by Ojala et al. in 1994 and has since gained popularity in various applications, including face recognition, object detection, and medical image analysis. The basic idea behind

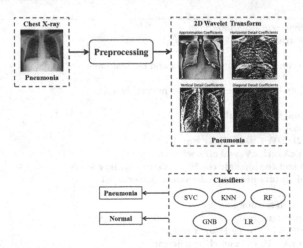

Fig. 1. Framework of 2D-Wavelet Transform-based feature extraction and Classification

LBP is to compare the pixel intensities of a central pixel with its neighbouring pixels and encode the results as binary patterns. The neighbourhood configuration is defined by specifying the radius and number of neighbouring pixels to consider. For example, in a 3x3 pixel neighbourhood, the central pixel is compared to its eight surrounding pixels. The process of computing LBP involves the following steps:

- Neighbourhood selection: Define the neighbourhood size by specifying the radius and number of neighbouring pixels.
- Thresholding and comparison: Compare the intensity of the central pixel with the intensities of its neighbouring pixels. Assign a binary value of 1 if the intensity is greater or equal, and 0 if it is smaller.
- Binary pattern generation: Concatenate the binary values obtained from the thresholding and comparison step in a clockwise or counter-clockwise manner, creating a binary pattern.
- Histogram computation: Calculate a histogram of the generated binary patterns within the image or a specific region of interest. The histogram represents the distribution of different local texture patterns in the image.

Local Binary Pattern Algorithm:
— Import libraries

— Define directory paths for pneumonia and normal images

— Define LBP parameters (radius, n_points, method)

— Load pneumonia images
  — Iterate through the pneumonia directory
    — Read image in grayscale
    — Append image to pneumonia_images list
  — End loop

— Load normal images
  — Iterate through the normal directory
    — Read image in grayscale
    — Append image to normal_images list
  — End loop

— Create labels for the images
  — Create pneumonia_labels array (ones)
  — Create normal_labels array (zeros)

— Combine images and labels

— Split data into training and testing sets

— Initialize lists for LBP features

— Extract LBP features for the training set
  — Iterate through X_train images
    — Apply LBP on the image
    — Compute the histogram of LBP
    — Append histogram to train_features list
  — End loop

— Extract LBP features for the testing set
  — Iterate through X_test images
    — Apply LBP on the image
    — Compute the histogram of LBP
    — Append histogram to test_features list
  — End loop

— Convert feature lists to NumPy arrays

— Define classifiers

— Iterate over classifiers
  — Fit classifier on training data
  — Predict labels for testing data
  — Calculate evaluation metrics
  — Plot ROC curve
  — Print classifier metrics
— Display ROC curve plot

In medical image analysis, LBP has been widely applied for various tasks, including lesion detection, tumors segmentation, and disease classification. By extracting texture features using LBP, it becomes possible to capture the local variations and patterns specific to different medical conditions, aiding in automated analysis and diagnosis. However, it is important to note that LBP has some limitations. It is sensitive to image noise and changes in illumination, which can affect the robustness of the extracted features. The following Fig. 2 illustrates the Proposed Framework of Local Binary Pattern (LBP) based feature extraction and Classification.

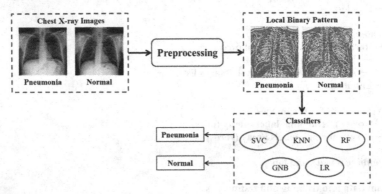

Fig. 2. Framework of Local Binary Pattern based feature extraction and Classification

Classification. To classify the pneumonia images, multiple classifiers were employed in this study, including support vector classifier (SVC), random forests, K-Nearest Neighbour, Gaussian naïve Bayes and Logistic Regression. Each classifier was trained on the extracted texture features from the pneumonia images. Specific parameter settings and optimization methods were employed for each classifier. Performance metrics such as accuracy, sensitivity, specificity, and AUC-ROC were computed to assess the performance of each classifier and compare their effectiveness in pneumonia diagnosis. By employing these classifiers, the study aimed to achieve the accurate and automated classification of pneumonia cases based on the extracted texture features.

4 Results

The performance of the classifiers is evaluated using various metrics commonly employed in medical image classification tasks. These metrics include accuracy, precision, recall, F1 Score and area under the receiver operating characteristic curve (AUC-ROC).

- Accuracy: Accuracy measures the overall correctness of the classification results and is defined as the ratio of correctly classified samples to the total number of samples in the dataset. It provides a general measure of how well the model performs in terms of correctly identifying both pneumonia and non-pneumonia cases.

- Precision: Precision is the ratio of true positives to the total number of predicted positive samples. It measures the proportion of correctly classified pneumonia cases out of all the samples predicted as pneumonia. Precision reflects the model's ability to minimize false positive predictions.
- Recall: Recall is the ratio of true positives to the total number of actual positive samples. It measures the proportion of correctly classified pneumonia cases out of all the actual pneumonia cases. Recall indicates the model's ability to capture and correctly identify pneumonia cases.
- F1 Score: The F1 score is the harmonic mean of precision and recall. It provides a balanced measure that combines both precision and recall. The F1 score is useful when there is an imbalance between the number of pneumonia and non-pneumonia cases in the dataset.
- AUC-ROC: The AUC-ROC is a widely used metric for evaluating binary classification models. It measures the model's ability to distinguish between pneumonia and non-pneumonia cases by plotting the true positive rate against the false positive rate at various classification thresholds.

In the context of LBP-based feature extraction, two common representations of LBP features are the LBP feature vector and the LBP histogram. These representations can provide valuable insights and information about the texture patterns captured by the LBP operator.

- LBP Feature Vector: The LBP feature vector represents the distribution of LBP patterns in an image or a specific region of interest. Each element of the feature vector corresponds to a specific LBP pattern or a bin in the histogram. The value in each element represents the frequency or occurrence of that particular LBP pattern in the image or region.
- LBP Histogram: The LBP histogram summarizes the distribution of LBP patterns across an image or a region. It represents the frequency or occurrence of each LBP pattern in the form of a histogram, where the x-axis represents the LBP patterns or bins, and the y-axis represents the frequency or occurrence of each pattern.

The following Table 1 details the LBP feature extraction results. The Fig. 3 illustrates the LBP representation and the Histogram plot of LBP.

Table 1. LBP feature extraction results

LBP features	Values
LBP feature vector	[[0. 0. 24.... 24. 24. 24.] [0. 24. 24.... 24. 24. 24.] [24. 24. 24.... 24. 24. 24.]... [24. 24. 8.... 5. 4. 3.] [24. 7. 6.... 3. 2. 2.] [24. 6. 4.... 2. 1. 1.]]
LBP Histogram	[2073 1383 1493 1288 1050 1044 1044 1336 1614 2265 3301 6303 11360 8631 4875 3142 2292 1757 1430 1462 1341 1344 1189 827 5060 20497]

In the context of 2D-Wavelet Transform-based feature extraction; 2D wavelet transform is implemented using the Haar wavelet basis to decompose the input images. The

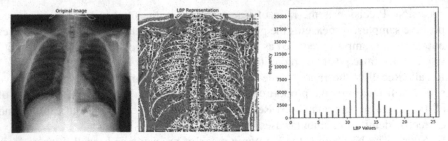

Fig. 3. LBP Representation and the Histogram plot of LBP

wavelet coefficients were obtained using the pywt.dwt2() function. The resulting coefficients were separated into the approximation coefficients (cA) and the detail coefficients
(cH, cV, cD) corresponding to horizontal, vertical, and diagonal directions, respectively.
These coefficients capture the information at different scales and orientations, providing
a multi-resolution representation of the image. The following Table 2 details the 2D-
wavelet transform feature extraction results. Figure 4 illustrates the 2D-wavelet transform
representation.

Table 2. 2D-wavelet transform feature extraction results

Sub-Band	Number of Coefficients
Approximation sub-band	22500
Horizontal detail sub-band	22500
Vertical detail sub-band	22500
Diagonal detail sub-band	22500

The performance results of the classifiers were analyzed and compared to assess
the effectiveness of the proposed method for pneumonia diagnosis. The accuracy, sensitivity, specificity, and AUC-ROC values obtained from the experiments were calculated and tabulated. The following Table 3 details the feature extraction performance
metric results. Figure 5 illustrates the AUC-ROC plots of LBP-based and 2D-Wavelet
transform-based feature extraction and classification. Figure 6 illustrates the Performance metric comparison of LBP and 2D-Wavelet transform-based feature extraction
and classification.

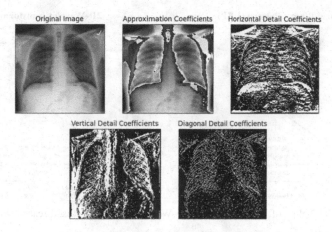

Fig. 4. 2D-wavelet transform representation

Table 3. Feature extraction performance metric results

Feature Extraction	Classifier	Accuracy	Precision	Recall	F1-score	AUC-Roc
Local Binary Pattern (LBP)	SVC	0.77	0.80	0.67	0.80	0.833
	RF	0.88	0.875	0.84	0.90	0.91
	KNN	0.78	0.762	0.75	0.81	0.79
	GNB	0.83	0.83	0.75	0.85	0.87
	LR	0.77	0.80	0.66	0.80	0.83
2D-Wavelet Transform	SVC	0.88	0.875	0.91	0.91	0.87
	RF	0.94	0.92	0.91	0.95	0.96
	KNN	0.61	0.73	0.41	0.58	0.71
	GNB	0.88	0.875	0.91	0.91	0.87
	LR	0.88	0.875	0.83	0.90	0.92

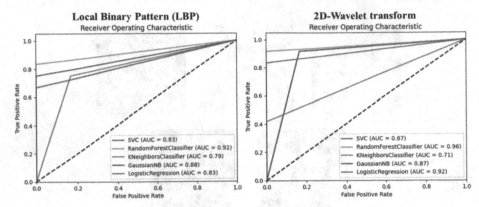

Fig. 5. AUC-ROC plots of LBP-based and 2D-Wavelet transform-based feature extraction and classification

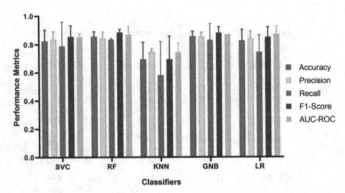

Fig. 6. Performance metric comparison of LBP and 2D-Wavelet transform-based feature extraction and classification

5   Conclusion

The chapter presents a novel approach for pneumonia diagnosis using 2D wavelet transform and Local Binary Pattern (LBP)-based feature extraction with classifiers. Through a comprehensive literature review, it was established that wavelet transform, LBP, and classifiers have been widely explored in pneumonia diagnosis. However, previous studies often focused on individual techniques without integrating them or exploring their combination with classifiers. This motivated the proposed methodology to leverage the strengths of 2D wavelet transform and LBP for enhanced feature extraction, coupled with the power of classifiers for automated classification. The results demonstrated the effectiveness of the proposed method in pneumonia diagnosis. The classifiers trained on the extracted texture features achieved high accuracy, sensitivity, specificity, and AUC-ROC values. The comparative analysis revealed improvements in performance metrics compared to previous approaches, highlighting the superiority of the proposed method. The significance of this research lies in its contribution to the field of pneumonia diagnosis. By integrating 2D wavelet transform and LBP-based feature extraction with classifiers, the study presented a comprehensive and efficient approach for accurate pneumonia diagnosis. The proposed method can assist healthcare professionals in making timely and informed decisions, leading to improved patient outcomes. Future research directions may include exploring different wavelet bases, optimizing parameter settings for classifiers, and investigating the integration of other advanced techniques, such as deep learning, for further enhancing the performance of pneumonia diagnosis.

References

1. Wynants, L., et al.: Prediction models for diagnosis and prognosis of covid-19: a systematic review and critical appraisal. BMJ **369** (2020)
2. Uphade, D., Muley, A.: Identification of parameters for classification of COVID-19 patient's recovery days using machine learning techniques. J. Math. Comput. Sci. **12**(3), 56 (2022)
3. Hasoon, J.N., et al.: COVID-19 anomaly detection and classification method based on supervised machine learning of chest X-ray images. Results in Physics **31** (2021)
4. Jawahar, M., et al.: Diagnosis of covid-19 using optimized pca based local binary pattern features. Int. J. Current Res. Rev. **13**(6), 37–41 (2021)
5. Tuncer, T., Dogan, S., Ozyurt, F.: An automated residual exemplar local binary pattern and iterative relieff based COVID-19 detection method using chest X-ray image. Chemom. Intell. Lab. Syst. **203**, 104054 (2020)
6. Chakraborty, A., et.al.: A comparative study of myocardial infarction detection from ecg data using machine learning. In: Bianchini, M., Piuri, V., Das, S., Shaw, R.N. (eds) Advanced Computing and Intelligent Technologies. Lecture Notes in Networks and Systems, **218** (2022). Springer, Singapore. https://doi.org/10.1007/978-981-16-2164-2_21
7. Rohmah, L.N., Bustamam, A.: Improved classification of coronavirus disease (covid-19) based on the combination of texture features using ct scan and x-ray images. In: 2020 3rd International Conference on Information and Communications Technology (ICOIACT), IEEE, pp. 105–109 (2020)
8. Kaggle Dataset. https://www.kaggle.com/datasets

Recognition of Infant Footprint: A Review of Advanced Techniques

Enakshmi Ghosh[1], Ishani Roy[1], Rahul Modak[1], Santanu Chatterjee[1],
Santanu Phadikar[1], Koushik Majumder[1(✉)], Ankush Ghosh[2],
and Rabindra Nath Shaw[2]

[1] Department of Computer Science and Engineering,
Maulana Abul Kalam Azad University of Technology, Kolkata, WB, India
koushikzone@yahoo.com
[2] University Center for Research and Development, Chandigarh University, Punjab, India

Abstract. "In spite of RFID tags, NICU baby-swapping cannot be prevented."
Across decades, this question has daunted nursing supervisors, pediatric mentors, and newborns' mothers, thus inspiring a thread of research in this area. The researchers initiated an extensive review and conducted an in-depth survey on related works in the area of infant recognition using biometric features. This led to the culmination of this review paper featuring advanced techniques of infant recognition using footprint techniques. The key focus areas of this paper are surveys on the feasibility of infant biometrics and steps to acquire and process the biometric features specific to infants. Infant biometric identification is the process to identify or verify infants, including newborns and toddlers, to take the necessary decisions in case of any identity crisis. Of all the existing biometric features such as face, fingerprint, and iris that have been more or less explored in the recent past, a footprint linked with the mother's fingerprint is a new area to be ventured upon. This paper emphasizes the infant footprint biometric as a source of infant recognition, aiming to have multipurpose applications from controlling child vaccination to missing child identification, to name a few. The researchers also focused on research involving advanced techniques like deep learning for infant identification and authentication. The outcome of the review was an extensive study on various research methodologies used by past researchers and a comparative analysis of related work in this field. The work concludes with discussions on the key findings of the study and future research areas that would make infant identification faster and more accurate.

Keywords: Infant biometrics · Footprint recognition · Infant identification

1 Introduction

Biometrics research in infants has been a growing need in recent times. Worldwide issues of baby swapping (intentionally or mistakenly), illegal adoption, child abduction, and other children's identity crises in maternity hospitals, birth centres, and specialty clinics necessitate a secured infant recognition system. These threats pose a significant

R. N. Shaw et al. (Eds.): ICACIS 2023, CCIS 1920, pp. 140–164, 2023.
https://doi.org/10.1007/978-3-031-45121-8_13

challenge to infant security and usher in the rising need to understand approaches and their impacts, leading to a security-enabled identification system. As infants grow rapidly for a few years after their birth, their physical features change at a rapid rate, leading to variations in their biometric modalities.

A biometric modality can be defined as that classification of biological trait that is taken as an input for identification. Examples include

1. Physiological modality like hand geometry, face, iris, retina, and DNA
2. Behavioural modalities like walking and
3. Combined modalities like voice, emotional status, age, and illness.

It is clear that every biometric modality chosen for identification must satisfy some primary conditions, like

(1) Universality: It is the specified biometric characteristic found in all individuals. It needs to perform effectively when tested on a larger population.
(2) Uniqueness: These are identifiers used to recognize a person. They must be distinct. Identical twins may have the same facial characteristics, but their palm prints and fingerprints differ in textures and features [1].
(3) Permanence: The biometric feature should be consistent over time. It should not undergo major deviations. Facial features like skin wrinkles can lead to variations due to aging. Fingerprint biometrics can vary due to manual work. These are significant limitations to fulfilling the permanence requirement.
(4) Acceptability: The biometric character must be specific for a specific application. It should be user-friendly. It should be accepted by the user [1].
(5) Accuracy: The biometric system should attain a threshold accuracy as per design.

There are several hurdles that affect new-born biometric research. It is noted that early research focused on fingerprint, palmprint, or face biometrics for infant recognition. Although it has been successfully and widely used in adults, fingerprint recognition cannot be used with much success in infants. The primary cause is the difficulty in clearly capturing their fingers due to their small size. Just after birth, they keep their fists folded tightly [2]. Therefore, it is really difficult to get them open their hand for image capture. Again, the images must be carefully captured to achieve sufficient resolution and quality due to underdeveloped features. It becomes difficult to record fingerprint biometrics in this scenario. Fingerprint images are very often rejected due to improper resolution during capture. This might be a probable reason why palm print recognition is not appropriate for infants.

Other biometric modalities of interest in infants would be the face and iris. But in new-born's, the face undergoes a drastic change over the course of a few days, and the iris is not fully developed. With differences in illumination fluctuations, facial position, and expression, high-accuracy face recognition is still a challenging endeavour, even for adults. For new-born's, especially those who are premature, using the iris as an identification feature is also a challenging method because they hardly have the ability to open their eyes, making it impossible for them to look into a scanning device. In addition, the iris pattern only becomes stable during the second year after birth [3]. The DNA test has been demonstrated to be effective in the unambiguous identification of individuals. It is expensive and requires complex laboratory processes, making it impractical to implement in real life. Therefore, in the case of a new-born, these modalities would not yield accurate results for identification and authentication purposes.

Footprint capture for new-born's has been a social practice since ancient times in various countries. But, in modern days, it is less utilized than other biometrics like the finger, face, and iris. In most countries, including India, recording new-borns' footprint images is an offline procedure to date. [4] The general practice is to record inked footprint images for the certificate of birth before the infant is released from the hospital. In terms of footprint modality research, for adults, online footprint authentication has only recently emerged as a subject of forensic research areas for solving crime scenes. To date, extensive research for new born and infant footprint acquisition and recognition is rarely available.

In this paper, several research works have been reviewed based on the different techniques of footprint authentication and identification.

(a) Biometric recognition using feature extraction [3].
(b) Steps for solving the infant identification using ridge-based biometrics [5].
(c) Mathematical modelling of footprint biometrics [6].
(d) Footprint-based image retrieval using transfer learning [7].
(e) Recognition of children's footprints using deep learning [8].

Finally, the impact of using deep learning techniques for footprint recognition is highlighted. In short, this paper brings together the various researches on infant biometrics using various techniques, like template matching, identification using fuzzy feature-set extraction, and identification using transfer learning models, under one umbrella.

The rest of the paper is organized as follows: In Sect. 2, technical research and surveys in the fields of biometrics and deep learning are reviewed. Section 3 provides a comparative analysis of related research works. This section presents discussions on the outcome of these researches, highlighting the mathematical modelling and metrics calculation for different biometric models. Section 4 and Sect. 5 identify future research directions and conclusions.

2 Literature Survey

2.1 Related Works

There has been some investigation in areas of biometric authentication using infant footprints in last couple of years. Parallelly, last few decades have seen a surge in deep learning techniques for several areas from healthcare to space research. In this section, information from multiple surveys and academic researches is concisely presented. In this paper several researches, surveys and reports were considered in the timeline of 2008–2022. The resources considered for review is presented in the order of their publication year with a brief overview of their work. The study began with reference to work of Weingaertner et al. [9] in 2008. Here a survey on feasibility of new-born biometric identification was presented. This case study investigated the ridge minutiae of face, footprint and palm of infants and analysed the images thus yielding an accuracy rate of 63.3% and 67.7%. This study opened up a new perspective for the creation of an automatic identification system for new-borns. This was followed by study of Wei Jia et al. [4] in 2010. They used several pre-processing method for image orientation and scale normalization and subspace approaches like PCA, LDA for recognition of newborn footprints. Their findings influenced several researches in 2013. Khamael Abbas Al-Dulaimi [3] in 2013 proposed a technique of human footprint recognition using feature extraction. In 2013, work of Kumar *et al.* [10] proposed a Footprint Recognition System (FPRS) highlighting the potential areas of employment of footprint as a recognition system for newborns. Balameenakshi *et al.* [11] presented their paper in 2013 IEEE Conference on Information & Communication Technologies. They pioneered the work of biometric recognition of infants where they proposed a complete approach of infant identification using footprint. They used several pre-processing techniques like particle filter, grey scale segmentation and mathematical morphology. The Gabor filter mechanism was responsible for the feature extraction process. Template matching techniques were subsequently utilized during the final footprint matching stages. The identification of new-born was further strengthened by including multiple modalities in the identification process. In 2015, Jain *et al.* [12] initiated a line of research focusing on the persistence of fingerprint recognition for infant and toddlers. Their research resulted in the creation of first biometric database for infant identification. This led to a series of further research works in 2017–19 by Basak *et al.* [13] in 2017, Liu [14] in 2018, Kotzerke *et al.* [15] in 2018, Kapase *et al.* [5] in 2018 and Nagwanshi *et al.* [6] in 2018.

Nagwanshi *et al.* [6] presented a mathematical approach by introducing a framework for a footprint-based identification system. The first ever modelling system using a standard algorithm for enrolment authentication and identification has been proposed in this work. Kotzerke *et al.* [15] investigated the steps to solve the infant biometric problem with ridge-based biometric features. The work of Kapase *et al.* [5] emphasized a multimodal biometric system for new-born recognition. Saggese *et al.* [16] used non-contact fingerprinting of newborns for their biometric recognition. They were the first to use a technology-centric development approach over traditional human-centred methods. This research was a Gates Open Research project, funded by the Bill & Melinda Gates Foundation in 2019.

On the other hand, with the advent of deep learning models like CNN and ANN, several studies were conducted in the area of infant footprint biometrics. Thus, a new research area was ushered in for the biometric identification of infants employing footprint biometrics involving deep learning techniques.

Chen *et al.* [7] published a report in 2021 in the Journal of Sensors on footprint image detection using ensemble deep neural network. They used transfer learning techniques for footprint image retrieval. His work was based on previous work by He *et al.* [17] *in* 2016. This report was published in the proceedings of the IEEE conference on computer vision and pattern recognition. This study focused on deep residual learning for image recognition. Another major contribution came from Kamble *et al.* [8]. They researched using children's footprints as a biometric recognition system using deep learning. This report was published in the IEEE Journal and was presented at the International Conference on Emerging Smart Computing and Informatics in 2022.

Ahsan *et al.* [18] in 2021 proposed an intelligent system for automatic identification of fingerprints using feature fusion. They used the Gabor filter and deep learning techniques for identification.

This paper presented some major areas of research related to infant biometrics and recognition. The overall intention of this paper is to highlight the application of deep learning techniques to infant footprint biometrics and their possible impact on improving prediction accuracy. This review can serve as a common platform for the health sector as well as technical researchers and stakeholders in both the medical and technical domains.

2.2 Methodologies Used in Reviewed Papers

After extensive survey of various surveys, research articles, and conference proceedings, the infant footprint biometric authentication and identification are broadly classified into

(a) Traditional approaches like morphology-based identification, template matching techniques, matching using fuzzy logic, and human footprint matching using feature extraction.
(b) Subspace Projection Techniques for Footprint Recognition.
(c) Deep learning approaches for footprint detection. Each of these approaches is discussed in the next section of the paper.

Traditional Approach of Infant Footprint Recognition

The traditional method for newborns involves capturing and analysing the unique characteristics of an infant's footprints. Ink-based Footprint Identification methods have been used for infant identification since ancient times and continue to be used today. This method involves applying ink to the infant's foot and then making a print on paper or card. The ink captures the pattern of ridges and valleys on the foot's surface, which can be analysed and used for identification purposes. This method has been used in hospitals and other medical centres for many years as a way to identify infants and prevent swapping. With the advent of the latest technologies, digital methods are used to capture the infant's footprints. The footprints are captured using a digital scanner or camera and the image is stored in a database for future identification purposes. This method is faster and more accurate than ink-based identification and is aimed at wider acceptance. With the wide spread use of automation in the technical domain, several approaches are being taken for software-based identification. The software uses algorithms to match the unique patterns of ridges and valleys on the skin surface and determine if there is a match with an existing record. This method is more efficient than manual identification and has been the subject of several research studies, both in the technical and medical domains. In this section of the study, some of the research works related to the traditional approaches of footprint biometric identification for infants are discussed. It is important to note that each of these traditional approaches has its advantages and disadvantages, and the choice of method depends on the specific application and requirements.

Structure/Morphology Based approaches.
Structural matching is a conventional method of biometric recognition that is considered in this section. Balameenakshi *et al.* [11] based their study on this technique. In their study, the authors used footprint features such as ridge bifurcations and line endings. The extracted features from the two patterns are then compared to generate the matching score. In their study, they used it for fingerprint and footprint matching. For example, a

pattern is framed out of the ridges and furrows on the surface of a fingertip or under the toe. The lines on the tip of a finger or under the toe are known as ridges. The spaces or gaps on either side of a ridge are known as valleys. The unique pattern of lines can either be a loop, whorl or arch. The most important features thus identified in fingerprints or prints are called the minutiae. These are usually known as the ridge endings and ridge bifurcations [10]. A ridge ending is the point where a ridge terminated. A ridge bifurcation is the point where a ridge separates into a branch ridge. An efficient minutia extracting approach uses a ridge map, thinning and post-processing. Some appropriate morphological functions are then used after the estimation of the ridges. The acquired images must be pre-processed to segment the undesired regions. Thus, a region of interest or ROI is cropped. The estimation of the ridges is performed using an efficient minutiae extraction algorithm [5]. The algorithm generates the ridge map. Next, thinning and post-processing activities are done using morphological functions. The minutiae information are expressed in a format of x and y coordinates along with the orientation angle [19]. An alignment-based pattern matching system is used. The process terminates with a similarity measure to determine the appropriate performance metric to use. The figure below (Fig. 1) shows the samples of ridges and bifurcations used for structural matching techniques in biometrics.

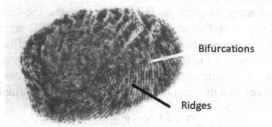

Bifurcations

Ridges

Fig. 1. Examples of Ridge Feature

Human Footprint Matching using feature extraction
In this section, the feature extraction techniques of image processing are considered. In this regard, many methods are used for biometric recognition. Gabor filters[1] are found to be the most effective and efficient method. They have been successfully applied to palmprint, face, fingerprint, and newborn footprint identification [11]. Gabor filter, filter bank, and transform functions are widely applied to image processing.

Feature extraction starts with identifying ridgelines. These are then followed by pixel identification, which ends when bifurcations are found. The end result of feature extraction is a template, which essentially consists of a list of features, each identified

---

[1] The Gabor filter has the following general equation form: $G(p,q;\lambda,\theta,\psi,\sigma,\gamma) = \exp(-((p'^2 + \gamma^2 q'^2) / (2\sigma^2))) * \cos(2\pi x' / \lambda + \psi)$ where, p and q are the spatial coordinates of the image, λ is the wavelength of the sinusoidal plane wave, θ is the orientation of the filter (in degrees), ψ is the phase offset of the sinusoidal plane wave, σ is the standard deviation of the Gaussian kernel.

by its coordinates with respect to the image. Shabil *et al.* [20] in their studies proposed a unique framework for the feature extraction process, as referred to in (Fig. 2). The framework considered the ridge orientation and appearance for the feature extraction process. Then Gabor filtering technique was applied on the selected features. This was followed by subsequent scanning and encoding. Some preset rules were applied and ridge minutia was detected at the final stage.

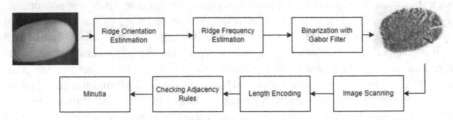

Fig. 2. Sample of Feature Extraction Process

Footprint Identification using Modified Sequential Haar Energy Transform (MSHET)
In this section the MHE approach for footprint recognition is considered. MHE stands for Modified Haar Energy mechanism. In MHE techniques, the vectors are calculated, stored in the database using Euclidean Distance (ED). The ED signifies the geometric distance between the initial point and center point of each image. This was a new method to extract features of footprint used by Al-Dulaimi *et al.* [3] where the researchers used the footprint input for determinant computation. In the recognition phase a threshold value, T, is used. To extract the required features, F (x, y), the formula below was used

$$F(x, y) \geq T \rightarrow F(x, y); \text{ Else, } F(x, y) \rightarrow 0 \tag{1}$$

The mathematical baseline can be further extended for feature selection in course of further study discourse (Fig. 3).

Fig. 3. Example (s) of minutiae pairs from Footprint Sample

Footprint Matching using fuzzy logic
In this section the fuzzy logic and neural network implementation for feature extraction in image processing is considered. Nagwanshi *et al.* [6] used set of fuzzy rules for feature

set generation. After normalization of the images, the feature set has been extracted. Some of the identified feature-set examples are shown if figure below (Fig. 4).

(a) Silhouette: A silhouette in footprint is defined as outline distance to foot midpoint, foot-length and the area within the silhouette polygon.
(b) Shape: A footprint shape is defined as the different types of foot widths and positions.
(c) Eigen-feet: An Eigen-feet is defined as projection of sampled footprint using feature space linked by some principal components.
(d) Minutiae: Minutiae of a footprint is defined by gathered footprint data using minutiae extractor on ball-print region or ridges under big toe. If, S be a biometric sample within the universe of discourse X.A feature extractor can be defined as E: X → F which maps each samples to its feature vector representation x ∈ F within the feature space. Here e_1, e_2,..., e_i denote different feature extractors such as illumination, Gaussian curvatures etc.

Fig. 4. Diagram of Foot print Silhouette

Template Matching technique for Footprint Recognition.
This section discusses one of the most popular methods for matching foot patterns. This is commonly known as template matching. It is based on comparing the pixel values of two images pattern. Every possible pattern sample is compared to the template pattern to determine the degree of similarity. Moreover, template matching eliminates the need for additional steps in the calculation of feature locations such as ridge ends and bifurcations [11].

There were no well-defined template matching algorithms for footprint matching. Liu [10] modified the algorithms for palmprint matcher and applied them for infant footprint matching study. The algorithm operates in following steps. In first step it classifies each minutia into one of the centroids using k-means clustering algorithm (with K = 32).

This step is offline. In the next step, the top N minutiae pairs with highest similarity are selected. Using local match propagation, more matching minutiae pairs are generated iteratively. With the large number of minutiae pairs the overall computation time was much reduced. In the last step, a final match score is generated which is the maximum score in match propagation of the minutiae pairs. Verifinger is commonly used to extract template from fingerprint. By default, Verifinger uses a proprietary template that uses other features in addition to standard minutiae features [21]. Jain et al. [12] used a protocol based on Fingerprint Verification Competition (FVC). They considered three scenarios (a) Single template per finger (b) Two template per finger (c) Fusion of two fingers. All results reported from these experiments are based on two finger fusion using one or two templates per finger taking into consideration the effect of age and effect of gender for each subject. In this experiment the rank-1 identification accuracy of matching against a single template came out 83.98% and 96.12%. For two templates the results improved the rank-1 identification accuracy to 84.95%. The rank-1 accuracy further improves to 91.26% and 99.03% by fusion of two different fingers. Due to these high rates of accuracy, template matching has been the most popular and extensively used by majority of studies till date.

Subspace Projection Techniques for Footprint Recognition
In this section, the advantages of online or digital image-based recognition methods are considered. Footprint recognition has been used for infant personal authentication for a long time. Usually, the footprints are collected with ink spread under the toe of the infant. It is then printed on the paper along with the mother's fingerprint for medical record. Nevertheless, with rising demand for fast and reliable newborn personal authentication, offline foot printing is no more a reliable choice. Besides inked footprints or bracelets serve as an identification measure only for the period of permanence of the child in the hospital unit. A study was conducted by Chicago's hospitals (USA) in which footprints collected were analyzed, concluding that 98% could not be used for identification. After providing training and the right equipment to the medical team, a new analysis of the collected footprints was performed, scaling the accuracy of image detection to 99%. But this identification was not based on dactyloscopy ridges. It used the creases of the foot which change during the first months of life.

Siddiqui et al. [18] developed an intelligent system that combined deep learning and the Gabor filter to classify fingerprint images into five distinct categories rather than using a minute matching method. A realistic solution for this task is an online system based on digital image acquisition and processing (Fig. 5). Typically, a digital capture sensor or optical sensor that can be connected to a computer for quick processing is used to capture footprint photos. An orientation and scale normalization preprocessing method were created to guarantee the quality of the images. The images were aligned using a given coordinate system and a region of interest (ROI) is clipped.

With the use of these Jia et al. [4] in their studies was able to recognize infants. The results were significantly superior than those of any earlier approach. In their experiments, they employed two palmprints of 30 randomly chosen infants, acquired on consecutive days within a time span (Time:24h and Time:48h). They were randomly numerated (from 1 to 60) and handed to three fingerprint experts to match the pairs. The results shown that with 19 out of 30 pairs properly identified, they achieved a score of

63.3%. Two of the 11 misclassified images were considered to be classification errors. When the matching test was conducted again with a fresh group of 30 infants drawn at random from the remaining 76, the experts correctly identified 20 of the 30 couples (67.7%), confirming the earlier identification rate.

Some subspace learning techniques like Principal Component Analysis (PCA) and Linear discriminant analysis (LDA) are used during the recognition stage to aid in recognition. PCA is used for reducing the image variables by selecting only the features which show maximum variance while LDA works on a similar principle as PCA and is used for dimensionality reduction while preserving inter-class discriminatory information. In [4], authors provided a comparative analysis of different algorithms like subspace learning with subspace methods and deep learning methods.

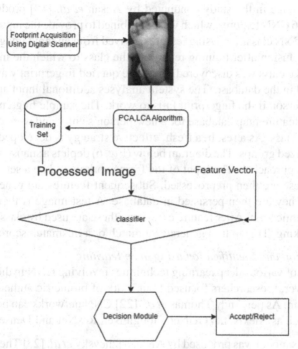

Fig. 5. Flow Diagram of Classifier Based Recognition Techniques Using PCA, LDA Algorithms

Footprint Recognition using Deep Learning Techniques

With the advancement of convolution neural networks (CNN), it has been found that various transfer learning models like VGGNet, GoogleNet, DenseNet and ResNet perform well in image retrieval and recognition in recent years. The accuracy of these models is also high. They have performed well in image classification and retrieval in several other domains of Image processing. Since the learning models are trained on a large number of images, their precision levels are also very high. The various techniques that are used for studies based on deep learning approach are.

– *Classification Techniques based Identification.*
– *Feature Extraction and Identification using deep learning*

Each of these are taken up for following section with the referred works.

Classification Techniques based Identification.
Multiclass classification was used in several investigation, and a classifier was trained using the training data. The different class levels were thought to be the Arch, Left-loop, Right-loop, Tented Arch and Whorl. Although there are other classification techniques, such as K-nearest Neighbor (KNN), decision trees (DT), and multiclass Support Vector Machines (SVM), CNN classifier was chosen because of its high level of classification accuracy. Image classes were taken from the fingerprint dataset and split into training and test datasets. Five classes of fingerprint picture data were used to extract CNN and Gabor features. Each image in the study conducted by Ahsan *et al.* [18] produced 72 Gabor features and 4096 CNN features, which were combined to provide the input feature vector for training the CNN classifier. Using features derived from an input image, the classifier generated a conclusion after training regarding the class to which the image belonged. At first, the image class was discovered. Then the queried fingerprint was matched with templates stored in the database. The system analyses additional input and keeps trying to identify the person if the fingerprint fails to work. The sample fingerprints were also uploaded to the feature map database for a new person's entry and were classified based on the specified class. As a result, a fresh, effective strategy is developed in accordance with the categorized groups. The diagram below (Fig. 6) depicts a snapshot of the process using classifier approaches. The input of the framework would be a set of 1...n images for training. These are then preprocessed. Subsequent features are generated using set of algorithms. They are then persisted in database. A test image is then passed to the system for authentication. After feature extraction these are used by classifier subsystem for decision making. This in turn generates a match or a mismatch score as output.

Feature Extraction and Identification using deep learning
With the advent of various deep learning techniques involving CNN in the arena of computer vision, several researchers focused their work of biometric authentication in this combined domain. As per Andy Thomas *et al.* [22] CNN networks can be classified into several types such as AlexNet, VGGNet, GoogleNet, ResNet and DenseNet model(s).

– AlexNet: This model was proposed by Alex Krizhevsky *et al.* [23] The network architecture consists of eight layers of learnable parameters. It consists of five convolution layers combined with max-pooling layers, three fully connected layers, eight pretrained layers. The first two layers have 4096 neurons each, and the third layer has 1000 neurons (corresponding to the 1000 classes in the ImageNet dataset). Alexnet produces a size of 4096-dimension for each image as a feature vector. The final layer of the network is a softmax layer that uses 1000 classes in the ImageNet dataset to generate the output.
– VGGNet:This is designed after AlexNet having some improvement in terms of architecture. The VGGNet architecture is characterized by its simplicity and depth. It has 16 or 19 layers (depending on the version) of convolutional and pooling layers, followed by three fully connected layers. The input to the network is an RGB image of size 224x224, and the output is a vector of probabilities for each of the 1000 object

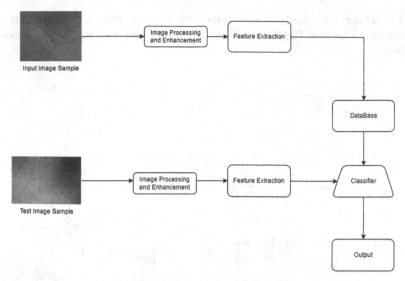

Fig. 6. Sample identification process using classifier approaches

categories in the ImageNet dataset. VGGNets comprises five blocks and three fully connected layers. Each block comprises some convolutional layers. It is followed by a max-pooling layer. This serves as a more in-depth network architecture built on AlexNet.

- ResNet: Alexnet works for fewer layers. With an increasing number of layers, a very common problem in deep learning gets invoked. This is called the Vanishing/Exploding gradient problem. This causes the gradient to become either 0 or too big. ResNet architecture (including Residual Block) was designed using the Tensorflow and Keras API. From the overall design perspective, it is made up of 34-layer plain network architecture that consists of (a)Residual Architecture consisted of Residual Blocks and skip connections. This is used to solve the vanishing/exploding gradient problem.(b)Residual block: The skip connection connects activations of a layer to other layers. This is turn skips some layers in between. Thus, a residual block is formed. Resnets are formed by arrangement of the residual blocks together.

Using these learning models, several studies were conducted referred in articles [6, 7, 18, 24].In this section, a sample framework from the works of Chen *et al.* [7] is presented. It explores different characteristics of VGGNet, ResNet and DenseNet models in their experiments for identification of infant using biometric features like finger and foot. Combined features of these models gave outstanding performance in terms of accuracy (98%). It has been found that all the proposed frameworks for footprint recognition using deep learning models would require the following basic steps.(A) Pre-processing (B) Model Training and Fine tuning (C) Feature Extraction using some deep neural models (D) Interpret the retrieved results in terms of several performance metrics. In this paper, some of these deep learning models have been explored for footprint recognition. The framework proposed by their works can be represented diagrammatically in figure below

(Fig. 7) where they have used CNN for training the footprint images using transfer learning techniques. VGGNet, ResNet and DenseNet features are used for features extraction and selection.

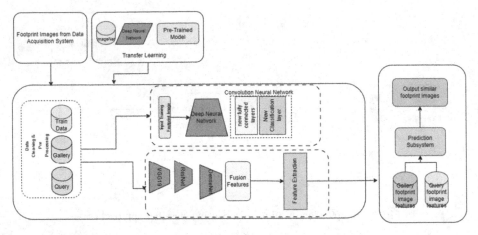

Fig. 7. Footprint image recognition using deep learning framework

The studies reveal that deep learning models have their performance benefits and drawbacks based on the accuracy and the computational time. In the next section, a performance comparison between the models is discussed to investigate the applicability of transfer learning in infant footprint biometric area.

3   Comparative Analysis

In this section, a comparative analysis of the researches in this domain is presented. Before going for a comparison, the papers have been classified in the following order for ease of study and analysis. (A) Recognition using Traditional Approaches (B) Footprint Acquisition using Subspace Approaches (C) Recognition using deep learning techniques. Here we compare the works that have been conducted in these areas with their major achievement and issues encountered in the course of the study.

In the papers [5, 15] the study reveals several morphology based approaches for footprint detection. Important biological features that are considered for the purpose of this study were skin ridges and the bifurcations between them. Other features that were studied were spaces between them known as valleys. Thus, a very important term called "minutia" was identified. This was referred in subsequent stages of researches by various scientists as basic step of every biometric research.

Another very useful research area explored was under [11, 20]. These studies revealed the application of the identified minutia now termed as features for further identification purpose. These studies used different filtering techniques for feature identification and selection-Gabor Filter, Transform Functions are some of them. These techniques proved to be very efficient and fast for feature retrieval and selection. Another contemporary research referred in [3] described a very significant approach of detection called Modified Sequential Haar Energy Transform where the extracted features are represented by feature vectors and Euclidean distance was used for measurement. A formula driven approach was used for this study purpose. Further these were stored in database for the course of study. A very popular approach of biometric authentication using stored templates is referred in studies [11, 12, 14]. Popular template matching approaches that were considered were (1)Single Template Matching (2)Two-template matching and (3)Fusion Template Matching. These matching techniques proved to be very efficient and effective for generation of output. They generated a score "Matching Score" that gave a Accept when a Match occurs and a Reject when Mismatch occurs. These studies paved the path on which current day researches were based. With the surge of advanced technologies various learning models were considered for the purpose for biometric identification. Under the current study several such references are reviewed that are discussed in the rest of the section. [4, 9, 25] focused on several subspace learning techniques -PCA and LDA for the purpose of biometric identification. PCA is an algorithmic approach used for selecting only the features which show maximum variance. LDA works on a similar principle as PCA and is used for dimensionality reduction of features. The output of these models was used by later works in [17, 18] for classifier-based feature selection that can be used by various CNN models for learning purpose. With the rising need of biometric authentication for infant security, several studies have been conducted using advanced techniques of deep learning(an effective strategy of machine learning).These explored deep learning models like AlexNet, ResNet and VGGNet. A series of researches on these and related topics were referred in [2, 6–8, 23, 26, 27]. Using these references the advantages and disadvantages of these models when used for biometric authentication were explored in depth. Next, a summary table is presented as a performance comparison based on measurable parameters like accuracy, computation time and training time [7, 8, 18, 24]. While studie [8, 24] shows that AlexNet used for ImageNet Classification has faster response time with low accuracy. Instead of focusing on accuracy the authors in [8] emphasized on class wise accuracy from each model. A very important factor was revealed in this study where the authors concluded that since the footprint crease pattern have ridge structure which is less concentrated than fingerprint ridge pattern. Hence, very deep features are not required for convolution layer. In [24], VGGNet model was explored which was more dense having reduced number of filters. This in turn lead the ability of learning more complicated features. VGG have moderate number of layers but the number of parameters required are yet higher. They found that Alexnet reached its highest training point after 1200 iteration while VGG achieved its highest point in 600 iteration. Thus, Vgg-16 and Vgg-19 are selected for identification of footprints in their study. With the use of transfer learning, the training phase required a large number of images [7, 8] explored ResNet, a deeper model that solves the problem of gradient disappearance due to increase of depth. Here the authors used a feature fusion approach using the three different models. The outcome of the study was a new feature vector of 5120 dimensions. Using ResNet, the authors derived a higher performance in terms of footprint image detection. They concluded that ResNet50 was more suitable for research content in this area. They used two metric learning models to calculate the similarity for their study.

After analysis of all the related study under this scope some major areas have been identified in the domain of infant biometric study. A large number of studies have demonstrated the use of performance metrics for better understanding and interpretation of results. There is also rising need of a mathematical approach of footprint modelling with use of proper algorithmic framework for the purpose of study. So in this section we provide some standard metrics used as a benchmark for result interpretation is presented. In addition some useful algorithmic approach for recognition and retrieval of footprint images are also discussed.

3.1 Mathematical Structures of Footprint Modelling

Majority of the studies showed that the basic steps that every research team follows for biometric authentication are a)**Image Acquisition** where are collected either using offline or pen -paper mode or using digital devices like mobile phones or sensors etc. Related studies shows that for infant biometric, in the images acquisition phase, data are collected in a timespan of several months due to rapid growth rate. The images are captured in a) normal b) special background. The time interval for two or more sets of data collection are 2-4 months or in two separate seasons. Image thus captured are cleaned and processed in the b)**Image Preprocessing** phase. The works of [11], shows that there are several key procedures employed for image processing post the acquisition phase like Particle Filter Processing, Executing the Clamp Function, Image Segmentation using Grey Scale, Morphology Study, ROI Extraction, Feature selection, Biometric storage in the database c) the results are calculated in the c) Matching stage either using template matching or employing deep learning techniques like AlexNet, DenseNet or Resnet. A score is calculated to verify whether a feature extraction stage matches a pattern pre-registered in the database. The system threshold value is then utilized to compare the matching score to, in order to determine whether or not the infant may be authenticated. A very important outcome of the study conducted in [6] was a three-stage algorithmic approach which have been referred to by majority of future research works. The generic structure of this approach in considered here for our discussion. I) Enrollment Stage: The enrollment algorithm would work in various substages as follows a) In the first step the algorithm would retrieve the required footprint data from the acquisition system. b) In the next step a template would be constructed containing the required details. c) In the last phase the features would be stored in the database. II) Authentication Stage: The authentication phase would commence with a) retrieval of the required footprint image from the acquisition system followed by b) Template construction. This commences with the verification stage in the database. If the query retrieves a match of the result-set from the template verification process then the result will generate a match else this would be rejected. Identification Stage using a Matching score: This is the final step of where to identify the result-set in accordance with matching score. With a match an acceptance occurs. With a non-matching score, a rejection occurs. The algorithm(s) are given special emphasis as these serves as the basis for many future researches [6].

Another feature that was noted for all the studies that are referred are some common metrics that are used for interpreting the results.[13, 16, 20] referred to some common measures of measurement using some common metrics like FTE,GAR,FRR etc. In this section a tabular representation is considered for evaluation (Table 1).

Table 1. Standard Metrics in Practice

Metric	Metric Name	Measurement (in Percentage)	Remarks
FTE	Failure to Control	FTE = (Number of failed enrollments / Total number of enrollment attempts)	A lower value of FTE indicates better population coverage
GAR	Genuine Accept Rate	GAR = (Number of authentic attempts accepted / total number of input attempts)	Higher value of GAR parameter generates better performance
FRR	False Reject Rate	FRR = (Number of genuine attempts rejected / Total number of genuine attempts)	A lower value of FRR indicates better performance of a biometric authentication system
FTC/FTA	Failure To Capture	FTC = (Number of forged or fake templates created / Total number of attempts to create forged or fake templates)	Lower value of FTC parameter generates better performance
TAR	True Acceptance Rate	TAR = (Number of genuine attempts identified/ Total number of genuine attempts)	Higher value of TAR parameter generates better performance
FAR	False Accept rate	FAR = (Number of fake attempts identified by the system/ Total number of fake attempts)	Lower value of FAR parameter generates better performance

Finally, the accuracy of all the studies is derived using the equation,

$$\text{Accuracy} = \text{Number of accurately matched samples} / \text{Total number of input samples} \tag{2}$$

All of the above empirical formulations indicate how biometric values can be interpreted mathematically from a biological perspective. In the remaining part of this section a comparison table is presented that discusses the methodologies, output and observation of each of the paper that are considered for the current review work (Table 2).

Table 2. Comparison of major resources and reference for Infant footprint recognition [2008–2022]

Authors	Methodology	Observations	Scope	Drawbacks
Al-Dulaimi *et al.* [3]	The researchers proposed a new technique called feature extraction. A method of calculating a desired threshold value. They used a NxN matrix to calculate the determinant value. This is used to calculate the center of each image. Finally, a training model is established using MSE criterion	The result is derived using Min(MSE) value between trained set and the verifying image. The mean square error between training set of foot and verified image were derived	Normalization of position and orientation of the input pair of footprint would yield higher matching score	The matching frequency and robustness of the technique was low
Jia *et al.* [4]	Online image acquisition & image preprocessing methods like image orientation and normalization were used. Learning techniques used for recognition are PCA and LDA	First technique of online footprint gathering for personal authentication of the newborns. First preprocessing method using coordinate system and ROI cropping was proposed	Images collected in one session in this study. But acquisition in multiple sessions would ensure better results	All the pictures were taken in one batch during the first two days after the infants birth. The main drawback for this work was the failure to obtain the second set of footprints from the same infant
Kapase *et al.* [5]	Fusion method of using mother's fingerprint newborn footprint was used here for successful authentication	The output was a fusion level matching by combining several single scalar score The final decision is based on fusion match score	Accuracy can be improved by a) larger database b) better image acquisition techniques	Single modality was used for the study purpose The accuracy can be further improved by using multiple modality

(*continued*)

Table 2. (*continued*)

Authors	Methodology	Observations	Scope	Drawbacks
Nagwanshi *et al.* [6]	A matcher framework for a biometric system based on footprints is suggested. Image normalization and feature extraction using fuzzy logic and neural networks are done during pre-processing	The researchers gave a generic architecture for a footprint biometric system that uses a standard algorithm for Enrollment, authentication and identification that makes use of fuzzy and neural sets	The featured metric footprint system is scheduled to begin operation in the near future with faster identification rates and more accuracy (based on researched hypothesis)	The featured metric footprint system is scheduled to begin operation in the near future with faster identification rates and more accuracy (based on re-searched hypothesis)
Chen *et al.* [7]	The researchers experimented the effect of CNN on footprint image retrieval. They stated an ensemble deep neural network approach for image retrieval based on transfer learning. They also explored the edge computing technology and developed a footprint acquisition system to gather the footprint data	They observed that VGGNet19, DenseNet121 and ResNet50 layers gave better feature representations of footprint images	The researchers proposed a larger dataset for future researches	The authors described some of the hindrances in terms of (a)small dataset which may affect the pre-training performance of the deep learning model (b)Construction of sample datasets can be taken up for consideration (c)At the same time, image background processing and different metric learning methods are scope of future work

(*continued*)

Table 2. (*continued*)

Authors	Methodology	Observations	Scope	Drawbacks
Kamble *et al.* [8]	The researcher used footprint crease pattern of children for recognition. Different deep learning algorithms were employed like VGG16, VGG19, ResNet50, AlexNet. The comparison of parameters used is done for all algorithms	A model which is a fine tuned, customized AlexNet model was proposed that reduces that reduces the number of parameters by 1,69,30,688	Multimodal and Multidomain approach can give better accuracy results. Longitudinal study of these modality needs to be carried	
Kotzerke *et al.* [15]	This work used the ridge features of the skin of the ball point under the toe as a measure of infant recognition. The main reason is that ball print image is easy to capture with more features and larger ridges than a fingerprint	The results of this work proved that value of ball prints was more accurate for infant identification, by themselves, or when fused with other biometrics	The work proposed a scope of upscale to larger populations. This may also be translated to other ridge-based biometrics features for infant identification	Small database, lack of good quality assessment algorithm and missing feature richness were some of limitations to theses study with further scope of improvement
Balameenakshi *et al.* [11]	Unique pre-processing methods for two scenarios a) normal b) special background ground	Some valuable observations including calculation of matching scores	The research proposed the use of multimodal system using mothers' fingerprint for verification in the tier 2 level	Some back-drops due to in-accurate image collections causing difficulty in precise ROI extraction

(*continued*)

Table 2. (*continued*)

Authors	Methodology	Observations	Scope	Drawbacks
Basak *et al.* [13]	A great initiative of the research team to aim to create a multimodal biometric database for future uses. The various tools used here a) Verilook face recognition SDK - to process face images, and the b) VeriEye SDK - to recognize irises. For c) NBIS NFSEG tool -fingerprinting image segmentation d) MINDTCT and Bozorth3 - for feature extraction and matching Then CMBD baseline results are reported	The database has several modalities-face, fingerprint, iris Sample size-more than 100 infants (ages Age group -18 months to 4yearsTime of collection -two multiple sessions months apart Thus first multimodal biometric (CMDB) database of young toddlers is proposed	More fusion biometrics like left and right iris or face with finger could be an attractive scope	Researchers faced several challenges associated with biometrics for young children, particularly when capturing fingerprints and irises
Saggese *et al.* [16]	Use of non-contact optical imaging of infant fingerprint	Resulted in a proposition of a hardware device to accommodate variations of several biometric features for infants b	The summary of the lessons learned is useful for future research work	Several issues faced by the researchers hindered the pace of data collection

(*continued*)

Table 2. (*continued*)

Authors	Methodology	Observations	Scope	Drawbacks
Ahsan *et al.* [18]	The team extracted a combined features using Gabor filtering technique and deep learning technique such as Convolutional Neural Network (CNN)	The outcome of the experiments multiclass classifier trained using the extracted features	Use of filtering technique in larger receptive field was suggested as a further scope in achieving better accuracy in the image segmentation	The authors presented some suggestion to improved their proposed models (a) Use of FusionNet for fingerprint detection (b) Application of DNN for image filters. (c) Use of Adaptive morphology to overcome performance issue
He *et al.* [17]	Deep The researchers used various residual nets like VGGNet on ImageNet Database	The results show that that these are easier to optimize and can gain more accuracy	Combining stronger regularization may lead to improvement in results in future	Training time was one of the concerns of the researchers which was overcome by a bottleneck design of the model
SHABIL *et al.* [20]	Evaluation of the significance of newborn babies' fingerprint recognition was done on some evaluation metrics	This study resulted in enhanced evaluation procedure for quality assessment. These are i) TAR-True acceptance rate ii) FRR-False Rejection Rate iii) FAR-False Acceptance Rate (FAR)	Scope of improving the evaluation process lies with use of quality indicators for biometrics. This can be enhanced with more precise algorithms	This report summarizes the main challenges and some discoveries during the collection and data processing of newborn fingerprints

4   Future Research Directions

There has been a rapid growth in the current market for deep learning techniques in various areas. Both biometrics and deep learning researchers are investing huge resources in research trends in this area. While quite a number of studies have already demonstrated the potential of employing deep learning techniques for biometric identification, the future of infant biometric research lies in this direction. So far, researchers have explored deep learning techniques like VGGNet, ResNet and AlexNet.They have compared the performance of these models in terms of computation time and accuracy.

- *Advanced Techniques of deep learning* - With the innovation of new arenas in deep learning, the scope of applying more advanced models to improve the prediction accuracy can be explored. Some of them are discussed below.

  - Inception Net: With the innovation of Inception Net (V3) models, the time required for classification is reduced drastically. This model can be pretrained using transfer learning as needed. The decrease in training time is due to the fact that the last layer of the model is trained to make it suitable for the application on demand. This model can be explored further for infant biometrics using results from existing models. This can help the footprint searches have higher accuracy and produce more efficient results.
  - Google Net is another model based on Inception Net's architecture. Key features of this model are that (a) the dropout layer (40%) is adjusted before the linear layer. (b) An additional layer called Auxiliary Classifiers is only invoked during training. Since this also offers a reduction in classification, this model can be trained on ImageNet for an increase in the identification accuracy of footprint images. These models can be focused upon for future study purposes.

- *Hybrid Technique for Human Footprint Recognition using biometric features of parents and child*: Studies by Kamble *et al.* [8] focused on unimodal feature footprint extraction using single models like VGG16 (accuracy 0.9394–1), VGG19 (accuracy 0.9797–1), and Resnet50 (0.9393–1). The proposed model attained 98% accuracy with 1,693,030,688 parameters. Chen *et al.* [7]explored Resnet50, VGGNet19, and DenseNet121 on a database of 5000 images using feature-fusion biometrics. They claimed to get better performance with this method. This model gave better performance when they were combined with Euclidean distance and cosine distance, yielding accuracy of more than 97%. They claimed that the fusion feature + cosine gave the best performance. From these propositions, it can be inferred that fusion features are very useful for future considerations. It can give more efficient results and a faster response when used with multi-modal features. Furthermore, employing hybrid techniques (parents' biometrics in fusion with infant biometrics) for generating the results can also be an efficient approach in this process. Thus, the scope of future work in this domain should be multimodal and multidomain in terms of feature selection and tuning several models to achieve the target.
- *Data Augmentation Approaches Using Generative Adversarial Networks (GAN):*. The studies referred to so far have one issue in common. They all reported that the availability of a footprint database in the case of infants is negligible. This is

a bottleneck for machine learning purposes. This has caused a hindrance to further research in this domain. A very recent innovation Generative adversarial networks (GANs) can be implemented to solve this problem. Using generative models of GANs, new footprint data instances can be created that resemble datasets. Further, they can be used for infant footprint identification by training a model to generate synthetic infant footprints that closely resemble the real ones. This can be attained by training a GAN on a dataset of real infant footprints and using the generator network to produce generated footprints that closely resemble the real ones. The discriminator network can then be used to distinguish between the generated and real footprints. The goal would be to train the generator to produce footprints that are so realistic that the discriminator cannot tell them apart from the real ones. Once the GAN has been trained, it can be used to generate new synthetic footprints that can be used for identification purposes.

5 Conclusion

To conclude, it is well observed that footprint modalities for infant recognition are not established procedures. Due to the rapid growth of children in the initial years, there have been large variations in biometric modalities such as face or fingerprint as compared to footprint.

In this paper, an extensive review of foot print-based biometrics for infant recognition has been considered. The scope of various machine learning algorithms using the CNN architecture for growth factor modelling in infants has also been reviewed. A comparative analysis of the different studies conducted in this field and their outcomes have been presented with an analysis of their respective achievements and limitations. The study concludes with a discussion on the scopes of future researches that has been revealed while conducting the review. This review work could serve as a source of essential information for upcoming research works in the field of biometric research.

Acknowledgement. The authors would like to express gratitude to Ms.Tandra Kabiraj,Part-Time Ph.D Scholar (NIMS University Rajasthan, Jaipur) and Assistant Professor(Nursing)-Techno India University for her time and support provided during this work. Her useful advice and suggestions were really helpful during the work.

References

1. JavaTPoint. Biometric System Functionality, 2011–2021, https://www.javatpoint.com/biometric-system-functionality, urldate = 2023–01–15
2. Masumoto, H., et al.: Accuracy of a deep convolutional neural network in detection of retinitis pigmentosa on ultrawide-field images. In: PeerJ **7**, e6900 (2019). https://doi.org/10.7717/peerj.6900
3. Al-Dulaimi, K.A.: Using feature extraction for human footprints recognition. International J. Comput. Appl. **64**(3) (2013)
4. Jia, W., Gui, J., Hu, R.X., Lei, Y.K., Xiao, X.Y.: Newborn footprint recognition using subspace learning methods. In: Advanced Intelligent Computing Theories and Applications: 6th International Conference on Intelligent Computing, ICIC 2010, Changsha, China, August 18–21, 2010. Proceedings 6, pp. 447–453. Springer Berlin Heidelberg (2010)

5. Kapase, T., Panpaliya, K. and Khandare, K.S.: Multi-Biometric System for Newborn Recognition
6. Nagwanshi, K.K., Dubey, S.: Mathematical modeling of footprint based biometric recognition. International of mathematical trends and technology (IJMIT) **54**, 49–61 (2018)
7. Chen, D., et al.: An ensemble deep neural network for footprint image retrieval based on transfer learning. Journal of Sensors, pp.1-9 (2021)
8. Kamble, V., Dale, M.: Deep learning for biometric recognition of children using footprints. In: 2022 International Conference on Emerging Smart Computing and Informatics (ESCI), pp. 1–6 (2022). IEEE
9. Weingaertner, D., Bellon, O.R.P., Silva, L., Cat, M.N.: Newborn's biometric identification: can it be done?. In: VISAPP (1), pp. 200–205 (2008)
10. Kumar, V.A., Ramakrishan, M.: Employment of footprint recognition system. Indian J. Comput. Sci. Eng. (IJCSE) **3**, 774–778 (2013)
11. Balameenakshi, S., Sumathi, S.: Biometric recognition of newborns: identification using footprints. In: 2013 IEEE Conference on Information & Communication Technologies, pp. 496–501. IEEE (2013)
12. Jain, A.K., Arora, S.S., Best-Rowden, L., Cao, K., Sudhish, P.S., Bhatnagar, A.: Biometrics for Child Vaccination and Welfare: Persistence of Fingerprint Recognition for Infants and Toddlers. *arXiv preprint* arXiv:1504.04651 (2015)
13. Basak, P., De, S., Agarwal, M., Malhotra, A., Vatsa, M., Singh, R.: Multimodal biometric recognition for toddlers and pre-school children. In: 2017 IEEE International Joint Conference on Biometrics (IJCB), pp. 627–633 (2017). IEEE
14. Liu, E.: Infant footprint recognition. In: Proceedings of the IEEE International Conference on Computer Vision, pp. 1653–1660 (2017)
15. Kotzerke, J., Davis, S.A., McVernon, J., Horadam, K.J.: Steps to solving the infant biometric problem with ridge-based biometrics. IET Biometrics **7**(6), 567–572 (2018)
16. Saggese, S., et al.: Biometric recognition of newborns and infants by non-contact fingerprinting: lessons learned. Gates Open Res. **3**(1477), 1477 (2019)
17. He, K., Zhang, X., Ren, S., Sun, J.: Deep residual learning for image recognition. In: Proceedings of the IEEE conference on computer vision and pattern recognition, pp. 770–778 (2016)
18. Ahsan, M., Based, M.A., Haider, J., Kowalski, M.: An intelligent system for automatic fingerprint identification using feature fusion by Gabor filter and deep learning. Comput. Electr. Eng. **95**, 107387 (2021)
19. Goodfellow, I., Bengio, Y., Courville, A.: Deep learning. Illustrated Edition. In: Amazon, MIT Press, p. 526 (2016)
20. Shabil, M., Fadewar, D.: Fingerprint Recognition of Newborns Baby: A Review
21. Han, X., Zhong, Y., Cao, L., Zhang, L.: Pre-trained alexnet architecture with pyramid pooling and supervision for high spatial resolution remote sensing image scene classification. Remote Sensing **9**(8), 848 (2017)
22. Thomas, A.: QUORA. What is max pooling in convolutional neural networks? Accessed = 2023–1–13 (2013). https://www.quora.com/What-is-max-pooling-in-convolutional-neural-networks/answer/Andy-Thomas-12?share=d3b8c024&srid=qf3d
23. Garg, C., et al.: Adaptive fuzzy logic models for the prediction of compressive strength of sustainable concrete. In: Bianchini, M., Piuri, V., Das, S., Shaw, R.N. (eds) Advanced Computing and Intelligent Technologies. Lecture Notes in Networks and Systems, **218**. Springer, Singapore (2022). https://doi.org/10.1007/978-981-16-2164-2_47
24. Abuqadumah, M.M.M., Ali, M.A., Abd Almisreb, A., Durakovic, B.: Deep transfer learning for human identification based on footprint: a comparative study. Periodicals of Eng. Natural Sci. **7**(3), 1300–1307 (2019)

25. Siddiqui, S., Vatsa, M., Singh, R.: Face recognition for newborns, toddlers, and pre-school children: a deep learning approach. In: 2018 24th International Conference on Pattern Recognition (ICPR), pp. 3156–3161 (2018). IEEE
26. Bodapati S., Bandarupally H., Shaw R.N., Ghosh A.: Comparison and analysis of RNN-LSTMs and CNNs for social reviews classification. In: Bansal J.C., Fung L.C.C., Simic M., Ghosh A. (eds) Advances in Applications of Data-Driven Computing. Advances in Intelligent Systems and Computing, **1319** (2021). Springer, Singapore. https://doi.org/10.1007/978-981-33-6919-1_4
27. Engelsma, J.J., Deb, D., Cao, K., Bhatnagar, A., Sudhish, P.S., Jain, A.K.: Infant-ID: fingerprints for global good. IEEE Trans. Pattern Anal. Mach. Intell. Intell. **44**(7), 3543–3559 (2021)

Method Comparison for Predicting Student Retention at a Private School in Indonesia

Abiella A. N. A. P. Panggabean[✉] and Pujianto Yugipuspito

Pelita Harapan University, Jakarta, Indonesia
01679210009@student.uph.edu

Abstract. Student retention is a significant indicator of a private school sustainability. This indicator is like the churn ratio in normal industries. This paper comparing several machine learning techniques to predict the student retention, i.e., random forest (RF), logistics regression (LR), support vector machine (SVM) and neural network (NN). Furthermore, this paper determined several predictors to student retention. This private school has levels from preschool to high school. The collected data includes student profile and demographic data parent's satisfactory survey from 2021 to 2023 that consists of 483 rows with 32 captured features. Next step is the feature extraction and then feature selection using Pearson correlation coefficient. The final data set is randomly divided into 70% for training and 30% for testing. This segregation is fixed for all machine learning methods. This research shown that the best method for this case is RF, almost similar with SVM, and the prominent predictors to student retention are Sibling Active, Learning Process, Individual Approach and Observation.

Keywords: Student Retention · Random Forest · Logistics Regression · Support Vector Machine · Neural Network

1 Introduction

Buying a product or service is more than just buying. For a customer, it means they experience and use it, and in return they get pleasurable level of fulfilment [1]. When customers feel satisfied with a product or service, they will purchase it again and recommend it through word of mouth which means they will retain. If they are not satisfied, they will complain about it or, worst-case scenario, they will not buy it anymore in the future and will not recommend it to others. In other words, eventually the customers will churn.

Customer churn happens when customers are not using a company's product or service anymore, but instead they use competitor's product or service [2]. Of course, every company does not wish to have churning customers, but rather the loyal ones who will repurchase their product. This type of customer is called retaining customers, the ones who are loyal, have positive attitudes towards the company, committed to repurchase, and willing to make recommendations. Companies are doing their best to retain their customers because it is more beneficial than acquiring the new ones. In fact,

R. N. Shaw et al. (Eds.): ICACIS 2023, CCIS 1920, pp. 165–176, 2023.
https://doi.org/10.1007/978-3-031-45121-8_14

if a company can retain just 5% of its customer, its profit will increase, and it can reduce marketing and operational costs while at the same time increasing its sales [3]. Unlike customer retention activities that can generate more profit if managed well, customer churn's downside is that it can cost more loss for the company. Therefore, a small improvement in customer retention and churn prediction can really help a company save a lot of money [4].

Both customer retention and churn are important for most companies from various industries, including the field of education. The benefits of education are numerous, for example it can make someone be a better person, brings confidence, ensures bright future, and helps with character building. In the long run, education can give self-preservation and success in someone's life [5]. The importance of education makes parents want to give their children the best education available.

According to some studies, parents are the key decision-makers in deciding which school for their children [5–7]. Parents will consider factors from their internal preference when choosing a school, such as their own education background, occupation, income, and even their family's ethnicity and religious background. Other factors that influence parents' decision-making come from the school itself, like academic quality, safety and discipline, school's strategic location, the distance from home to school, curriculum, school's environment, students' performance, and of course teacher's quality [6, 7]. If a school provides excellent service in each factor, it can cause satisfaction for the parents and make them want to enroll their children to that school. This also applies to parents who want to re-enroll their children to the same school for the next academic year, which can be called as customer retention in education. This research calls it student retention.

Student retention and churn prediction is necessary for schools because it can identify students who are most likely to churn [8–11] and help school management to evaluate and improve its service, learning system, facility, and even Customer Relationship Management (CRM) strategy [8, 10, 12]. This prediction also can show the causes or factors behind retain or churn behavior [9]. Other studies use factors like academic performance, attendance, family, financial condition, behavior, parent involvement, and demographics (age, gender) as variables to predict student retention and churn.

This research raises a case study of a private school that has a target of student retention or re-enrollment. Usually at the beginning of an academic year, the school's management makes a list of student retention. In this list, the management will mark the ones who will most likely continue their education in the next academic year and who will quit. The list is made solely from daily observation on parents done by the customer service team, which means the result validity cannot be ensured. Also, it is challenging for the school to come up with the right customer relationship management strategy to overcome student retention issues.

The research is conducted to replace the manually made prediction and instead will try to use machine learning models to predict student retention, and to determine which feature is the best predictor to student retention. In the future, there will be no need for this school to use prediction based on assumption anymore, but instead they can get a more precise result of prediction through machine learning, anticipate the parents and students who are showing signs of not continuing their education in the next academic year, and make a better customer relationship management strategy. The experiment will use machine learning models such as Random Forest (RF), Logistic Regression (LR), Support Vector Machine (SVM), and Neural Network (NN), and then compare the four models to determine which one is the most optimal machine learning for student retention predictions.

2   Literature Review

2.1   Customer Retention and Churn in Education Sector

Customer retention means the number of active customers who continue to buy products or services from a company [13, 14]. It is more profitable for a company to retain its customers, because attracting new customers costs more than retaining the existing ones [4, 15–17]. Not to mention, losing customers means a loss of opportunity because sales are reduced. In fact, just a 1% increase in customer retention has a significant impact of increase to the company's profit by 5% on average [13, 16, 18, 19].

As for customer churn, it is the likelihood of customers to stop buying from a company in each time period and switch to another business provider or competitor that sells better and cheaper products or services [2, 18, 20, 21]. Churning is a result of customer's low satisfaction level, not to mention the fierce competition between businesses vying to make the best product or service [16].

There are many studies that have raised this topic and used the telecommunications sector as a research object. Tsai and Lu [19] combined two different neural network techniques to predict customer churn: artificial neural network and self-organizing maps (SOM). Kraljević and Gotovac [17] also used neural network to predict prepaid customers churn in telecommunication services. Other sectors that uses machine learning for customer retention and churn predictions are in the retail sector [22, 23], human resources sector [24, 25], finance sector [13, 26], and of course the education sector.

Several studies called it Educational Data Mining (EDM), the application of data mining techniques to explore educational data to understand the context of learning process and other educational issues [27]. EDM extracts information about the students and process it to help school management to predict course enrollment, student performance, student dropout or churn, and many more [28]. Student dropout means the students who quit school [29], which is kind of similar to the meaning of customer churn. Student dropout is a threat for schools because it makes them lose revenue each year and possibly costs more resource and time [30, 31].

Alkhasawneh and Hobson [32] did a research of student retention prediction using Neural Network. They argued that student retention prediction gives useful information for schools during the advising and student recruitment process. In 2016, Aulck et al. [30] made an experiment of student dropout modeling using data from University of Washington, USA. They tried to analyze student dropout amongst a small, homogenous population using Logistic Regression, k-Nearest Neighbors, and Random Forest. The result shows that Logistic Regression is the strongest predictor of student dropout. Another study [33] used Logistic Regression, Random Forest, k-Nearest Neighbors, and Multilayer Perceptron model to reduce student dropout rates, and resulted in Logistic Regression and Multilayer Perceptron as the most superior model in the experiment.

2.2 Machine Learning Models for Student Retention and Churn Prediction

According to the findings from past studies of student retention and churn, Random Forest, Logistic Regression, Support Vector Machine, and Neural Network are popular amongst other machine learning models. Therefore, this research uses those four models too.

Random Forest is a tree-based learning algorithm which is known for its low tendency to over-training and its high accuracy [34]. It is a popular and powerful machine learning algorithm that offers significant benefits in the domain of student retention and churn prediction. With its ability to handle large and complex datasets, Random Forest excels in capturing intricate relationships between various factors affecting student retention. Its strength lies in its robustness against overfitting and noise, resulting in more accurate predictions and reduced false positives.

Logistic Regression is a classifier that estimates the probability of a binary output target [27]. It is one of the most widely used statistical techniques that holds several benefits in student retention and churn prediction. It identifies the relations between the output target or dependent variable with a set of independent variables, and computes the occurrence of an event happening based on predictors and weights [28, 35]. In the case of student retention and churn, Logistic Regression can identify the relationship between variables like student performance, student engagement, socio-economic background, and parents' involvement with student retention, and can point out which variable is the key driver of retention or churn. Additionally, Logistic Regression handles both categorical and continuous variables effectively, making it suitable for diverse data types commonly found in educational settings.

Support Vector Machine is a supervised learning algorithm that analyze data for regression and classification [27]. It is a powerful machine learning algorithm that offers several benefits in the context of student retention and churn prediction. It works by finding the optimal hyperplane that separates the data into two classes with maximum margin [8]. To achieve this, Support Vector Machine transforms the input data into a higher-dimensional feature space using a kernel function. This transformation helps in finding a decision boundary that can effectively separate the students who will retain and the students who will churn. The choice of the kernel function depends on the nature of the data and the problem at hand.

Neural Network is an algorithm that transforms inputs into desired outputs using highly inter-connected networks of relatively simple processing elements neurons [36]. The power of Neural Network lies in its ability to automatically learn complex patterns and relationships in data, making it a key component in deep learning models that tackle tasks requiring sophisticated modeling capabilities. Neural Network enables schools to gain a deeper understanding of the factors driving student churn and develop targeted strategies to improve student retention.

3   Research Methodology

This research design is an adopted Design Science Research (DSR) [37], that consists of five process steps as shown in Fig. 1.

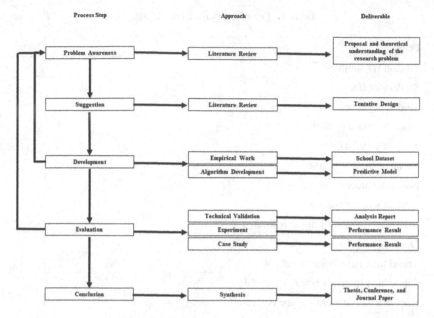

Fig. 1. Steps of data science research.

3.1 Data Collection

This research is using a private dataset from a private school in Jakarta, Indonesia to predict student retention for the academic year of 2023–2024 based on data from the academic year of 2021–2022. The collected data is from two years before the actual enrollment in question because the enrollment itself will start in the second term of the academic year of 2022–2023. Therefore, it is necessary to use the data from the two years prior so that the school management can come up with the right CRM strategy during the first term to maintain student retention.

3.2 Data Pre-processing

Data pre-processing or data preparation is a phase that is done before the actual prediction experiment. Several steps are taken to prepare the data before continuing to model development and experiments. Data cleaning is applied to transform raw dataset into a format that was more compatible for the modeling process later [35]. A tool called Orange3 [41] is used to handle data pre-processing up until the experiment.

All data from four separate datasets are joined. There are 483 rows obtained, which means there are 483 students who should re-enroll in the academic year of 2023–2024. Initially, there are 32 features captured, including the output variable which the student retains or not. There are more features added through features extraction, so the total of features is 37, as shown in Table 1.

Table 1. Features obtain from dataset.

No.	Feature	Note
1	Student ID number	
2	Student's name	
3	Student's gender	
4	Student's place of birth	
5	Student's birthdate	
6	Name of student's father	
7	Name of student's mother	
8	Student's home address	
9	Area which student's home is located	selected
10	Distance from home to school	
11	Travel time from home to school	
12	City which student's home is located	
13	Region which student's home is located	
14	Zip code of student's home	
15	Parent's email	
16	Parents phone number	
17	Parents phone number	
18	Parents phone number	
19	Student's religion	
20	Student's nationality	
21	The school branch (location) which the student studies at	
22	Grade of the student	
23	The date when the student became a member of the school	
24	The duration of the student being a member of the school	
25	The date when the family became a member of the school	
26	The duration of the family being a member of the school	
27	Student has special needs or not	
28	Student has sibling(s) who is currently active student(s) and will still be in academic year of 2023–2024	Selected
29	Student has sibling(s) who is currently active student(s) and will also need to re-enroll in academic year of 2023–2024	Selected
30	Student has sibling(s) who left the school in the middle of a level (did not graduate)	

(*continued*)

Table 1. (*continued*)

No.	Feature	Note
31	Student has sibling(s) who graduated from the school	
32	Parent's satisfaction in school's learning process	Selected
33	Parent's satisfaction in teacher's interaction with student	Selected
34	Parent's satisfaction in teacher's individual approach towards student's learning needs	
35	Parent's commentary and critique	
36	Customer service team's observation on parents' daily behavior	Selected
37	Student re-enroll to academic year of 2023–2024 or not	Target

3.3 Evaluation Methods

The commonly used performance metrics to evaluate student retention and churn predictions are [9, 16, 38–40]:

1. Confusion Matrix is matrix used to compare prediction results with the actual class depending on a positive and negative value.
2. AUC is the area under the Receiver Operating Characteristics (ROC) curve that ranges from 0 to 1. A model with AUC value closer to 1 is considered a better model.
3. F-Measure is the harmonic mean of precision and recall. F-measure is used as a single metric for evaluating classifier performance.
4. Accuracy is the proportion of the total number of predictions that were correct. Accuracy is used to measure the total proportion of the students whose final status, retain or churn, is correctly predicted by a model.
5. Precision is the proportion of the predicted positive cases that were correct. Precision is used to determine the proportion of the students that were actual churners among all those that the technique predicted as churners.
6. Recall is the proportion of positive cases that were correctly identified.

These metrics assess the effectiveness of machine models in various tasks, including classification, regression, and clustering. The selection of the appropriate metrics depends on the specific task and the desired evaluation criteria. It is common to consider multiple metrics together to gain a comprehensive understanding of the model's performance and to select the best model for a given task. Careful consideration of the performance metrics helps in selecting the most appropriate model and fine-tuning it to achieve optimal performance of retention and churn predictions.

4 Experiment and Results

The focus on this stage of experiments is to identify the students that will re-enroll in the academic year of 2023–2024. The experiment uses four machine learning models for prediction: Random Forest, Logistic Regression, Support Vector Machine, and Neural

Network. The cleaned dataset is trained using these models. Then, the trained models are used on the testing data for evaluation. The steps are as follows:

1. Train each model and make predictions on training data,
2. Use the "Test and Score" widget in Orange3 for validation. Apply k-fold cross validation with a 'K' value of 10,
3. Use the trained models to make predictions on testing data and compute the performance metrics to get the most optimal model,
4. Rank the features to know the top three features on both trained and tested models.

4.1 Random Forest Parameters

The parameters used in Orange3 for this Random Forest (RF) model are as follows:

1. Number of trees: 70
2. Number of attributes considered at each split: 3
3. Replicable training: Yes
4. Limit depth of individual trees: 3
5. Do no split subsets smaller than: 2

4.2 Logistics Regression Parameters

The parameters used in Orange3 for this Logistics Regression (LR) model are as follows:

1. Regularization type: Lasso (L1)
2. Strength (C): 3

4.3 Support Vector Machine Parameters

The parameters used in Orange3 for this Support Vector Machine (SVM) model are as follows:

1. Cost: 0.10
2. Regression loss epsilon: 0.10
3. Kernel: Linear (x,y)
4. Numerical tolerance: 0.0010
5. Iteration limit: 100

4.4 Neural Network Parameters

The parameters used in Orange3 for this Neural Network (NN) model are as follows:

1. Neurons in hidden layers: 250
2. Activation: ReLu
3. Solver: Adam
4. Regularization: 0.5
5. Maximal number of iterations: 50
6. Replicable training: Yes

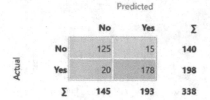

Fig. 2. Confusion matrix of Random Forest model.

Table 2. Confusion matrix of training model.

Case	RF	LR	SVM	NN
Predicted (No) – Actual (No)	125	120	112	119
Predicted (No) – Actual (Yes)	15	19	28	21
Predicted (Yes) – Actual (No)	20	20	19	15
Predicted (Yes) – Actual (Yes)	178	179	179	183

Table 3. Confusion matrix of testing model.

Case	RF	LR	SVM	NN
Predicted (No) – Actual (No)	47	46	47	42
Predicted (No) – Actual (Yes)	6	7	6	11
Predicted (Yes) – Actual (No)	6	6	6	2
Predicted (Yes) – Actual (Yes)	86	86	86	89

4.5 Confusion Matrix Results

In these experiments, each method will produce confusion matrix for training and testing data. A typical result is shown a Fig. 2, the case of Random Forest. The complete results are tabulated in Table 2 and Table 3 as training and testing respectively.

The maximum number of true and minimum number of false are achieved by the Random Forest model then Support vector machine model.

4.6 Evaluation Results

The results of Area Under ROC Curve (AUC), Classification Accuracy (CA), F1 score, Precision and Recall are shown in Fig. 3. Random Forest model give the best result. Followed by Support Vector model.

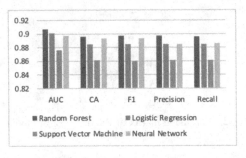

Fig. 3. Evaluation results.

5 Conclusion

To predict student retention, this research uses four machine learning models (Random Forest, Logistic Regression, Support Vector Machine, and Neural Network). Data is collected from a private school located in Jakarta, Indonesia. The data includes information like demographic data, enrollment data, parents' satisfaction survey data, and an observation of parents' behavior.

The data goes through a pre-processing phase, and then the four models are trained using the cleaned dataset. The models are evaluated, and their performances are compared using accuracy and AUC as the chosen metrics. The analysis results reveal that for the training model, Random Forest is the best machine learning model to predict student retention. But when applied to the testing data, the best machine learning model to predict student retention is Random Forest followed by Support Vector Machine. Nevertheless, all machine learning models in this research are showing good results.

References

1. Date, P.U.B., Type, P.U.B., Price, E.: An Overview of Customer Satisfaction Models Interim Director of Research (2000)
2. Roozbahani, Z., Minaei, B., Qiasi, R., Roozbehani, Z., Minaei-Bidgoli, B.: Predict Customer Churn By Using Rough Set Theory and Neural Network (2013). https://www.researchgate.net/publication/308399969
3. Bowen, J.T., Chen, S.: The Relationship Between Customer Loyalty and Customer Satisfaction, pp. 213–217 (1999)
4. Abbasimehr, H., Setak, M., Tarokh, M.J.: A neuro-fuzzy classifier for customer churn prediction. Int. J. Comput. Appl. **19**(8), 35–41 (2011)
5. Frempong, J.: Importance of Education in Human Life: A Holistic Approach, pp. 23–28
6. Altenhofen, S., Berends, M., White, T.G.: School choice decision making among suburban. High-Income Parents **2**(1), 1–14 (2016). https://doi.org/10.1177/2332858415624098
7. Alyani, N., Mohamed, M., Bachok, S.: An assessment of factors influencing parents' decision making when choosing a private school for their children : a case study of Selangor, Malaysia : for sustainable human capital. Procedia Environ. Sci. **28**(SustaiN 2014), 406–417 (2015). https://doi.org/10.1016/j.proenv.2015.07.050
8. Sansone, D.: Beyond early warning indicators: high school dropout and machine learning. Oxf. Bull. Econ. Stat. **81**(2), 456–485 (2019). https://doi.org/10.1111/obes.12277

9. Chung, J.Y., Lee, S.: Dropout early warning systems for high school students using machine learning. Child. Youth Serv. Rev., p. #pagerange# (2018). https://doi.org/10.1016/j.childy outh.2018.11.030

10. Hassan, M.M.: Prediction of School Drop outs with the help of Machine Learning Algorithms (2020)

11. Lee, S., Chung, J.Y.: The machine learning-based dropout early warning system for improving the performance of dropout prediction. Appl. Sci. **9**(15) (2019). https://doi.org/10.3390/app 9153093

12. Baker, R.S., Berning, A.W., Gowda, S.M., Zhang, S., Hawn, A.: Predicting K-12 dropout. J. Educ. Students Placed Risk **25**(1), 28–54 (2020). https://doi.org/10.1080/10824669.2019. 1670065

13. Wanganga, G., Qu, Y.: A deep learning based customer sentiment analysis model to enhance customer retention and loyalty in the payment industry. In: Proceedings - 2020 International Conference on Computational Science and Computational Intelligence, CSCI 2020, pp. 473–478 (2020). https://doi.org/10.1109/CSCI51800.2020.00086

14. Almohaimmeed, B.: Pillars of customer retention: an empirical study on the influence of customer satisfaction, customer loyalty, customer profitability on customer retention. Serbian J. Manag. **14**(2), 421–435 (2019). https://doi.org/10.5937/sjm14-15517

15. Verbeke, W., Martens, D., Mues, C., Baesens, B.: Building comprehensible customer churn prediction models with advanced rule induction techniques. Expert Syst. Appl. **38**(3), 2354–2364 (2010). https://doi.org/10.1016/j.eswa.2010.08.023

16. Vafeiadis, T., Diamantaras, K.I., Sarigiannidis, G., Chatzisavvas, K.C.: A comparison of machine learning techniques for customer churn prediction. Simul. Model. Pract. Theory **55**, 1–9 (2015). https://doi.org/10.1016/j.simpat.2015.03.003

17. Kraljević, G., Gotovac, S.: Modeling data mining applications for prediction of prepaid churn in telecommunication services. Automatika **51**(3), 275–283 (2010). https://doi.org/10.1080/ 00051144.2010.11828381

18. Ghorbani, A., Taghiyareh, F.: CMF: a framework to improve the management of customer churn. 2009 IEEE Asia-Pacific Serv. Comput. Conf. **1**, 457–462 (2009). https://doi.org/10. 1109/APSCC.2009.5394085

19. Tsai, C., Lu, Y.: Customer churn prediction by hybrid neural networks. Expert Syst. Appl. **36**(10), 12547–12553 (2009). https://doi.org/10.1016/j.eswa.2009.05.032

20. Xie, Y., Li, X., Ngai, E.W.T., Ying, W.: Customer churn prediction using improved balanced random forests. Expert Syst. Appl. **36**(3), 5445–5449 (2008). https://doi.org/10.1016/j.eswa. 2008.06.121

21. Tsai, T.Y., Lin, C.T., Prasad, M.: An intelligent customer churn prediction and response framework. In: Proceedings of IEEE 14th International Conference on Intelligent Systems and Knowledge Engineering, ISKE 2019, pp. 928–935 (2019). https://doi.org/10.1109/ISK E47853.2019.9170380

22. Seymen, O.F., Ölmez, E., Doğan, O., Er, O., Hiziroğlu, K.: Customer churn prediction using ordinary artificial neural network and convolutional neural network algorithms: a comparative performance assessment. GAZI Univ. J. Sci. **36**(2), 720–733 (2022). https://doi.org/10.35378/ gujs.992738

23. Kumar, M., Singh, P.A.J., Handa, D.: Literature Survey on Educational Dropout Prediction, pp. 8–19 (2017). https://doi.org/10.5815/ijeme.2017.02.02

24. Dolatabadi, S.H., Keynia, F.: Designing of customer and employee churn prediction model based on data mining method and neural predictor. In: 2nd International Conference on Computer and Communication Systems, ICCCS 2017, pp. 74–77 (2017). https://doi.org/10. 1109/CCOMS.2017.8075270

25. Ben Yahia, N., Hlel, J., Colomo-Palacios, R.: From big data to deep data to support people analytics for employee attrition prediction. IEEE Access **9**, 60447–60458 (2021). https://doi.org/10.1109/ACCESS.2021.3074559

26. Alizadeh, M., Zadeh, D.S., Moshiri, B., Montazeri, A.: Development of a customer churn model for banking industry based on hard and soft data fusion. IEEE Access **11**, 29759–29768 (2023). https://doi.org/10.1109/access.2023.3257352

27. Palacios, C.A., Reyes-Suárez, J.A., Bearzotti, L.A., Leiva, V., Marchant, C.: Knowledge discovery for higher education student retention based on data mining: machine learning algorithms and case study in chile. Entropy **23**(4), 1–23 (2021). https://doi.org/10.3390/e23040485

28. Wan Yaacob, W.F., Mohd Sobri, N., Nasir, S.A.M., Wan Yaacob, W.F., Norshahidi, N.D., Wan Husin, W.Z.: Predicting student drop-out in higher institution using data mining techniques. In: Journal of Physics: Conference Series **1496**(1), 012005 (2020). https://doi.org/10.1088/1742-6596/1496/1/012005

29. Sultan, E., Norshahriel, M., Rani, A., Filzah, N., Radzuan, M., Huay, L.: Predictive analytics on university student dropouts from online learning due to MCO. Knowl. Manag. Int. Conf. 2021, pp. 117–123 (2021)

30. Aulck, L., Blumenstock, J.: Predicting Student Dropout in Higher Education (2016)

31. Malsa, N., et al.: Framework and smart contract for blockchain enabled certificate verification system using robotics. In: Bianchini M., Simic M., Ghosh A., Shaw R.N. (eds) Machine Learning for Robotics Applications. Studies in Computational Intelligence, **960** (2021). Springer, Singapore. https://doi.org/10.1007/978-981-16-0598-7_10

32. Alkhasawneh, R., Hobson, R.: Modeling Student Retention in Science and Engineering Disciplines Using Neural Networks, pp. 660–663 (2011)

33. C.S. Engineering. Machine learning approach for reducing students dropout rates (2019)

34. Heredia-Jimenez, V., et al.: An early warning dropout model in higher education degree programs: a case study in Ecuador. In: CEUR Workshop Proc., vol. 2704, pp. 58–67 (2020)

35. Perez, B., Castellanos, C., Correal, D.: Applying data mining techniques to predict student dropout: a case study. In: 2018 IEEE 1st Colombian Conference on Applications in Computational Intelligence ColCACI 2018 - Proc., pp. 1–6 (2018). https://doi.org/10.1109/ColCACI.2018.8484847

36. Thammasiri, D., Delen, D., Meesad, P., Kasap, N.: A critical assessment of imbalanced class distribution problem: the case of predicting freshmen student attrition. Expert Syst. Appl. (2013). https://doi.org/10.1016/j.eswa.2013.07.046

37. Mduma, N.: Data Driven Approach for Predicting Student Dropout in Secondary Schools (2020)

38. Ahn, J., Hwang, J., Kim, D., Choi, H., Kang, S.: A survey on churn analysis in various business domains. IEEE Access **8**, 220816–220839 (2020). https://doi.org/10.1109/ACCESS.2020.3042657

39. Lykourentzou, I., Giannoukos, I., Nikolopoulos, V., Mpardis, G., Loumos, V.: Computers & Education Dropout Prediction in E-learning Courses Through the Combination of Machine Learning Techniques, **53**, 950–965 (2009). https://doi.org/10.1016/j.compedu.2009.05.010

40. Sani, N.S., Nafuri, A.F.M., Othman, Z.A., Nazri, M.Z.A., Nadiyah Mohamad, K.: Drop-Out Prediction in Higher Education Among B40 Students. Int. J. Adv. Comput. Sci. Appl. **11**(11), 550–559 (2020). https://doi.org/10.14569/IJACSA.2020.0111169

41. Demsar, J., et al.: Orange: data mining toolbox in python. J. Mach. Learn. Res. **14** (2013)

Distribution and Semantics of Terms with the Component 'White' in the Bulgarian Language: A Statistical Approach

Velislava Stoykova[(✉)] [iD]

Institute for the Bulgarian Language "Prof. Lyubomir Andreychin", Bulgarian
Academy of Sciences, 52, Shipchensky proh. blvd, bl. 17, 1113 Sofia, Bulgaria
vstoykova@yahoo.com
http://www.ibl.bas.bg

Abstract. The chapter presents a statistical search and Big Data approach to Bulgarian language data from the electronic text corpus for studying the distribution and semantics of terms with the component 'white'. The technique employs the Sketch Engine search approach by scoring for searching the bgTenTen12 Corpus, and several search steps to extract the semantic relations by the generation of the keyword search. The obtained results are subsumed with respect to the standard classification and typology of the obtained color terms and are analyzed concerning the modifier's semantic features. The related conclusions imply both the specific and global cultural context of terms' formation and usages.

Keywords: Artificial Intelligence · Big Data · Data Mining and Knowledge Discovery · Natural Language Processing · Fuzzy Logic

1 Introduction

Colors accompany human beings from ancient times. Contemporary anthropologists claim that the way colors are named in a specific culture implies the human's perception of colors from the local natural landscape. Thus, the terms colors are named are culturally specific and reflect the related typical customs, beliefs, and social behavior.

Consequently, colors have a primary function in human perception of the world and the way they are named is a sign of basically old, stable, and unconscious patterns that reflect the related symbolic meaning. Thus, studying color terms and their semantic motivation and relations can reveal important unconscious mechanisms of human perception of the world.

Further, we shall study the distribution and semantics of the terms with the component *white* in the Bulgarian language using a Big Data approach to discover their semantic relations and analyze them in the context of contemporary global culture.

R. N. Shaw et al. (Eds.): ICACIS 2023, CCIS 1920, pp. 177–187, 2023.
https://doi.org/10.1007/978-3-031-45121-8_15

2   Colors from Different Perspectives

Colors have been studied from different perspectives. For example, in physics, colors are regarded as a physical phenomenon, i.e. a light with a fixed wavelength. Alternatively, in linguistics and mainly in lexical semantics, colors have been studied using the nomination theory interpretations [8], i.e. analyzing them with respect to the main semantic feature standing behind their nominating (naming).

Additionally, in psycho-linguistics, colors have been studied from the point of view of the reaction they invoke in people to find the basic unconscious symbols and prototypes they assign. Finally, in terminology, colors are regarded as terms for the color (color terms) as well as terms with a color component, and using specific approaches (mainly knowledge-based [1]) terms are described and classified according to their semantic relations, typology, and classification as the primary approach to terminology from its early beginning [12] is to describe the domain of conceptual knowledge [5].

Thus, we study and analyze the distribution and semantics of terms containing the word *white* by using statistical scoring for the term's extraction, description, and typology.

2.1   Colors and Color Terminology

Thus, in our study, we make a principal difference in interpreting color as human perception and regarding color as a physical phenomenon analyzed as light with a fixed wavelength (visible light) and the subsequent ways of measuring it. However, the color attributes such as hue, saturation, lightness, and brightness that are measured physically might play a significant role in human color perception and color naming, and we shall take into account for them to outline color classification and typology.

Further, in our study, we regard color as a linguistic phenomenon, i.e. using related language theories for the interpretation and analysis of naming, functions, and usage of colors in the natural language.

2.2   Linguistic Approaches to Colors

One of the first research in the area [6,13] was focused on studying the universal language characteristics of the colors and their classification, made from the point of view of psycho-linguistics based on experiments on the human perception of colors in 20 languages, including Bulgarian. The definitions of the basic colors (color terms) used by various cultures, the ways of their appearance and stages of formation, the interconnection between them, and the established hierarchy was outlined.

Thus, the Basic Color Term (BCT) refers to a word (or phrase) that reflects human's perception of colors, which is the main color name. In classical color terms studies [6], within the BCTs, it is outlined an internal organization and hierarchy of colors. The BCTs are mostly monolexemic words as white, black, red, green, blue, yellow, brown, etc., which are accepted as abstract color terms.

That color classification system differentiates languages that are divided into seven stages in the formation of their BCTs and additionally accounts for the intensity of color by relating them as deep/pale. Thus, colors can vary in many of their characteristics as hues, saturation, and brightness. All these variations are expressed in the language by naming the colors according to light/dark, brightness/shades, and deep/pale, respectively.

Alternatively, the color names (color terms) might be studied in the onomasiological framework, in light of the nomination theory [8]. Thus, they are subsumed into primary (basic, abstract) as white, black, red, green, etc., and secondary (indirect, descriptive) as lilac, purple, cyclamen, rose ashes, etc. presenting also compound color terms.

Consequently, both abstract and descriptive color terms are formed in various stages of the continuous development of different cultures and are a result of language development itself. Thus, color terms are also examined and analyzed concerning their cultural interconnections and differences [18] in languages and cultures presenting the basis for evaluating their symbolic meaning for outlining their correct translation.

For the Bulgarian language, the color terms that have been studied outlining their symbolic meaning and function from the perspective of cultural context were studied in detail by M. Almaleh [2,3].

3   The Distributional Semantics Model

The first studies on colors as an object of linguistic analysis employ the statistical approach using the word association measure. However, recent linguistic research uses similar approaches and electronic text corpora [7] as a reliable database for studying words' distributions and associations. Thus, the Distributional Semantics Model (DSM) is a reliable approach that interprets the word's semantics as vector representations of its statistical word associations. That approach is semantically oriented as it employs statistical search, and accepts the resulting query keyword as connected to its statistically related (collocated) words. Consequently, the DSM uses frameworks that regard statistical similarity (or distance) as significant for semantic similarity (or distance) [4] of a related keyword.

Basically, the DSM approaches and techniques employ extraction of statistically-significant words of a searched query keyword regarding the search result as semantically relevant. Thus, the generation of common words to a related keyword is regarded as significant for generating relevant semantic information on the keyword's variability and functionality within the searched electronic text corpus. The approach adopts metrics and scoring for the extraction of various types of keyword semantic relations using the word similarity measure.

Thus, we employ the DSM approach to analyze the distribution and semantics of the word *white* studying the search query results by employing the statistical functions of the Sketch Engine software [11] and using the linguistic data of bgTenTen12 [10] electronic text corpus.

4   The Sketch Engine

The Sketch Engine (SE) [11] is a search machine that processes electronic text corpora by employing statistical search. It performs the extraction of statistically-similar words in order to outline semantically similar words and allows the comparison of results between several corpora. It uses software that allows a search for keywords, concordances, collocations, and co-occurrences for a related keyword.

The keywords are ranked on the base of their frequency and are extracted using statistical scoring. Thus, the collocations and co-occurrences are words that are most probably to be found with the related keyword. They are evaluated by estimation of their probability employing the techniques of $T-score$, $MI-score$, and $MI^3 - score$ incorporated into the SE. For them, the related terms are N - corpus size, f_A - number of occurrences of the keyword in the whole corpus (the size of the concordance), f_B - number of occurrences of the collocated keyword in the whole corpus, f_{AB} - number of occurrences of the collocate in the concordance (number of co-occurrences). The used formulas are as follows:

$$T - Score = \frac{f_{AB} - \frac{f_A f_B}{N}}{\sqrt{f_{AB}}} \tag{1}$$

$$MI - Score = log_2 \frac{f_{AB}N}{f_A f_B} \tag{2}$$

$$MI^3 - Score = log_2 \frac{f_{AB}^3 N}{f_A f_B} \tag{3}$$

As a result, the SE software allows the extraction of horizontal semantic relations such as synonymy, antonymy, and meronymy. Also, the vertical relations as hierarchy presented by hyperonymy and hyponymy are extracted as well.

Further, we analyze the results of the employment of the statistical approach already described in [16,17] to study the distribution and semantics of terms with the component *white* in the Bulgarian language. We use the SE search techniques and scoring to generate the keyword semantic clusters by the estimation of concordances, collocations, and thesaurus. We use statistical search by employing retrieval and clustering of statistically similar words of the keyword *white*.

5   The bgTenTen12 Corpus

The bgTenTen12 Corpus is created as a part of the TenTen Family Corpora which are multilingual corpora crawled from the web [10] and sized more than 10 million words per language. The corpus was compiled by crawling texts from the web employing the *SpiderLing* tool and includes web text materials of linguistically valuable texts.

CONCORDANCE

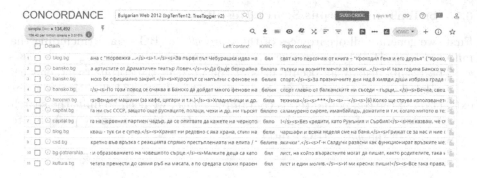

Fig. 1. The results from the concordance search of the word *white* (BG - бял).

The technique of creating the bgTenTen12 Corpus consists of web text downloading, cleaning texts from linguistically valueless content using *jusText* software, tokenization, and removing duplicated texts using *Onion* software. Further, the corpus was divided into specific domain genres according to the related text styles and topics. Then, the corpus was lemmatized and tagged with Bulgarian language part-of-speech tagger and finally annotated using the TenTen Family Corpora metadata to be suitable for language-specific searches.

According to its volume, the bgTenTen12 Corpus consists of texts at about 705 156 683 words, subsumed into several journalistic genres of Bulgarian newspapers, and is representative of contemporary Bulgarian journalistic. It is uploaded into the SE, which allows various types of processing.

6   The Distribution and Semantics of Terms with the Component 'White'

Further, for the semantic analysis, we follow the theory of prototypes [9,14] and mainly the understanding of colors as universals, which are represented symbolically by their prototypes (objects) as well as the framework of culturally specific interpretation of colors and their transition [18]. Moreover, the theory of prototypes was examined over the classifications (of objects) [15], which is fully compatible with the basic terminological interpretations.

We also follow the related terminology used as Basic Color Terms (BCTs) - for the different colors, Prototype Terms (PTs) - for the prototypes of a related color, Rivals Terms of Prototypes (RTs) - for the rivals of the prototypes terms, and Terms for the Basic Features of the Prototypes (TBFPs), which was employed in [2,3] for semantic analysis.

Thus, we shall use a statistical scoring of SE to extract the terms with the component *white*, and later to analyze the results according to the above accepted classification of terms semantically related to *white* color.

6.1   bgTenTen12 Corpus Search Results

First, we generate all occurrences of the word *white* (BG - бял) (including the inflected forms [17]) by generating its concordances as shown in Fig. 1.

The results display all occurrences of the word in the corpus together with their related quantitative contexts and sources, which are 134 492. However, for extraction of the compound terms containing *white*, we need to limit the search to the generation of related collocations or words, which are most probable to be found with the *white* (BG - бял).

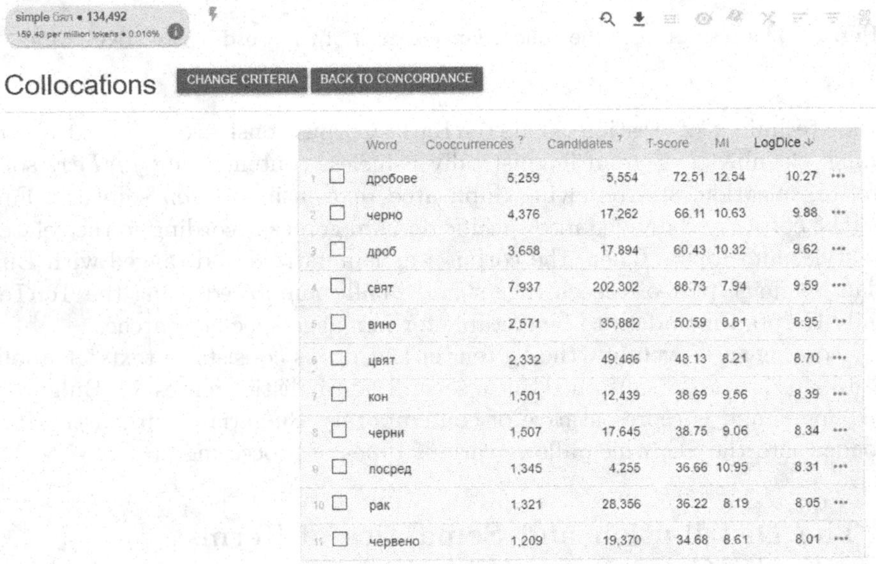

	Word	Cooccurrences	Candidates	T-score	MI	LogDice ↓	
1	дробове	5,259	5,554	72.51	12.54	10.27	•••
2	черно	4,376	17,262	66.11	10.63	9.88	•••
3	дроб	3,658	17,894	60.43	10.32	9.62	•••
4	свят	7,937	202,302	88.73	7.94	9.59	•••
5	вино	2,571	35,882	50.59	8.81	8.95	•••
6	цвят	2,332	49,466	48.13	8.21	8.70	•••
7	кон	1,501	12,439	38.69	9.56	8.39	•••
8	черни	1,507	17,645	38.75	9.06	8.34	•••
9	посред	1,345	4,255	36.66	10.95	8.31	•••
10	рак	1,321	28,356	36.22	8.19	8.05	•••
11	червено	1,209	19,370	34.68	8.61	8.01	•••

Fig. 2. The results from the collocation candidates search for the word *white* (BG - бял).

Figure 2 presents the first 11 collocations search results, and they include *black* (BG - черно), *lung* (BG - дроб), *world* (BG - свят), *wine* (BG - вино), *color* (BG - цвят), *horse* (BG - кон), *red* (BG - червено), etc.

However, the results present the most frequent terms with a modifier *white*: lung (BG - бял дроб), the white world (BG - бял свят), white wine (BG - бяло вино), white color (BG - бял цвят), white horse (BG - бял кон) as well as white-black (BG - бяло-черно), white-red (BG - бял-червен), etc. Within them, only one term presents a color name i.e. *white color* (BG - бял цвят), which is BCT, whereas the other results present terms with a component of *white*.

Thus, we extend the analysis by visualizing more collocation candidates as well as more semantic relations (assigned with different colors) of the word *white* as presented in Fig. 3.

Fig. 3. The visual presentation of semantic relations of the word *white* (BG - бял).

Among the results, we outline more collocations: bread, shirt, dress, paper, spot, etc. that can be regarded as RTs forming the compound terms like: white bread (BG - бял хляб), white shirt (BG - бяла риза), white dress (BG - бяла дреха), white paper (BG - бял лист), white spot (BG - бяло петно).

Similarly, we study the prepositional occurrences of the keyword *white* with *like*. The results from Fig. 3 (orange marked) show that the co-occurred words are *snow* (BG - сняг), *milk* (BG - мляко), and *cheese* (BG - сирене), which are PTs as well as *canvas* (BG - платно) and *angel* (BG - ангел), which are RTs of the prototypes, and all they are assigned with the semantic feature of *purity*.

Also, according to the semantic relation *and/or* (green marked) results are: black (BG - черен), red (BG - червен), green (BG - зелен), yellow (BG - жълт), blue (BG - син), brown (BG - кафяв), purple (BG - лилав), pink (BG - розов), orange (BG - оранжев), and gray (BG - сив), which together with *white* form 11 colors system and are BCTs. Additionally, the results include beige (BG - бежев), creamy (BG - кремав), silvery (BG - сребрист), flowery (BG -цветен), etc.

The first results also outline some color relations like *white-black* and *white-red*, which from the point of view of the classical color studies imply the formation of a language triple color system (white, black, red) [6]. Thus, we extend our theoretical assumptions to analyzing color transitions of *white*, i.e. *macro-white* as presented in [18], and we regard *white* as extending its scope by relating it to *red* and searching for *and/or* semantic relation between them.

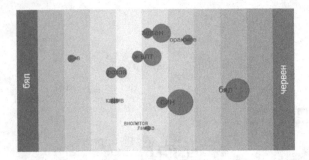

Fig. 4. The visual presentation of semantic relation *and/or* of words *white-red* (BG - бял-червен).

Figure 4 presents the visualized results and contains colors that are most probably to be collocated with *white* or *red*, respectively. Thus, grey (BG - сив) tends to be closer to *white*, and *white* is closer to *red* (BG - червен). The other presented colors as blue (BG - син), green (BG - зелен), yellow (BG - жълт), pink (BG - розов), and purple (BG - лилав) express relatively similar closeness to both *white* and *red*.

More sophisticated statistics can be used to extract more complex semantic relations of the keyword and its related words that share common collocations. Thus, if two words have a common collocation, they are semantically related. That relations are mostly hierarchical and form a thesaurus. Consequently, we employ the search for common collocations of the keyword *white* to extract more complex semantic relations, to build a thesaurus.

The results presented in Fig. 5 contain the most frequent collocated words that form the core of the semantic cluster and are similar to the results already obtained, i.e. BCTs. However, the results also include *bright* (BG - светъл), *warm* (BG - топъл), *soft* (BG - мек), *tender* (BG - нежен), *golden* (BG - златен), *transparent* (BG - прозрачен) that can be regarded as attributes of colors and *light* (as PT of *white*). Also, the results include other types of terms as *pure* (BG - чист), which is a BFPT, *beautiful* (BG - прекрасен) as well as *healthy* (BG - здрав) that also are semantically related to *white*.

From the statistical analyses of the distribution and semantics of *white*, we can conclude that the word *white* as presenting a color is a BCT that has *light*, *snow*, *milk*, and *cheese* as PTs. Additionally, the PTs have a semantic feature *purity*, which is BFPTs. Thus, *white* symbolizes *light*, *pure*, *beautiful*, and *healthy* things. Some researchers regard *white* as having a semantics of inclusiveness since *light* (PT of *white*) includes all colors, as our results also improved, and more than this. Consequently, *white* has very complex semantics that possesses the attributes of the colors themselves as brightness and transparency, as well as symbolize the feelings of warmness and tenderness. It is possible to analyze the semantics of *white* by revealing its religious symbols as presented in [3].

Fig. 5. The visual presentation of thesaurus of the word *white* (BG - бял).

Thus, the terms with a component *white* in the contemporary Bulgarian language present attributive collocations and express a semantics that relates to the BFPTs of *white* as in the *white dress* (white uniform) (BG - бяла дреха), which symbolizes the healthy institutions, in *white paper* (BG - бял лист), which symbolizes the purity, in *white bread* (BG - бял хляб), which symbolizes purity, unmixedness. Also, they express the semantics of nothing as in the *white spot* (BG - бяло петно), which symbolizes the lack of something. Finally, the terms with the component *white* express the semantics of the BCT as in *white wine* (BG - бяло вино) and a *white horse* (BG - бял кон).

7   Conclusion

The analysis of search results show that the distribution, semantics, and use of terms with the component *white* in the standard Bulgarian language employs a complex algorithm that includes various steps of statistical search using the SE scoring to extract concordances, collocations, semantic relations, and thesaurus in a big text corpus of linguistic data in Bulgarian.

The presented search results outline that the distribution, semantics, and use of terms with a component *white* (BG - бял) are closely connected to the complex semantics of the color term for *white* as a BCT. Also, the results include terms of type PTs (light, snow, milk, etc.) and TBFPs (purity). The results clearly show that the old and basic prototypes and their semantic features for

186   V. Stoykova

white are preserved in the standard Bulgarian language and are semantically active and productive, except for religious meaning due to the process of globalization.

Thus, the terms with component *white* can be semantically derived and related to the meaning of the BCT, its PTs, RTs, and the TBFPs. Further, it would be good to employ the same approach to study terms with components from different colors or languages since the presented technique is language-independent.

References

1. Alexiev, B.: Knowledge-Oriented Terminography. Avangard Publishing Co., Sofia (2011)
2. Almalech, M.: Colour as cultural unit: challenges and developments. In: Thellefsen, T., Sørensen, B. (eds.) Umberto Eco in His Own Words, pp. 206–213. De Gruyter Mouton, Berlin (2017)
3. Almalecth, M.: The Light in the Old Testament. Kibea, Sofia (2010). (in Bulgarian)
4. Baroni, M., Lenci, A.: Distributional memory: a general framework for corpus-based semantics. Comput. Linguist. **36**(4), 673–721 (2010)
5. Bergenholtz, H., Agerbo, H.: Types of lexicographical information needs and their relevance for information science. J. Inf. Sci. Theory Pract. **5**(3), 15–30 (2017)
6. Berlin, B., Kay, P.: Basic Color Terms: Their Universality and Evolution. The University of California Press, Berkeley and Los Angeles (1969)
7. Brezina, V.: Statistics in Corpus Linguistics: A Practical Guide. Cambridge University Press, Cambridge (2018)
8. Čermák, F.: Types of language nomination: universals, typology and lexicographical relevance. In: Braasch, A., Povlsen, C. (eds.) Proceedings of the 10th EURALEX International Congress, pp. 237–247, Center for Sprogteknologi, København (2002)
9. Heider, E.R.: Universals in color naming and memory. J. Exp. Psychol. **93**(1), 10–20 (1972)
10. Jakubíček, M., Kilgarriff, A., Kovář, V., Rychlý, P., Suchomel, V.: The TenTen corpus family. In: 7th International Corpus Linguistics Conference CL, pp. 125–127 (2013)
11. Kilgarriff, A., et al.: The sketch engine: ten years on. Lexicography **1**, 7–36 (2014)
12. Lineai, K.: Systema naturae sive regna tria naturae systematice proposita per classes, ordines, genera, and species. apud Theodorum Haak, Lugduni Batavorum, Leyden (1735)
13. McNeill, N.: Colour and colour terminology. J. Linguist. **8**(1), 21–33 (1972)
14. Rosch, E.: Natural categories. Cogn. Psychol. **4**, 328–350 (1973)
15. Rosch, E., Mervis, C.B., Gray, W., Johnson, D., Boyes-Braem, P.: Basic objects in natural categories. Cogn. Psychol. **8**, 382–439 (1976)
16. Stoykova, V.: Bulgarian noun - definite article in DATR. In: Scott, D. (ed.) AIMSA 2002. LNCS (LNAI), vol. 2443, pp. 152–161. Springer, Heidelberg (2002). https://doi.org/10.1007/3-540-46148-5_16
17. Stoykova, V.: Extracting and analyzing terms with the component 'Green' in the Bulgarian language: a big data approach. In: Abraham, A., Bajaj, A., Gandhi, N., Madureira, A. M., Kahraman, C. (eds) Innovations in Bio-Inspired Computing

and Applications. IBICA 2022. Lecture Notes in Networks and Systems(LNNS), vol 649, 245–254. Springer, Heidelberg (2023). https://doi.org/10.1007/978-3-031-27499-2_23

18. Wierzbicka, A.: The meaning of colour terms: semantics, cultures and cognition. Cogn. Linguist. 1(1), 99–150 (1990)

Sanskrit OCR System

Jyoti Madake, Yuvraj Yedle[✉], Vaibhav Shahabade, and Shripad Bhatlawande

Department of Electronics and Telecommunication Engineering, Vishwakarma Institute of
Technology, Pune, India
{jyoti.madake,yuvraj.yedle20,vaibhav.shahabade20,
shripad.bhatlawande}@vit.edu

Abstract. The use of optical character recognition technology has become
increasingly important for researchers in recognition techniques. Recognition of
Sanskrit character is a challenging area in pattern recognition, character recognition is used to convert printed or handwritten text into machine-encoded text.
The proposed system explores the effectiveness of three distinct feature extraction methods, namely Discrete Cosine Transform (DCT), Histogram of Oriented
Gradients (HOG) and Scale-Invariant Feature Transform (SIFT), for character
recognition. Each method is applied separately to a dataset of handwritten characters and evaluated for accuracy. Also the combination of SIFT + DCT, SIFT
+ HOG and DCT + HOG is used for comparison in order to check whether the
combinations are effective or not compared to individual methods. For the Sanskrit
OCR system it is observed that DCT gives the highest accuracy of 98.7%.

Keywords: Sanskrit OCR · SIFT · DCT · HOG · SVM

1 Introduction

Sanskrit is an ancient Indian language, has been used for millions of years in many areas
of study and research, such as scientific research, philosophical thought, and literature
etc. Researchers from all over the world are giving more attention to their research of
these ancient documents or papers. Because of a lack of qualified experts and challenges
with imaging old manuscripts, texts written in Sanskrit became tough to keep and make
available. The progress of OCR (optical character recognition) technology, the technique
of digitizing and preserving ancient texts for future generations, has experienced an
important evolution.

With the growth of digital content, the demand for powerful optical character recognition (OCR) engines has increased.OCR works by analyzing document images by page,
word, and character, and identifies the characters by comparing them to image patterns.
It is possible to recognise characters in printed and handwritten documents. Sanskrit
includes more consonants and modifying characters than other offline related writing
systems, making it harder to identify Sanskrit characters from handwritten writings. As
is generally known, the Sanskrit script of India is an old Indo-Aryan language with a
significant literary legacy.

R. N. Shaw et al. (Eds.): ICACIS 2023, CCIS 1920, pp. 188–200, 2023.
https://doi.org/10.1007/978-3-031-45121-8_16

Historically used to write Sanskrit. Much of the Sanskrit literature on science, technology and poetry is the product of a vibrant literary heritage. Sanskrit language contains 48 letters, containing 15 vowels and 33 consonants.

Feature extraction is one of the key step in OCR, many paper use CNN to recognize the sanskrit text.In this context, various feature extraction techniques have been used for Sanskrit OCR, such as Discrete Cosine Transform (DCT), Histogram of Oriented Gradients (HOG) and Scale-Invariant Feature Transform (SIFT).

2   Literature Survey

By using a convolutional neural network (CNN) Sanskrit characters are digitized using OCR (optical character recognition) technology. In this paper [1] For calculating pixel intensities to identify letters in the image, the image segmentation algorithm is used. An OCR for Devanagari script using a novel approach of using Convolutional Neural Networks as classifiers, which are found to be more suitable for multi-class image classification than SVMs and ANNs. The OCR system is efficient with regard to the size of the fonts, style, image quality, and contrast, which makes it the best choice for digitizing old and badly maintained content [8].

OCR for Sanskrit divides compound words into subwords to determine correctness using fundamental Sandhi rules. A minimum set of words with a maximum length and a minimum edit distance are utilized as the criteria in a greedy approach. This helps detect out-of-vocabulary words and generate suggestions [2]. The paper [3], a feed-forward architecture is used by the OCRopus system, making it easier to add other layout analysis and text recognition modules and easier to test, evaluate, and optimize. The feed-forward approach reduces coupling between components and eliminates the difficulty of statistically modeling backtracking. This paper [4] tells the Character recognition involves several steps including pre-processing like binarization, noise reduction, normalization, and skew correction, another step is segmentation (splitting the image into individual characters), feature extraction (extracting important features from the character images), and classification (using techniques such as artificial neural networks to identify the characters). The mean squared error and classifier accuracy are used for determining the accuracy.

Automatic speech recognition system for Sanskrit language a speech corpus was created from various sources and was processed to obtain uniform format. The system uses HMM models and N-gram language models. In this paper [5, 16] the Viterbi algorithm is used to decode the speech observations. In this paper [6] the system proposes for recognizing handwritten Hindi/Sanskrit characters. Starts with pre-processing for clean character image, then the system followed by feature extraction using the Freeman chain code (FCC). The segmentation step uses a genetic algorithm for character segmentation, and the recognition model uses Support Vector Machine (SVM) classifiers for higher level classification accuracy. Handwritten Character Recognition (HCR) techniques, Neural networks, Support Vector Machines and Convolutional Neural Networks are the main techniques used for recognition [7, 13, 20]. Synthetic Minority Over-sampling Technique (SMOTE) is used [9] to solve the imbalance distribution problem in pattern recognition, which can negatively affect performance. The technique generates synthetic samples for each class by combining the original sample with its k nearest neighbors. When a class only has one sample, Gaussian noise is added to create a new sample before using SMOTE. This ensures that there is more than one sample per class for SMOTE to work with. Recognizing handwritten Devanagari characters using image processing techniques and pattern recognition algorithms [10]. The images are first pre-processed and standardized. Afterward, characters are roughly divided into three categories based on whether or not a vertical bar is present. A system [11] designed to recognize and classify different scripts, including alphabetic, non-alphabetic, and connected scripts.It also can handle moderate distortions and artifacts in documents, making it suitable for real-life applications. The authors express interest in linking their research to language identification for multi-language scripts and using the script identification templates for OCR. Combining script identification, language identification, and OCR would lead to a more effective system.

It involves collecting and preprocessing handwritten numeral images, dividing them into zones, computing average pixel distance, and extracting 250 features. The recognition in this paper [12] is performed using Support Vector Machine (SVM). The authors used 4000 numeral images collected from 40 different writers and achieved efficient character recognition. In this paper [14] an algorithm has been developed to convert English text to Hindi (transliteration) using Hindi language Unicode mapping. The algorithm uses a virtual keyboard or typing method and has been tested with good accuracy. The approach and analysis used to develop the OCR program for Devnagri script are discussed in the paper [15]. This shows that despite the complexity of the script, it is possible to develop an OCR program that accurately recognizes the individual characters. The correlation method and OCR using artificial neural networks. The correlation method involves preprocessing an image, segmenting it into characters, and comparing it to preloaded templates to recognize the character. The OCR using ANNs involves training an artificial neural network to recognize characters through example inputs [17]. The authors of paper [18] used a test dataset of 430 scanned images and manually annotated text, and a training set generated synthetically from digitized Sanskrit text with added distortions. The training set was divided into 20–80 split for development and training. Evaluation metrics used were Character Recognition Rate, Word Recognition Rate, and F1-Score.

Script identification is a multi-class classification problem solved using the LSTM network [21]. The LSTM network is trained to identify a class-label which is targeted for all alphabets in a given language or script. The method avoids the vanishing gradient problem and allows for individual characters of both recognition and localization simultaneously.

In this paper [22] the survey of different feature extractions like HOG,CNN,LDA, MSD, DCT,LBP,KPCA, GLAC,HMM as well as different classifier like SVM, KNN, ANN, SOM, FUZZY,CNN,RNN etc. is done. A summary of the improvements made in the last 20 years in the area of OCR. The paper [23] main topic is handwritten OCR approaches, and it is arranged chronologically beginning in 1993. The survey aims to give insight into the various techniques used in international OCR research and how they can be improved in the future. OCR techniques include Feature Extraction, Matrix Matching, Structural Analysis etc. [24]. Artificial Neural Networks and the components of an OCR system, include some methods like pre_processing, Post_processing, location and segmentation, feature extraction, and optical scanning. Neural networks are deemed the most efficient OCR technique due to their ability to recognize characters through abstraction [19]. The characters were isolated using a contour tracing algorithm, sorted, and sent for moment computation. Raw, central, and normalized central moments of order three or less were calculated for each character. The moment generating algorithm was optimized to reduce computation time [25].

3 Methodology

The Proposed system block Fig. 1 Explain the steps of Sanskrit character recognition.The proposed system contain several steps starting from

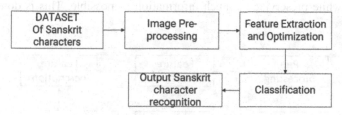

Fig. 1. Proposed System Flow

3.1 Dataset and Pre-Processing

The dataset contains 300 images of each devanagari character. It has 36 classes, each class for individual characters. All the images in the dataset are binarized for extracting features. The size of images is 64 x 64. From the dataset some sample images are shown in Fig. 2 where (a) and (b) are images before preprocessing and, (c) and (d) are images after preprocessing i.e. Binarization and Gaussian blur.

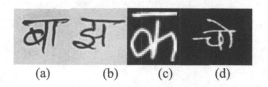

(a)   (b)   (c)   (d)

Fig. 2. Dataset images

After this the Gaussian blur is used to improve the quality by reducing noise, removing small unwanted details and smoothing out uneven lighting from the images.

3.2 Feature Extraction

For extracting features from preprocessed images DCT (Discrete Cosine Transform), HOG (Histogram of Oriented Gradients) and SIFT (Scale-Invariant Feature Transform) are used.

Feature Extraction using SIFT (Scale-Invariant Feature Transform) for Sanskrit Characters

As shown in Fig. 3 Features are detected by analyzing the pre-processed image at different scales and orientations. Once features have been detected, they are described in terms of their visual properties. After this descriptor is generated for each feature that captures its unique visual characteristics. Next a subset of features is selected from the available data. The goal is to choose the most relevant and informative features that will help the machine learning algorithm make accurate predictions. Then reducing the number of features while preserving as much information as possible. This is done by using k-means.

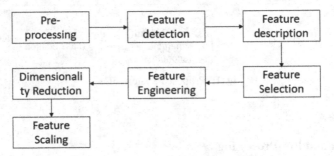

Fig. 3. Steps for implementing SIFT algorithm

Algorithm I. represents the feature extraction using SIFT for feature vector generation. After this for the Dimensionality reduction process k-means is used as shown in Algorithm II in that 8 clusters are used to reduce the feature vector.

Algorithm I : SIFT Feature extraction Method

Input: Images (10800)
Output: Feature Vector (204876 x 128)

Initialization
        1. Path of images
        2. every image in dataset
        3.   rescale
        4.   initialize SIFT
        5.   Key Points extraction
        6.   Description
        7. end
        8. append to csv
Return feature vector (204876 x 128)

Then the csv file of the reduced feature vector is saved for checking the accuracy of the model.

Algorithm II: Feature dimensionality reduction

Input: Feature Vector (204876 x 128)
Output: Optimized Feature Vector (10800 x 8)

    Initialization
    1.   Path of images
    2.   for every image in path
    3.   K means prediction (n_clusters=8)
    4.   dump model
    5.   append to csv
    6.   end
    7. reduction of vector size
Return Optimized feature vector (10800 x 8)

Feature Extraction using DCT (Discrete Cosine Transform) for Sanskrit Characters

DCT method is used to transform an image from one domain to another domain (spatial domain to the frequency domain). A set of spatial data points are transformed into a set of frequency coefficients using a mathematical procedure.

The transform is applied to each block of pixels separately after dividing the image into blocks of pixels. A formula based on the block size is used to apply the DCT to each block of pixels. The extracted features of 64 x 64 images are then normalized and obtained by the feature vector of size 10800 x 64.

For dimensionality reduction the PCA method is used and reduces components to 15. The final feature vector size for extracted DCT features is 10800 x 15 as shown in Algorithm III.

Algorithm III: DCT Feature extraction Method

Input: Images (10800)
Output: Feature Vector (10800 x 15)

Initialization
         1. Path of images
         2. every image in dataset
         3.   rescale
         4.   compute DCT feature
         5.   normalize extracted features
         6.   implement PCA(n_components=15)
         7. end
         8. append to csv
Return feature vector (10800 x 15)

Feature Extraction using HOG (Histogram of Oriented Gradients) for Sanskrit Characters

In Fig. 4, First step is the image processing, after that the images are divided into small cells and compute the gradient orientation for each pixel in each cell. The gradient orientations are binned into a set of predefined orientation bins. Then the next, histogram of gradient orientations for each cell is found by counting the numbers of gradient orientations that place into each orientation bin.In the last HOG feature extraction is normalized the histogram values across a group of blocks.

By combining the normalized histograms of the cells in an image, a HOG feature vector is obtained which represents the image. This feature vector can be used for character recognition tasks.

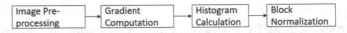

Fig. 4. Steps for implementing HOG algorithm

Algorithm IV. Shows the algorithm for feature extraction using HOG and using PCA the dimensionality reduction is done in HOG to reduce the feature vector.

Algorithm IV: HOG Feature extraction Method

Input: Images (10800)
Output: Feature Vector (10800 x 15)

Initialization
        1. Path of images
        2. every image in dataset
        3.   rescale
        4.   Implement HOG
        5.   implement PCA(n_components=15)
        6. end
        7. append to csv
Return feature vector (10800 x 15)

Feature Extraction using a Combination of Algorithms for Sanskrit Characters:
As shown in Fig. 5 SIFT + DCT, SIFT + HOG and DCT + HOG are combined to
check the accuracy, for that the csv file of SIFT and DCT are combined and the same
process is done for the remaining two. After doing this the feature vector for SIFT +
DCT is generated as 10800 x 23, SIFT + HOG is 10800x23 and for DCT + HOG is
comes 10800 x 30.

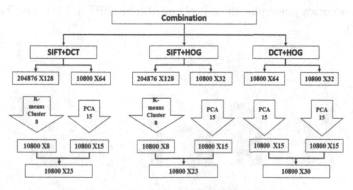

Fig. 5. Combination of SIFT, DCT and HOG

4 Result and Discussion

The entire dataset is divided in ratio 80–20%, 80% is for training dataset and 20% is
for testing dataset. To check the accuracy of the proposed model, a dataset(80% training
and 20% testing) is given to different classifiers. In this model we use Light gradient
boosting machine(LGBM), Random Forest (RF), K-nearest Neighbors(KNN), Support
vector machines(SVM-RBF), support vector machines(poly with degree 3) and Decision
Tree(DT) classifiers.

The maximum accuracy for SIFT, as shown in Table 1, is 74% from the SVM classifier. For DCT, it comes from 98.7% from SVM(Poly) and for HOG, it comes from 62% from LGBM.

Table 1. Classifiers on SIFT,DCT, HOG,SIFT + DCT, SIFT + HOGand DCT + HOG

CLASSIFIER	ACCURACY (SIFT) %	ACCURACY (DCT)%	ACCURACY (HOG)%	ACCURACY (SIFT + DCT)%	ACCURACY (SIFT + HOG)%	ACCURACY (DCT + HOG)%
DT	62.03	71	51	65	58.14	45.92
RF	69.07	70	60	67.96	66.03	63.33
SVM(RBF)	71.9	92.8	51	71.1	70.4	55.4
KNN	66.85	26	52	67.77	66.29	40
SVM(Poly)	71.7	**98.7**	59	69.8	69.8	50.2
LGBM	67	96	62	69.44	67.97	61.11

We coupled SIFT + DCT, SIFT + HOG and DCT + HOG to test the accuracy effectiveness.

Before Splitting the dataset to train and test, the features are saved in a csv file, we combine those csv files and check if the accuracy is increased.

After the combination we find that the accuracy is not significantly increased compared to the individual implementations of SIFT, DCT and HOG as shown in Table 5, the highest accuracy among the three is obtained from SIFT + DCT with 71.1% from SVM(RBF).

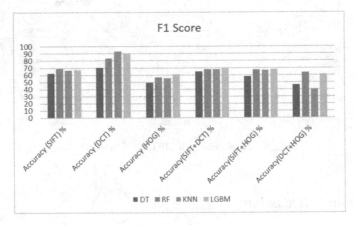

Fig. 6. F1 Score

Figures 6, 7 and 8 represent bar charts of F1 Score, Precision Score and Recall Score for all feature extraction methods which are mentioned in Table 1, the classifiers used for this are DT, RF, KNN and LGBM.

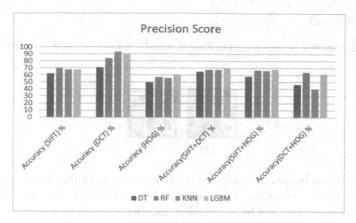

Fig.7. Precision Score

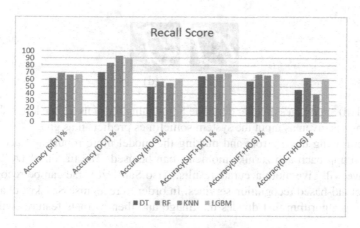

Fig. 8. Recall Score

The highest accuracy of F1 Score is observed at 93.45% which is obtained by DCT in KNN classifier and the lowest accuracy is obtained by DCT + HOG in KNN which is 40%.

As shown in Fig. 7 and Fig. 8 the highest accuracy for Precision and Recall obtained from KNN classifiers by DCT is 93.51% and 93.39% respectively.

4.1 Actual Result:

Below are the sample images from the dataset which look similar with minor differences:

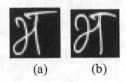

(a)   (b)

(a) and (b) are images of bha.When (b) is given as input then the model predicts the correct result by giving the correct label as bha, but when (a) is given as input the model gives inaccurate result by giving label ma. This happens because both the letters are nearly the same, the only difference is that bha has a curve on the upper right corner.

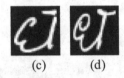

(c)   (d)

(c) and (d) are images of letter dha. The Same thing happens for the letter dha. When the (c) image is given as input the system sometimes predicts it as gha.

For optimizing these errors and making the model more robust and accurate, the CNN based approach and zernike moments can be used. The fusion of DCT and one of the above will give more accurate results. Also Sanskrit verse can be recognised in future by cloud-based recognition services. In order to recognise Sanskrit characters, a segmentation algorithm that divides the image and then extracts features will also be used.

5 Conclusion

The proposed system recognizes the Sanskrit characters. Also the paper proposes the comparison study between the SIFT, DCT and HOG feature extraction. After applying different Classifiers, we can say that HOG and SIFT are not that efficient for character recognition as compared to DCT.

Additionally, the combination of SIFT + DCT, SIFT + HOG, and DCT + HOG are used for comparison to see if the combinations are any more or less effective than the individual methods and We found that the accuracy is not increased effectively. The maximum accuracy of the trained model is 98.7% obtained in DCT feature extraction.

Different Algorithms are needs different pre-processed dataset. After applying Prewitt or sobel on the database the accuracy is suddenly falling down but SIFT requires Gaussian blur for removing the noise from images.

References

1. Avadesh, M., Goyal, N.: Optical character recognition for Sanskrit using convolution neural networks. In: 2018 IAPR 13th International Workshop on Document Analysis Systems (DAS), pp. 447452 (2018)
2. Adiga, D., et al.: Improving the learnability of classifiers for sanskrit ocr corrections. Computational Sanskrit & Digital Humanities, p. 143 (2020)
3. Breuel, T.M.: Applying the OCRopus OCR system to scholarly sanskrit literature. Sanskrit Computational Linguistics: First and Second International Symposia Rocquencourt, France, October 29-31, 2007 Providence, RI, USA, May 15-17, 2008 Revised Selected and Invited Papers. Springer Berlin Heidelberg (2009)
4. Dineshkumar, R., Suganthi, J.: Sanskrit character recognition system using neural network. Indian J. Sci. Technol. **8**(1), 65 (2015)
5. Anoop, C.S., Ramakrishnan, A.G.: Automatic speech recognition for Sanskrit. In: 2019 2nd International Conference on Intelligent Computing, Instrumentation and Control Technologies (ICICICT)
6. Dwivedi, N., Srivastava, K., Arya, N.: Sanskrit word recognition using Prewitt's operator and support vector classification. In: 2013 IEEE International Conference ON Emerging Trends in Computing, Communication and Nanotechnology (ICECCN)
7. Babu, N., Soumya, A.: Character recognition in historical handwritten documents–a survey. 2019 International Conference on Communication and Signal Processing (ICCSP)
8. Habib, S., Shukla, M.K., Kapoor, R.: OCR recognition system for degraded urdu and devnagari script. In: 2019 International Conference on Contemporary Computing and Informatics (IC3I)
9. Wei, H., Gao, G.: A holistic recognition approach for woodblock-print Mongolian words based on convolutional neural networks. 2019 IEEE International Conference on Image Processing (ICIP)
10. Hanmandlu, M., Murthy, O.R., Madasu, V.K.: Fuzzy Model based recognition of handwritten Hindi characters. 9th Biennial Conference of the Australian Pattern Recognition Society on Digital Image Computing Techniques and Applications (DICTA 2007), 454461
11. Hochberg, J., et al.: Automatic script identification from document images using cluster-based templates. IEEE Transactions on Pattern Analysis and Machine Intelligence **19**(2), 176–181 (1997)
12. Rajashekararadhya, S.V., Vanaja Ranjan, P.: Support vector machine based handwritten numeral recognition of Kannada script. In: 2009 IEEE International Advance Computing Conference
13. Chandure, S.L., Inamdar, V.: Performance analysis of handwritten devnagari and MODI character recognition system. 2016 International Conference on Computing, Analytics and Security Trends (CAST)
14. Jain, L., Agrawal, P.: English to Sanskrit transliteration: an effective approach to design a natural language translation tool. Int. J. Adv. Res. Comput. Sci. **8**(1), 1–10 (2017)
15. Karnik, R.R.: Identifying devnagri characters. In: Proceedings of the Fifth International Conference on Document Analysis and Recognition. ICDAR'99 (Cat. No. PR00318)
16. Singla, S.K., Yadav, R.K.: Optical character recognition based speech synthesis system using LabVIEW. J. Applied Res. Technol. **12**(5), 919–926 (2014)
17. Charles, P.K., et al.: A review on the various techniques used for optical character recognition. International J. Eng. Res. Appl. 2(1), 659–662 (2012)
18. Krishna, A., et al.: Upcycle your OCR: Reusing OCRs for Post-OCR Text Correction in Romanised Sanskrit. arXiv preprint arXiv:1809.02147 (2018)
19. Singh, A.K., Gupta, A., Saxena, A.: Optical character recognition: a review. Int. J. Emerg. Technol. Innov. Res. 3(4), 142–146 (2014)

20. Deshpande, P.S., Malik, L., Arora, S.: Characterizing handwritten Devanagari characters using evolved regular expressions. TENCON 2006 IEEE Region 10 Conference

21. Ul-Hasan, A., et al.: A sequence learning approach for multiple script identification. In: 13th International Conference on Document Analysis and Recognition (ICDAR) (2015)

22. Mridha, K., et.al.: Deep learning algorithms are used to automatically detection invasive ducal carcinoma in whole slide images. In: 2021 IEEE 6th International Conference on Computing, Communication and Automation (ICCCA), Arad, Romania, pp. 123–129 (2021). https://doi.org/10.1109/ICCCA52192.2021.9666302

23. Berchmans, D., Kumar, S.S.: Optical character recognition: an overview and an insight. In: 2014 International Conference on Control, Instrumentation, Communication and Computational Technologies (ICCICCT)

24. Rao, N.V., et al.: Optical character recognition technique algorithms. J. Theoretical & Applied Information Technol. **83**(2) (2016)

25. Cash, G.L., Hatamian, M.: Optical character recognition by the method of moments. Computer Vision, Graphics, and Image Processing **39**(3), 291–310 (1987)

Information Technology and Fintech Innovation and Its Effect on Indian Financial Services

Deepa Chauhan[1], Anup Kumar Srivastava[1]([✉]), Mridul Dharwal[1], Aarti Sharma[1], and Subrata Sahana[2]

[1] School of Business Studies, Sharda University, Greater Noida 201310, Uttar Pradesh, India
{deepa.chauhan2,anupkumar.srivastava,
mridul.dharwal}@sharda.ac.in
[2] Sharda School of Engineering and Technology, Sharda University, Greater Noida, India

Abstract. Fintech is a supply of creativity and a quickly expanding financial industry, yet little is understood about how facts era facilitates to fintech innovation. We discovered that records technology performs a critical function in nearly all factors of business fashions, organizing resources and techniques to offer individualized monetary offerings to customers efficaciously. This paper highlights the fintech innovation as well as information technology and its effect on Indian finance services. Fintech enables users to conduct transactions in a digital format that is more secure. Fintech services have the advantage of lowering operating expenses and making the customer experience more pleasant. India's fintech industry is the world's fastest expanding. Fintech services will alter the Indian financial sector's habits and behaviors.

Keywords: Fintech Innovation · Payment · Information technology · Security · Digital Transformation

1 Introduction

FinTech is a new term coined to describe financial services-related technology innovation. Governments are currently working to define FinTech, which is a broad term that lacks one. A wide range of benefits may be gained through FinTech technology, including enhanced performance and cost reductions. People's methods of making financial contributions are being reworked by advances in technology. The short form of the word "financial era" is "Fintech," which refers to an industry made up of firms that employ generations to transmit green financial services. As we enter the second decade of the twenty-first century, this mode of transport is becoming increasingly popular. As a result, new start-up companies are striving to replace the old transaction device with new, more successful tactics, such as leveraging the latest technology in the financial industry for mobile payments, loans and even for asset management. P2P lending, peer-to-peer pricing generation and virtual wallets are some of the more common examples of generation in economic transactions. Blockchain and cell banking are further examples of this generation. As a result, financial transactions will be more efficient and beneficial. They also aid to cut down on the prices that clients have to bear.

Fintech innovation is very different from traditional technological innovation. Many fintech solutions are not disruptive, but instead are built to provide existing solutions in a much more efficient and user-friendly way. For example, a fintech solution may use an existing payment system to provide users with a faster and more secure way to make payments. In this case, the problem is well-defined (i.e. providing a faster and more secure payment system), but the domain is not well-defined (i.e. the specific payment system being used). This means that Chesbrough's approach is not suitable for this type of innovation.

In contrast, the Lean Startup methodology is more suitable for fintech innovation. This approach focuses on quickly creating and testing solutions to problems, in order to determine whether or not they are viable. This allows fintech companies to quickly develop solutions to problems and test them in order to determine if they are successful. This is beneficial for fintech innovation, as it allows companies to quickly develop and test solutions to problems and determine whether or not they are successful, without investing too much time or money.

After the United States and China, India's FinTech market is now the world's third-largest FinTech ecosystem. However, due to limited financial service penetration, India remains an unexplored market. FinTechs in India have a lot of room to develop because of these untapped prospects and a favorable ecosystem.

The Indian financial services industry has been growing rapidly, with FinTech playing a significant role in driving growth. The increasing digitalization of the country has made it easier for consumers to access financial services, which has helped to boost the growth of the FinTech sector. BLinC Insights projects that the Indian financial services industry will be valued $500 billion in 2021, with the FinTech market contributing $31 billion to that total. Because India is increasingly becoming a digital society, the financial technology industry there is expanding at a lightning-fast rate.

FinTech sector in India is indeed expected to grow rapidly in the coming years, with a projected compound annual growth rate of 22%. This makes India one of the fastest-growing FinTech markets in the world, and it is already considered to be the third-largest FinTech ecosystem after the US and China. This growth is driven by a combination of factors, including a large and growing population of tech-savvy consumers, a supportive government policy environment, and a strong entrepreneurial ecosystem.

According to the graph that follows, the investment technology sector accounts for 28% of the 6,386 FinTech companies, while the payments sector accounts for 27%, the lending sector accounts for 16%, banking infrastructure accounts for 9%, and other sectors account for 20% (Fig. 1).

2 Literature Review

People across the world rely heavily on finance, particularly the banking industry, in their day-to-day activities. FinTech is a new age of financial services that have emerged since the traditional banking era of the previous century. Because it hasn't beenwell-researchedd, this industry presents a challenging environment for businesses. Many traditional financial technologies have undergone substantial changes over the past decade, and newer types of financial technology (FinTech) are presently a hot topic in the media

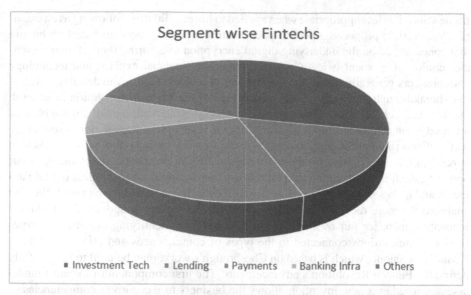

Fig. 1. Fintech Segmentation (Source: BLinC Insights)

and in the hands of financial investors. FinTech businesses are typically founded by former bank employees who were laid off following the 2008 financial crisis, according to Bellamy (2013). New enterprises and business models can be created by combining traditional financial services with cutting-edge technologies. A bank, for example, may assign certain obligations to these individuals. As a result, they only offer a limited subset of the services offered by a big financial services company (Bellamy 2013).

Consequently, they may concentrate on enhancing the quality of their offerings to customers. From USD 4.05 billion in 2013 to USD 12.2 billion in 2014, (Scan et al. 2015) found that investments in FinTech firms and start-ups surged. Investment in the company nearly doubled to USD 22.2 billion in 2015 (Dickerson 2016). These facts suggest that the industry is well-known in the financial world, which provides fertile ground for new ideas and research. FinTech also opens up new avenues for individual empowerment, such as more transparency, lower costs, and the removal of middlemen, all of which are made possible by the technology. Additionally, FinTech is having an effect on banks that fear losing their market share in favour of start-ups providing alternatives to traditional banking services and are working to join the FinTech revolution. When it comes to business, money, and technological innovation, the term "FinTech" is frequently bandied around as if it meant something completely different to everyone. This uncertainty is seen by both the intended external consumers and the FinTech industry experts. Uncertainty may stem in part from the FinTech industry's relative novelty and rapid growth.

Chesbrough (2003) defined a "disruptive innovation" is described as a new approach to a known problem when the problem itself is not well-defined but the domain around it is. When both the domain and the challenge are clear, we speak of a "sustainable innova-tion." While this method of technical innovation is helpful in terms of the fundamental frameworks, it is less appropriate when applied to fintech. Take the following as an example. Vora (2015) proposed a peer-to-peer electronic payment system based on bitcoin that concentrated on the underlying digital encryption to assuring those digital currencies could not be spent twice. Computer scientists, financial experts, and technology entrepreneurs generally agree that the concept of a blockchain is the defining "disruptive, breakthrough technical logical innovation" of the Fintech Revolution in general. (Shrivas and Yeboah 2019). However, in Chesbrough's innovation matrix, these phrases are used when neither the application area nor the issue to which a solution is sought are well-defined (breakthrough innovation) (disruptive innovation). So, while blockchain is recognised as disruptive by the innovation matrix (a reasonable assessment, in our opinion), the first publication to explain its use merely applies it to cashless digital payments and makes no claims regarding its generality. Those would have to wait. We also analyzed the more recent work by (Pisano 2015), who gave an updated 2x2 technical innovation map, for our own evaluation technique for identifying the different types of fintech innovations connected to the types of consequences and effects they have. Pisano's technique, which is based on Chesbrough's work, may be used to successfully define the Fintech Revolution's advancements. The first component of Pisano's model assesses whether a new invention allows the business to use current competencies or necessitates the acquisition of new technical skills. The second dimension, on the other hand, determines whether an existing business model may be used or whether a new one must be developed. Routine innovation, according to the author, is defined as the utilization of existing technological competencies inside an existing business model. A radical innovation, on the other hand, allows the company to keep its present business model while developing new technical skills; however, a disruptive innovation allows the company to keep its existing technical skills but must change gears to develop a new business model.

Even though there has been a lot of research on financial services and banking, there have been little studies on FinTech. As new FinTech startups spring up like mushrooms overnight and revolutionise the industry, today's research environment is wide and unfamiliar. This upheaval has inspired our inquiry into FinTech's relationship with the real world. Information technology (IT) scholars have paid scant attention to media presentations on many aspects of IT (Zavolokina et al. 2016). It's hard to argue against the importance of the popular media in observing and reflecting the public's sentiments, but we believe that it also has a significant impact. Therefore, we feel this study merits researchers' attention, and we claim that this research is valuable for finance researchers (especially those interested in financial innovation research) and multidisciplinary social science researchers (such as media and business researchers). On the other hand, this kind of analysis remains a mirror of the current reality. For this study, most of the data came from databases in English-speaking nations in North America and Europe. An overview of the places, persons and their goals and ambitions, as well as the organisations and connections that characterise and sustain the phenomena, motivated by a surge in media attention on FinTech, is provided. Besides that, we bring out important disputes concerning FinTech and its role in the current climatic conditions.

In the financial services industry, fintech firms are often micro, small, or medium-sized firms having a clear vision on how to deliver new services or improve on already existing ones. Typically, they are start-ups in the field of financial technology, which is continually expanding in scope. Fintech companies are often financed through a combination of venture capital and crowdsourcing. Fintech start-ups may potentially improve the efficiency of the monetary machine, according to some experts (Vlasov 2017; Vovchenko et al. 2019).With an increasing number of people throughout the world unable or unable to utilize traditional banking services, FinTech, which provides similar services but is more efficient, cheaper, and lucrative than banks, is growing in popularity. Banks face operational risks and long-term consequences as a result of these trends (Novokreshchenova et al. 2016; Thalassinos and Thalassinos 2018). A worldwide management consulting, technology services, and outsourcing business), fintech is one of the fastest-growing sectors of the financial system. Investments in the company have grown rapidly, reaching $12,2 billion in 2014, up from only $930 million in 2008. Europe has seen the most increase (Skan et al. Boniecki 2015).

The definition of "FinTech" is ever-changing as new technology entrepreneurs enter the market and adapt existing technologies to meet the demands of an ever-changing society. FinTech, on the other hand, is a financial service that employs cutting-edge technology to meet the needs of tomorrow's fast, mobile, and technologically-savvy consumers (Dapp 2017). In contrast, the term "FinTech" is used to describe the businesses that deliver these services. There is space for more clarification on the meaning of the word "FinTech" as it stands now. We believe that understanding the roots of FinTech will help academics and professionals alike evaluate the opportunities and risks associated with this development. The importance of the financial sector means that financial innovation—defined as the introduction of a new entity with the goal of reducing risks and costs or providing a product, service, or instrument that better meets the needs of involved parties than existing options—plays an important role in economic expansion (Berger et al. 2012). Recent technological advancements in the financial services industry have prompted widespread media and corporate interest in related societal concerns, which in turn frames a concept like FinTech.

Objectives of the Study

1. To understand the meaning of information technology and financial innovation in India.
2. To understand the effect of information technology and financial innovation on financial services.

3 Research Methodology

The goal of this study is to assess the current level of information technology and fintech's effects on Indian financial services. The study is entirely based on secondary data gathered from a variety of websites, academic publications, and other sources.

3.1 FinTech and Its Effect on Indian Financial Services

The FinTech sector in India is at a very early stage of development, but it is growing rapidly due to a large market base, a thriving startup culture, and supportive government policies and regulations. The growth of FinTech has the potential to transform the traditional banking and financial services industries in India, addressing challenges such as low penetration, limited credit score records, and a cash-driven transaction economy. The success of FinTech in India will depend on collaboration between regulators, market operators, and traders. Inventions and advancements in financial technology The FinTech sector in India, which is still in its infancy, is thriving because to the support of a large market base, an inventive startup culture, and favourable government laws and rules. It's an exciting time to be an entrepreneur, with both traditional banks and non-banking financial institutions (NBFCs) catching up. This recent turmoil has had a broad impact on the banking and financial services businesses. Financial technology (FinTech) has the ability to relieve the issues faced by traditional financial institutions in India, such as poor penetration, limited credit score records, and a cash-driven transaction economy, among other things. The Indian banking and financial services industry may change if all parties, including regulators, market operators, and traders, work together.

Individuals and businesses may now obtain finance more quickly and simply thanks to peer-to-peer (P2P) lending services, which use alternative credit scoring methods and data assets to connect healthy lenders with suitable borrowers through the internet. Lend box, Fair cent, i2iFunding, Chillr, Shiksha Financial, Gyan Dhan, and Market Finance are a few examples.

Equity Funding Services: While crowdfunding methods are growing increasingly popular, obtaining project cash can be difficult. These services are targeted towards startups and small enterprises that are just getting started. Just a few examples are Start51, Wish Berries, and Ketto.

Money in international crypto-currency When compared to 19 other economies, India, a more traditional country where currency transactions still prevail, has made little development in the usage of digital economic money, including "bitcoin." Uno coin, Coin safe, and Zeb pay are three of the few Indian bitcoin exchange companies that have recently surfaced.

Developments in Blockchain Technology in India: There are a number of domestic firms that have lately shown an interest in blockchain and its supporting protocols, which are presented in the form of an enigmatic record. After doing research on whether or not BCT can be implemented in the Indian banking and financial sector using a White Paper that covers the relevant time period, issues, worldwide examples and possible areas of adoption in India, IDRBT released its findings. This White Paper includes details of the Institute's Proof-of-Concept on the applicability of BCT to an exchange financing application, which was carried out with the active participation of the NPCI, banks, and the answer issuer in order to obtain first-hand experience with the implementation. These findings are contained in the White Paper. As a result of the favorable results of the Proof of Concept, BCT's short-term implementation in India's currency market appears to be viable.

Cross-Border Payments: BCT allows for real-time agreement while also reducing operational and liquidity expenses. A lack of tampering with BCT data reduces the risk of fraud. Smart contracts prevent operational errors by documenting the tasks of financial institutions to guarantee that a suitable budget is exchanged. Because of the cheaper expenses, BCT makes it possible for senders and recipients to communicate directly with each other via bank-to-bank transfers for low-value transactions. Sub-processes of the syndicated loan agreement.

Syndication of Loans: The distributed ledger's monetary information may be used to automate underwriting processes. The implementation of KYC rules can also be automated in real time. BCT can offer an international fee reduction option for syndicated loans in the system execution and agreement sub-processes.

Capital Markets: Off-exchange mistakes are reduced or eliminated, back-office operations are simplified, and agreement times are decreased with BCT clearing and settlement techniques.

BCT Banking Operations in India Indian banks have asserted that BCT may be used effectively in their operations, such as for international remittances or for other purposes in the past several years. According to them, it has the potential to become an integral part of their banking operations on a much larger scale. In a blockchain transaction, the approval is visible to all parties, unlike in traditional change transactions in which files are authorised and physically transferred. Records can't be tampered with, and fresh entries are the most effective way to add new information.

3.2 Developments in the Payments Landscape in India

There has been a lot of innovation in India's financial sector thanks to the use of financial technology. Coins have given way to new forms of payment in India, reflecting a normal rise in the country's economy. Immediate Payment Service (IMPS)—real-time payments to the end consumer via several options, including most recently the Unified Payments Interface (UPI) – have all made significant progress in their respective sectors (UPI).

Process Innovation India has adopted Aadhaar, which gives all Indians with a unique identification number, and the National Payments Corporation of India has built an AEPS, a safe and convenient channel for micropayments. Merchants may utilize a fingerprint scanner to download the app on their smartphone and use it to process payments. The program's goal is to eliminate the need for a card or PIN while making purchases.

Wallets NEFT, RTGS, and many more digital fee systems are examples of traditional bill payment methods. Card payments are also accepted (debit and credit score). Non-financial institution consumers wanted the opportunity to utilize electronic payment methods and current financial institution customers wanted a level of security that limited their exposure. This led to a need for prepaid fee devices, such as physical cards or e-wallets. With the advent of bank and non-bank payment wallets (Paytm, Mobi Kwik, Oxygen, Citrus Pay, and many more), the way Indians pay their bills has altered forever. Chillr, for example, is a peer-to-peer money transfer service that doesn't require bank account details. Personal virtual wallets based on the NPCI's IMPS infrastructure have been offered by several major banks. Additionally, the social networking aspects of these virtual wallets have been included. The Online to Offline (O2O) version, promoted by Digital Innovators, makes it possible to make digital payments at brick-and-mortar establishments.

BHIM is an acronym for "Bharatiya (Bharat Interface for Money) NPCI released BHIM on December 30th, 2016, a smartphone app based on the Unified Payment Interface (UPI). Faster e-bill processing through banks is one of the goals of the movement away from cash transactions. Even though only one account at a financial institution can be active at any given time, customers can see their current balances on BHIM and pick which account to use for transactions when using the mobile app. In order to facilitate in-service transactions, QR codes can be generated for a charge by users.

Robot suggestion is a new sort of software that can help you manage your finances. A set of principles is used to provide automated investment recommendations. Those who don't need or can't afford the services of a financial expert, or who don't have sufficient assets, can use it as a suitable monetary counsellor. Each customer's portfolio is custom-built by a robo-adviser.

An acronym for software that helps individuals keep track of their finances: personal monetary management (PFM). The term "generational budgeting" has been shortened to "GBM." It helps you keep track of your finances by aggregating debts owed to many businesses. Using it, clients may evaluate their earnings and expenditures, keep to their budgets, and avoid getting into debt.

Low-cost banking and financial planning platforms are well-positioned to disrupt established investment banking strategies. Companies began to attack and infiltrate the business models of big finance institutions. In the beginning, they looked at personal and small business finances.

3.3 Other FinTech's

Diverse FinTech's are companies that offer services other than traditional banking, such as financial accounting and asset management. Coverage includes search engines and assessment websites as well as technology as well as infrastructure. Financial generating businesses have also taken over the insurance market. In this area, distribution is the primary focus for the vast majority of businesses. Apps like this are being used by these companies to reach out to their target audience. They aren't your standard insurance company; instead, they have a lot of latitude. In order to compete in the heavily regulated insurance industry, startups are trying to join up with established insurance companies. Comparative search engine evaluation sites In this part, you'll find search engines like Google that allow you to compare various financial products and services offered by different vendors.

As part of the sub-segment of technology, information technology (IT) and infrastructure, financial technology (Fintech) companies are included.

3.4   Factors Motivate for Adopting Financial Technologies

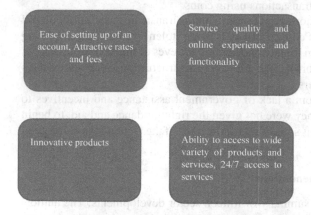

Ease of setting up of an account, Attractive rates and fees

Service quality and online experience and functionality

Innovative products

Ability to access to wide variety of products and services, 24/7 access to services

3.5   Major Barriers for Adopting Financial Technologies

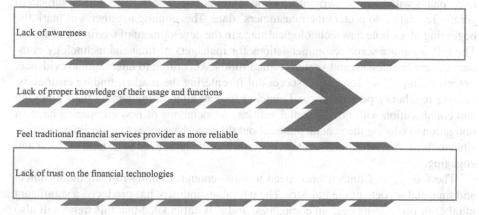

Major Barriers for Adopting Financial Technologies

Lack of awareness

Lack of proper knowledge of their usage and functions

Feel traditional financial services provider as more reliable

Lack of trust on the financial technologies

3.6   Challenges of Fintech in India

Despite the fact that there are many changes in fintech, it is a challenging path to take. The following is a list of potential impediments in the development of Fintech enterprises.

1. It is not always simple to access and carry out transactions in the Indian market due to the rigorous regulatory environment meant to prevent fraud. It creates a significant hurdle for new entrants. They must complete a number of requirements prior to the commencement of operations.
2. Even if people have bank debts, they are still plagued by poor internet access. As a result, humans are more likely to choose a currency transaction over an online transaction. Leaving aside the issue of opening a bank account and having access to the internet, the majority of the Indian populace lacks the monetary literacy required to pursue it.

3. It may be difficult to exchange the conservative approach of dealers and consumers who deal with day-to-day transactions using coins.
4. Various scams based on a shortage of funds in online transactions are a difficult pill for consumers to swallow. People's money is being stolen by fraudsters exploiting the period, and this has been a major endeavor in the eyes of fintech businesses. As a result, businesses must work hard to improve infrastructure and make themselves more appealing to customers.

Five. Fintech in India suffers from a lack of government assistance and incentives to preserve their activities. They were not given the right guidance and aid, to begin with, despite the fact that it is something for the good of the United States' financial system as well.

3.7 Conclusions and Recommendations

The study provided a high-level summary of fintech sector developments. The authors are certain that the cornerstone for the construction of digital monetary organisations of a new era will be new fintech technologies, mixed with existing bank services and achievements. Financial technology is predicted to displace traditional banking practises; banks will adopt modern information systems, and fintech firms will be subject to greater regulation to protect their customers' data. This coming together will mark the beginning of a whole new technological stage in the development of the financial sector. The following are some recommendations for managers of financial technology companies, new businesses, and venture capital funds. According to international evidence, fintech startups have been more successful in entering the market, finding customers, gaining regulatory permission, and enticing traders after strengthening their lobbying and collaboration with governmental entities. Associations of new companies have an obligation to educate the general public about the fintech services that are already accessible to them. Advertisements created by fintech companies need to be both efficient and engaging.

The founders of fintech firms need to have enough training in both the technical and financial aspects of the industry. The payments industry has produced a significant number of prosperous start-up companies, and it is anticipated that this trend will also prevail in other areas of the financial industry. Exceptional steps need to be taken in order for the government and other regulatory agencies to make even more of an effort to encourage the financial technology business.

References

Berger, A.N. et al. (ed.): Oxford Handbook of Banking, 3rd edn. Oxford University Press (2012)
Bellamy, C.: Throwing down the gauntlet. World Policy J. 30(1), 19–21 (2013)
Chesbrough, H.: Open Innovation: The New Imperative for Creating and Profiting from Technology. Harvard Business Press, Boston Massachusetts (2003)
Dapp, T.F.: Fintech: the digital transformation in the financial sector. In: Osburg, T., Lohrmann, C. (eds.) Sustainability in a Digital World. CSEG, pp. 189–199. Springer, Cham (2017). https://doi.org/10.1007/978-3-319-54603-2_16
Dickerson, P.S.: The evolving role of a nurse planner. J. Contin. Educ. Nurs. 47(10), 437–439 (2016)

Ishwari, C.: India's FinTech market size at $31 billion in 2021, third largest in world: Report. The Economic Times, January 10 (2022). https://bfsi.economictimes.indiatimes.com/news/fintech/indias-fintech-market-size-at-31-billion-in-2021-third-largest-in-world-report/88794336. Accessed 22 June 2022

Novokreshchenova, O.A., Novokreshchenova, N.A., Terehin, S.E.: Improving Bank's customer service on the basis of quality management tools. Euro. Res. Stud. J. **0**(3B), 19–38 (2016)

Skan, J., Dickerson, J., Masood, S.: Future of FinTech and Banking–Accenture. Accenture. Com (2015)

Shrivas, M.K., Yeboah, T.: The disruptive blockchain: types, platforms and applications. Texila Int. J. Acad. Res. **3**, 17–39 (2019)

Khurana, A., Puri, H.: Impact on economy with the emergence of block chain. Global J. Manage. Sustain. **1**(1). https://doi.org/10.58260/j.mas.2202.0101

Report of the Working Group on FinTech and Digital Banking. RBI Fintech Working Paper.PDF (2017). Accessed 22 June 2022

Thalassinos, E.I., Thalassinos, Y.: Financial crises and e-commerce: how are they related. SSRN Electron. J. (2018)

Vlasov, A.V.: The evolution of e-money. Eur. Res. Stud. J. **20**(1), 215–224 (2017)

Vovchenko, N.G., Andreeva, O.V., Orobinsky A.S., Sichev, R.A.: Risk control in modeling financial management systems of large corporations in the digital economy. Int. J. Econ. Bus. Admin. **1**(1), 3–15 (2019)

Vora, G.: Cryptocurrencies: are disruptive financial innovations here? Mod. Econ. **6**, 816–832 (2015)

Zavolokina, L., Dolata, M., Schwabe, G.: The FinTech phenomenon: antecedents of financial innovation perceived by the popular press. Finan. Innov. **2**(1), 1–16 (2016). https://doi.org/10.1186/s40854-016-0036-7

Application of Neural Networks and Genetic Algorithms in Establishing Logical Rules for Evaluating the Edibility of Mushroom Data

Ishita Johri[1] , Musiri Kailasanathan Nallakaruppan[1]([✉]) ,
Balamurugan Balusamy[2], Geetha V[3], and Veena Grover[4]

[1] School of Information Technology and Engineering, Vellore Institute of Technology,
Vellore, Tamil Nadu, India
`ishita.johri2019@vitstudent.ac.in` `nallakaruppan.mk@vit.ac.in`
[2] Associate Dean-Student Engagement, Shiv Nadar University, Delhi-National
Capital Region (NCR), Noida, India
`balamurugan.balusamy@snu.edu.in`
[3] Department of Computer Science, School of Applied Sciences, REVA University,
Bangalore, India
[4] Department of Management, Noida Institute of Engineering and Technology,
Greater Noida, India

Abstract. The cultivation of mushrooms for commercial purposes has had a notable impact on the global economy, as evident from recent agricultural data. The mushroom industry is rapidly becoming one of the most lucrative industries in India and around the globe. This has led to a rise in popularity of mushroom farms and cultivation. The objective of this study is to determine the logical rules for edibility of mushrooms based on 22 biological characteristics. To achieve this goal, two different approaches were utilized. The first approach involved using Back Propagation Neural Networks that were constructed using data mining techniques. This method is distinct from a simple Decision Tree as it doesn't require listing rules one by one. The cost function of the neural networks is based on the standard MSE (mean square error) plus a convergence controller. The Neural Network can be perceived as a tree-like logical graph, with a weight of 1 representing a strong positive correlation, -1 indicating a strong negative correlation, and 0 signifying no correlation. As a result, the top 4 logical rules account for every possible outcome based on most coverage. In the second approach, a Decision Tree is combined with a Genetic Algorithm (GA) for feature selection. The accuracy of the decision tree, which is constructed from the GA's feature selections, feeds back into the GA's fitness function. This method provides an alternative way of identifying edible mushrooms based on their biological characteristics.

Keywords: Neural Network · Genetic Algorithm · Mushroom classification · Logical rules

ⓒ The Author(s), under exclusive license to Springer Nature Switzerland AG 2023
R. N. Shaw et al. (Eds.): ICACIS 2023, CCIS 1920, pp. 212–220, 2023.
https://doi.org/10.1007/978-3-031-45121-8_18

1 Introduction

Mushroom production has become one of India's fastest-growing agricultural industries, not only in India but also globally. While white button mushrooms are commonly grown by Nepalese farmers and Countries such as China, the United States of America, the Netherlands, and Italy are among the top mushroom producers worldwide. The cultivation of mushrooms in India takes place in dark chambers, but this requires careful attention to variables such as temperature, humidity, and lighting. The growers must also provide regular watering and thorough inspection of the fungi to ensure proper identification. Mushroom poisoning is a significant cause of mortality and morbidity in many parts of the world. Identifying and categorizing deadly mushrooms has become crucial worldwide. Machine Learning (ML) technology has emerged as a powerful tool for identifying and categorizing various things, including mushrooms. As such, it is a promising solution to the problem of mushroom identification and categorization.

Given their 22 biological characteristics of 23 species of mushrooms present in the dataset, I explore the dilemma of determining the logical rules for whether mushrooms are safe to eat or not. The general public always assumes that they will be able to visually recognise specific rules for the categorization of foods. Yet, there is no surefire way to tell if a mushroom is safe to eat; unlike poison oak and ivy, there is no "leaflets three, let it be" rule for mushrooms. Thus, I want to see if I can't glean any simple rules with broad applicability. If people adhered to these logical rules, they would be able to make quick, accurate assessments with ease.

2 Related Work

The authors of the research [5] offered an Internet of Things (IoT) and Machine Learning (ML)-based solution to automate the agricultural irrigation system in order to resolve crop-specific irrigation, soil erosion, and over-irrigation issues. Various sensor modules were employed for monitoring purposes linked to a WSN, and Machine Learning (ML) was used to anticipate the quantity of irrigation required depending on the weather and the crops. Using GSM and IoT, the authors of the cited article [6] created a prototype of an intelligent chicken farm surveillance system. Their prototype was capable of detecting unlawful door openings, fire (smoke) detection, and temperature monitoring. They have used IoT for the collection of sensor data and GSM for the notification systems. By assessing the soil types, the authors of the research [7] devised a strategy for selecting suitable crops in order to increase total agricultural production. This system was powered by a raspberry pi and relied on IoT and cloud computing. In the study cited as reference [8], the authors presented a system for regulating agricultural fields by monitoring temperatures and humidity using a variety of sensors. Their plan was to remotely monitor changes in climate and moisture and adjust the irrigation system, temperature, and humidity automatically if certain parameters deviate from their reference values. The authors of the study [9] presented a method to semiautomate various agricultural and poultry-farming tasks in order to decrease human labour. The device might be used in chicken farms for feeding, managing temperature, and eliminating gas from the soil. Alternatively, it might be used to prepare soil, spray water on plants, and fertilise in agriculture. The authors of the research [10] showed a system to monitor and automatically regulate a variety of physical factors in mushroom cultivation. They had concentrated mostly on the mushroom cultivation cooling system. They employed a Peltier air conditioner with honey pads to achieve efficient cooling. In addition, they demonstrated via a cost comparison that their system is more cost-effective than conventional solutions. In the article cited in footnote [11], the authors addressed many forms of automated regulating and monitoring strategies for mushroom farming in order to assist a business in selecting the most appropriate methodology. The authors of publications [3–9] had exclusively worked on IoT for agricultural automation. Specifically, authors of studies [10] employed IoT for the automation of mushroom farms, but none used Machine Learning (ML) approaches to categorise the mushrooms as edible, inedible, or toxic. The authors of the research [12] created a categorization system for mushrooms utilising the attribute "texture" and a machine learning (ML) technology. They discovered that the SVM classifier was superior to Logistic Regression, KNN, Decision Tree, Ensemble, and Linear Discriminant classifiers by achieving 76.6% accuracy. In the research cited in [13], the scientists examined mushroom behavioural characteristics to determine the best characteristic for identifying various mushroom species. Using the PCA and DT technique, they determined that 'odour' was the characteristic with the greatest ranking in terms of classification precision. In the paper [14], the authors contrasted three prevalent classification algorithms: DT (C4.5), SVM, and NaveBayes. They experimented on the Lepiota Agaricus family of mushrooms and used data from the UCI Machine Learning (ML) library. Both the C4.5 and SVM algorithms were accurate to a perfect degree. In terms of speed, however, C4.5 fared better than SVM. The authors of the research [15] compared classification algorithms for edible and non-edible mushrooms. They compared and analysed the performances of the ANN, ANFIS, and Naive Bayes approaches. ANFIS performed with the highest accuracy and lowest mean absolute error among them. In the second spot was ANN. In addition, they discovered that the accuracy increased with the size of the training set.

2.1 Challenges Present in Existing System

Despite being efficient at classification, the existing systems did not give us a clear insight of what features are necessary in mushroom classification and most of the system only focuses on image classification as edible or poisonous mushroom. Hence, to bridge this gap I have suggested a model to extract simple to understand logical rules from mushroom data to identify mushrooms as edible or poisonous. It can be seen as a more practical approach for mushroom classification in general.

3   Methodology

The mushroom dataset [2] consists of hypothetical sample descriptions that match 23 different species of gilled mushrooms belonging to the families Agaricus and Lepiota. Each species is classified as either absolutely safe to consume, absolutely poisonous, or of unknown edibility and not advised for consumption. I have assumed mushrooms absolutely poisonous and of unknown edibility as one class. People always have the expectation that they will be able to perceive certain guidelines for the classification of edible items with just their naked eyes [11]. In spite of this, there is no foolproof method for judging whether or not a mushroom is edible, So, my goal is to try to extract, if there are any, some simple rules that have a high application value. People would be able to make instant, reliable judgements if they followed these possible rules [12].

The use of a Decision Tree, which is admittedly a method that is theoretically deterministic, allows us to obtain all of the logical principles for this type of situation. Nevertheless, the complexity of this extraction method grows exponentially with each step. A decision tree with 22 different qualities is extremely difficult to solve. Here, mt idea is to make extensive use of interpretable neural networks, which will allow us to weed out irrelevant details. In a perfect scenario, we wouldn't have to think about too many characteristics, and we have a clear notion of how those main characteristics relate to edible status. Edibility, when viewed as a binary property (either edible or poisonous), is an asymmetric characteristic. This is something that should be pointed out. In other words, a false negative result (incorrectly identifying something as dangerous) is often tolerable, whereas a false positive result (incorrectly identifying something as edible) might be deadly! When we are faced with a choice, we would prefer to reduce the overall accuracy rather than risk missing even a single potentially dangerous sample. 8124 instances are included in the primary data set, along with 22 attributes and one class (all nominally valued). Before implementing a neural network classifier, I quantify the values using a data mining technique. Following that, I built a back propagation neural network with a single hidden layer. In order to solve an issue involving binary classification, just one output neuron is required. A new auxiliary term is introduced into the cost function in order to account for the conventional MSE [1].

Mathematically, it is

$$\frac{\lambda}{2} \cdot \sum_{i,j} W_{i,j}^2 (W_{i,j} - 1)^2 (W_{i,j} + 1)^2,$$

where W is the weight between input and hidden layer. After training, the weights should be formalised so that they are the nearest integer (i.e. $1, 0$ or -1). In fact, W is a sparse matrix, which indicates that the values of many attributes are not significant to the mushroom's suitability for consumption. Given the circumstances, enumerating and combining all relevant variables works nicely [14].

3.1   Dataset Description and Preprocessing

Data mining offers a wide range of methods to quantify nominal values but there are no benchmarks available for comparison like we cannot claim that the size or length of mushrooms with brown caps is better than those with red caps. Therefore, here I have suggested performing a Dimensional Discretization [25]. Firstly, we create a list of unique values for each attribute, and then form a Euclidean space with a size equivalent to the number of unique values. The quantized value is a vector where all coordinates are -1, except for the corresponding location which is 1, representing the unique value. We treat the missing value as an additional, unique and meaningful value. After setting unique values for each attribute, we make Euclidean space. For example, for the cap-shaped attribute, the unique nominal values are sunken=s, bell=b, conical=c, flat=f, knobbed=k, and convex=x, in total 6.

For edibility, I assign a value of 1 to indicate edible and 0 to indicate poisonous. In conclusion, each instance is a 126-dimensional vector with 125 variables and 1 class. These vectors will be fed into neural networks as input and target. After discretization, we randomly select 20% of the instances as the test set, with the rest as the training set i.e. 80%.

3.2   Model Description

The Back-Propagation Neural Network Algorithm. The structure of the Back-propogation (BP) Neural Networks model that is being proposed here consists of one input layer with 125 variables (each of which is equal to 1 or -1), one hidden layer with undefined units, and precisely one output neuron. The cost function is :

$$E(W) = \text{MSE}(Output, Target) + \frac{\lambda}{2} \cdot \sum_{i,j} W_{i,j}^2 (W_{i,j} - 1)^2 (W_{i,j} + 1)^2$$

where $\text{MSE}(Output, Target)$ is the mean squared error between the output and target values, and λ is a regularization parameter.

When $W_{i,j} = 1$, -1 or 0, the second term derives its minimal (0), and the cost function turns back to MSE. Because of this property, all the weights approach one of 1, -1, 0 during the training process with a proper λ. Meanwhile, the weights between the hidden layer and the output layer should be frozen at 1. Given that the binary class was encoded as the numbers 1 and 0, the Sigmoid function will serve as a great option for the activation function used on the output layer. The classifier just has to establish a threshold, which is often located somewhere close to 0.5, and then compare the output to the threshold. If the output is more than the threshold, then the substance is classified as 1 (edible); otherwise, it is toxic. Overall, MSE is adequate for classification and performs very well for adjusting weights. This network cannot have a large number of hidden units and must be between 1–5. It is because finally we want to derive logical rules after interpreting the neural network topological implicits might arise when there are numerous hidden neurons. I've tried here with a range of parameters including a small number of hidden units (1–3) and the activation of the hidden layer (Tanh function, Sigmoid function, etc.). Meanwhile, I finetune λ from 0.001 to 1 and fixed the learning rate when needed following the strategy to change λ dynamically. At the preliminary stage of training, our main target is to make correct classifications, λ should be small in case it influences the correct classification. With training carrying on, the accuracy will gradually reach a plateau, then the primary goal becomes forcing the weights to converge at an integer (1, 0 or -1), and λ will matter during this phase. Through all kinds of attempts, the best setting of parameters can stably lead to 100% accuracy on the training set itself. The data set is big enough (8124 instances), so the cross validation is unnecessary. Therefore, we can say that the result are reliable to some extent.

GA + DECISION TREE. While Back-Propogation network is good for classification, adding an auxiliary weight term to the cost function changes the prior distribution of weights, making certain values more likely. This approach is discussed previously but the flaw is that the new term cannot be interpreted and only serves to adjust parameters otherwise accuracy can depreciate. Decision Trees are the most intuitive method for logical extraction, but they are not suitable for this classification task due to the complexity of large trees. To overcome this problem, Genetic Algorithm (GA) can be used for feature selection. The DNA structure used for GA consists of a 22-dimensional binary array, where positive values indicate which features are in use. Ideally a good setting is with control parameters as POP SIZE = 50, DNA POSITIVE = 3, 4, 5, CROSS RATE = 0.8, MUTATION RATE = 0.05 N, GENERATIONS = 10 and depth = 6.

Parameter	Meaning
DNA SIZE = 22	number of bits in DNA
POP SIZE	population size
DNA POSITIVE	max number of positive genes
CROSS RATE	DNA crossover probability
MUTATION RATE	mutation probability
N GENERATIONS	generation size
depth	max depth of Decision Tree

After defining the necessary parameters, we used a combination of GA Feature Selection and Decision Tree algorithms to build an accurate model. The accuracy of the Decision Tree is used as the fitness function for the GA. To prevent the number of selected features from becoming too large, we added a "Depressing step" after crossover and mutation to ensure that only DNA POSITIVE genes have a value of 1. We also implemented other exception handling procedures such as initialising the DNA when there is no positive value (1) and terminating the algorithm when the accuracy reaches 100%. The best accuracy achieved was 99.7046% on the entire dataset (training + testing) with DNA POSITIVE = 3. Using at least 4 features can result in 100% accuracy, but adding a 5th feature can simplify the Decision Tree topology.'

4   Results and Discussion

The purpose of this work is to establish clear logical rules for determining the edibility of mushrooms. This study aims to extract crisp logical parameters for mushroom identification and classification. All variables in the dataset are nominal or categorical values so we first quantize them. Vectorized Discretization is then performed for Data preprocessing. Next, for classification we have discussed two methods. First one, using Back-Propogation Neural Network with auxilary cost function term to force weight convergence. Second, Genetic algorithm along with Decision Tree can be utilized for logical rule extraction and feature selection.

BP Neural network implemented with 1 input layer, 125 variables equal to 1 or −1, 1 hidden layer with undefined units and 1 output neuron. The classifier simply set threshold and if Output>threshold then 1(edible); otherwise 0(poisonous). Finally, we get 100% accuracy on testing set. Using Decision Tree to derive distinct rules, we get top 4 rules based on most coverage giving 100% accuracy. Out of the 12 distinct rules, top 4 rules extracted are :

diagram.png

Second model suggested here is Genetic Algorithm with Decision Tree where GA is for feature selection and then decision tree for construction of trees based on selected features. It gives us 99.7046% accuracy on training + testing set for selected features equal to 3 and accuracy equal to 100% when number of features increased to 4 or 5 for complexity.

Finally we can say genetic algorithm implemented with decision tress model is better as is gives more information and help with manually changing attributes or features like DNA POSITIVE. Even though it runs slower than neural networks but it eliminates poor performance as number of features or complexity increases.

5   Conclusion

The purpose of this work is to establish clear logical regulations for determining the edibility of mushrooms. Since all variables are categorical, they must first be quantified through Vectorized Discretization. Two distinct methods were implemented for classification purposes. The initial approach involved training back-propagation neural networks with an auxiliary cost function term to enforce weight convergence. The second method utilised Genetic Algorithm for feature selection in conjunction with Decision Tree. Essentially, logical rule extraction is a process of feature selection, where significant features are chosen, and conditional logical rules are created. Therefore, GA is a more feasible approach in comparison to neural networks. The BP neural network method primarily relies on parameter adjustment and can perform poorly and require enhancements in complex situations. In contrast, GA + Decision Tree does not encounter this issue. GA provides more explicit information and facilitates manual alteration of a crucial parameter, DNA POSITIVE. However, GA runs slower than neural networks, possibly due to the need to train numerous Decision Trees.

References

1. Duch, W., Adamczak, R., Grabczewski, K.: Extraction of logical rules from training data using backpropagation networks. In: The 1st Online Workshop on Soft Computing, pp. 19–30 (1996)
2. Lincoff, G.H.: The audubon society field guide to north american mushrooms. Tech. rep. (1989)
3. Schlimmer, J.C.: Concept acquisition through representational adjustment (1987)
4. Alkronz, E.S., Moghayer, K.A., Meimeh, M., Gazzaz, M., Abu-Nasser, B.S., Abu-Naser, S.S.: Prediction of whether mushroom is edible or poisonous using back-propagation neural network. Int. J. Acad. Appl. Res. (IJAAR) 3(2), 1–8 (2019)
5. Breiman, L.: Random Forest. Mach. Learn. 45(1), 5–32 (2001)
6. Chitayae, N., Sunyoto, A.: Performance comparison of mushroom types classification using k-nearest neighbor method and decision tree method. In: 3rd International Conference on Information and Communications Technology (ICOIACT), Yogyakarta, Indonesia (2020)
7. Chumuang, N., et al.: Mushroom classification by physical characteristics by technique of k-nearest neighbor. In: 15th International Joint Symposium on Artificial Intelligence and Natural Language Processing (iSAI-NLP), IEEE Xplore, Bangkok, Thailand (2020)
8. Han, J., Kamber, M., Pei, J.: Data Mining: concepts and techniques. Morgan Kaufmann (2012)
9. Han, J., Kamber, M., Pei, J.: Classification: Basic Concepts and Advanced Methods in Data Mining: Concepts and Techniques (3rd ed.). Morgan Kaufmann Publishers, pp. 327–442 (2012)
10. Ismail, S., Zainal, A.R., Mustapha, A.: Behavioural Features For Mushroom Classification in IEEE Symposium on Computer Applications and Industrial Electronics (ISCAIE). Penang, Malaysia (2018)
11. Jayanthi, S.K., Sasikala, S.: REPTree classifier for identifying link spam in web search engines. ICTACT J. Soft Comput. (IJSC) 3(2), 498–505 (2013)
12. Kalač, P.: Chemical composition and nutritional value of European species of wild growing mushrooms: a review. Food Chem. 113(1), 9–16 (2009)
13. Roupas, P., Keogh, J., Noakes, M., Margetts, C., Taylor, P.: The role of edible mushrooms in health: evaluation of the evidence. J. Functional Foods 4(4), 687–709 (2012)
14. Martínez-Carrera, D., Ares, G., Deliza, R.: Mushroom consumption as a source of vitamins and minerals in a developed country. Food Res. Int. 103, 388–397 (2018)

15. Martínez-Carrera, D., Ares, G., Deliza, R.: Sensory evaluation of fresh mushrooms: a comparison between trained assessors and consumers. Food Qual. Prefer. **72**, 1–11 (2019)

16. Balouiri, M., Sadiki, M., Koraichi, S.I.: Methods for in vitro evaluating antimicrobial activity: a review. J. Pharm. Anal. **6**(2), 71–79 (2016)

17. Silva, E.M., Rogez, H., Larondelle, Y.: Optimization of extraction conditions for phenolic compounds from guava (psidium guajava l.) leaves. Separation Purification Technol. **55**(3), 336–342 (2007)

18. Essien, E.E., Ikpeme, E.V.: Proximate and Mineral Composition of Pleurotus pulmonarius (Fries) Quelet (Agaricomycetideae) Harvested from the Federal University of Technology, Akwa Ibom State. Nigeria. Int. J. Med. Mushrooms **16**(4), 375–381 (2014)

19. Felluga, B., Marconi, S., Raggi, L., Perini, C., Della Bella, L., Lucchini, G.: Cultivated and Wild Mushrooms: Comparison of Nutritional Composition. Food Chem. **230**, 142–150 (2017)

20. Ribeiro, B., Pinho, P.G., Andrade, P.B., Baptista, P., Valentão, P.: Fatty acid composition of wild edible mushrooms species: a comparative study. Microchem. J. **88**(2), 161–166 (2008)

21. Barros, L., Baptista, P., Ferreira, I.C.F.R.: Effect of lactarius piperatus fruit body maturity stage on antioxidant activity measured by several spectroscopic techniques. Food Chem. **101**(1), 193–201 (2007)

22. El-Debaiky, S.A.: Mushroom cultivation and application of mushroom cultivated solutions in spinach crop production. American-Eurasian J. Sustain. Agric. **5**(2), 109–117 (2011)

23. Gargano, M. L., et al.: Medicinal Mush (2017)

Multiple Linear Regression Based Analysis of Weather Data: Assumptions and Limitations

Savita Bansal and Gurwinder Singh[✉]

Department of AIT-CSE, Chandigarh University, Mohali, Punjab, India
{savita.e14045,gurwinder.e11253}@cumail.in

Abstract. Multiple linear regression is a statistical technique that is widely used in many fields, including weather forecasting. The primary aim of this chapter is to investigate the assumptions and limitations of multiple linear regression in analyzing weather data. Therefore, the main assumptions of multiple linear regression, including linearity, normality, independence, and homoscedasticity have been examined for weather data analysis. Also the limitations of multiple linear regression are explored in weather data analysis, such as multicollinearity, outliers, and model selection. The mean square error (MSE) and its rooted version (RMSE), and the mean absolute error (MAE), and the R-squared are employed to investigate the data (10 years with 4018 samples) for evaluating regression analysis. Finally, some recommendations and best practices to overcome these limitations and improve the accuracy of weather data analysis using multiple linear regression have been suggested to facilitate different stakeholders.

Keywords: Multiple Linear Regression · Limitations of Linear Regression · Regression Learner

1 Introduction

Water, one of our natural resources, is essential to all living organisms. It is utilized in many different sectors, including energy production, residential use, agriculture, and industry. The amount of precipitation in a particular area determines and is directly proportional to how much water is available in that area. Drought is caused by no rain, while flooding is caused by heavy rain. Rainfall is one important meteorological factor that affects many parts of our everyday lives. Due to its complexity and enduring uses, such as flood prediction and monitoring pollutant concentration levels, rainfall forecasting has recently earned the highest research relevance.

Traditional techniques like statistical methods have been used to predict rainfall for years. These methods examine the relationship between rainfall, geographic coordinates (like latitude and longitude), and other meteorological parameters (like pressure, temperature, wind speed, and humidity). However,

R. N. Shaw et al. (Eds.): ICACIS 2023, CCIS 1920, pp. 221–238, 2023.
https://doi.org/10.1007/978-3-031-45121-8_19

it is challenging to predict the forecast due to the complexity of the relationship between the weather, geographical conditions, and rainfall. Existing studies depend on sophisticated statistical calculations that are frequently very expensive, financially and computationally, or are no longer applicable beyond a certain limit. Long-term rainfall prediction and short-term rainfall prediction are the two sorts of rainfall forecasts. Predictions can provide precise results. Creating a model for predicting long-term rainfall is a big challenge.

Every year, people all around the world experience natural disasters like floods and droughts because of this. In India, the economy is primarily depends upon agriculture, the accuracy of rainfall predictions is important. Although, due to climate change and many other factors, significant and unanticipated changes in weather patterns are not consistent and may vary from one demographic region to another. Due to the atmosphere's dynamic character, applied mathematics techniques cannot guarantee reliable precision for a statement about precipitation. Some researchers have used regression to predict precipitation using machine learning techniques and data mining, while others have used artificial neural networks to predict the rainfall. This area of research has huge potential and looks to eventually bring about greater accuracy in weather predictions.

1.1   Literature Review

D.T. Deshmukh et al. [4] analyzed the trends that occurred in climatic variables like rainfall, rainy days, and temperature using Mann Kendall and t-test. Data has been taken from the India Meteorological Department (IMD), Pune, as a foundation for crop production sustainability over the last three decades, from 1975 to 2005, for the Yavatmal district of Vidarbha. The authors analyzed the data using regression analysis and correlation analysis. Bar graphs and scattered diagrams are used and fitted the regression lines using Microsoft Excel to show the flow of data at 5% level of significance.

Vittal et al. [19] concluded that the yearly mean rainfall data for the study zones showed a statistically negligible upward trend in some years and a decreasing trend in others on the mean annual rainfall, according to the findings of the linear regression analysis. The results of the ANOVA and Tukeys tests showed a significant difference between the zones and seasons. The above analysis enables farmers to make wiser judgements and use rainwater as effectively as possible in different zones and seasons. The authors collected the data to determine the patterns of rainfall in the ten districts of Telangana. They divided it into two parts: South districts and North districts. According to the authors' investigation, these zones saw oscillatory rainfall.

Manickam Valli et al. [18] primarily focused on the assessment of changes occurring in the periodic distribution of rainfall for determining the monthly, seasonal, and annual distributions, variations, and trends in 10 districts of Andhra Pradesh using a 30-year record of monthly precipitation. Regression analysis is used to investigate how changing weather parameters impact climatic circumstances. When the slope values from regression were derived for the ten districts, Karimnagar had the most significant negative value, and Guntur had the most significant positive value. The Climate Predictability Tool is used to forecast rainfall for the districts of Karimnagar and Prakasam from 2011 to 2015. Compared to Karimnagar, located in a single agro-climatic zone, Prakasam has distinct agro-climatic zones.

Vikas Kumar et al. [10] discussed to create a system for predicting rainfall more accurately using machine learning classification techniques. Their research paper aims to predict the amount of rain that is expected at a specific location using data input from users. The parameters include the time, place, the highest and lowest temperatures, humidity, wind direction and speed, evaporation, and other elements. The parameters related to rainfall are trained using the KNN, Decision Tree, Random Forest, and Logistic Regression techniques. Finally, compared the results of the performance of these four algorithms.

Chalachew Muluken Liyew et al. [11] worked on the dataset gathered from the regional meteorological office in Bahir Dar City, Ethiopia for the purpose of evaluating the effectiveness of three machine learning algorithms (Multivariate Linear Regression, Random Forest, and Extreme Gradient Boost). The major goal of their work is to apply machine learning approaches to identify the important atmospheric variables that generate rainfall and predict the amount of daily rainfall. Relevant environmental variables were chosen using the Pearson-correlation method and then used as inputs for the machine learning model. The performance of the machine learning model was evaluated using Mean absolute error and Root mean squared error approaches. The results indicated that Extreme Gradient Boosting is better than other machine learning algorithms.

R. Khavse et al. [9] observed that annual total mean rainfall and the annual mean maximum temperature have exhibited an increasing trend that is statistically insignificant at the 5% significance level for meteorological data of Labandi area, Raipur district of Chhattisgarh from 1971 to 2013 approximately three decades. For the importance of the temperature and rainfall trends, statistical techniques like regression analysis and the coefficient of determination R2 were applied.

The impact of climate on traffic accidents has been the subject of a number of studies. According to research by Pisano et al. [15], fog contributes to about 2% of all traffic accidents, while about 75% of weather-related collisions take place on wet roads. In their study on weather-related fatal crashes, Ashley et al. [3] found that the vast majority of such incidents happened on highways in the early morning hours during the coldest times of the year. Similarly, they found that a whopping 70% of fatal weather-related accidents take place if the relevant government agency hasn't issued a visibility-related-advisory.

Numerous other studies have been conducted on the effects of fog or smoke on vehicle collisions; these include Pisano et al. [15], Ashley et al. [3], Trick et al. [17], Hassan and AbdelAty [7], Mueller and Trick [14], Ahmed et al. [2] and Theofilatos and Yannis [16] Results from these research show that driving in fog can be dangerous. Reduced visibility may be to blame for the rise in danger, since drivers have a harder time observing their surroundings, including other vehicles, pedestrians, bikers, and fixed objects.

Among the most effective methods for making predictions are by [5,8,12,20] and reviewed by [6,13] as well. Some techniques can model complicated relationships and predict visibility by learning from the large amount of meteorological data (hourly data from weather monitoring stations).

1.2 Motivation

The motivation for this chapter is to provide a comprehensive understanding of the assumptions and limitations of multiple linear regression in analyzing weather data. This understanding can help researchers and practitioners in the field of weather forecasting to use the technique more effectively and accurately. Additionally, by highlighting the limitations of the technique, the chapter can also inspire future research in developing more advanced statistical techniques to improve weather data analysis. Ultimately, the goal of this chapter is to contribute to the advancement of weather forecasting and the development of more accurate models for predicting weather patterns.

1.3 Objectives

As weather forecasters and meteorologists need statistical techniques, such as multiple linear regression, to analyze weather data and make predictions as well as agricultural experts who rely on weather forecasting to plan crop cultivation and harvesting activities, the following objectives are considered:

- To investigate the assumptions of multiple linear regression in analyzing weather data, including linearity, normality, independence, and homoscedasticity.
- To examine the limitations of multiple linear regression in weather data analysis, such as multicollinearity, outliers, and model selection.
- To provide recommendations and best practices to overcome the limitations of multiple linear regression in weather data analysis and improve the accuracy of weather forecasting.
- To contribute to the understanding of the use of multiple linear regression in weather forecasting and provide insights into its assumptions and limitations.
- To highlight the importance of considering the assumptions and limitations of multiple linear regression in weather data analysis and encourage researchers to use appropriate statistical techniques to analyze weather data.

2   Data Understanding

To conduct a multiple linear regression-based analysis of weather data, the first step is to gain a thorough understanding of the data. This involves exploring and analysing the data to identify patterns, trends, and relationships among the variables. To do so, the descriptive statistics to summarize the main characteristics of the variables are considered, which include measures such as mean, median, standard deviation, and range. Additionally, graphical representations such as histograms, scatterplots, and boxplots are used to visualize the data and identify any outliers or anomalies.

2.1 Dataset

For this purpose, data of 10 years period 2012–2022 with a total of 4018 samples representing different characteristics (such as cloud cover, humidity, pressure, temperature, visibility, and precipitation etc.) is collected from source [1]. Then, the collected data goes through some basic steps, such as data cleaning, integrating and exploring the data, removing irrelevant or inconsistent data points, filling in missing data points, fixing mistakes, and transforming the data so it used for analysis.

2.2 Statistical Summary

Figure 1 mentions a statistical summary of parameters, which is helpful in descriptive analysis and beginning an investigation of large data sets. The upper and lower quartiles, median, lowest and maximum values, and mean are the five numbers that make up a summary. Each corresponds to the given meteorological data variables: maximum temperature, minimum temperature, total snow, sun hour, UV index, moon illumination, dew point, heat index, wind chill, wind gust, cloud cover, humidity, precipitation, and pressure.

	maxtempC	mintempC	totalSnow_cm	sunHour	uvIndex
count	4018.000000	4018.000000	4018.0	4018.000000	4018.000000
mean	33.767297	21.314087	0.0	11.208362	7.088850
std	8.351880	8.289623	0.0	2.272327	1.868551
min	12.000000	3.000000	0.0	3.800000	3.000000
25%	27.000000	14.000000	0.0	9.700000	6.000000
50%	35.000000	23.000000	0.0	11.600000	7.000000
75%	40.000000	28.000000	0.0	13.600000	9.000000
max	53.000000	39.000000	0.0	14.100000	11.000000
	moon_illumination	DewPointC	FeelsLikeC	HeatIndexC	WindChillC
count	4018.000000	4018.000000	4018.000000	4018.000000	4018.000000
mean	46.117222	9.934545	28.119960	28.217521	27.036336
std	31.274575	8.365050	9.769565	9.625110	8.684649
min	0.000000	-16.000000	7.000000	9.000000	7.000000
25%	18.000000	4.000000	20.000000	20.000000	20.000000
50%	46.000000	9.000000	29.000000	29.000000	29.000000
75%	73.000000	17.000000	37.000000	37.000000	34.000000
max	100.000000	26.000000	48.000000	48.000000	44.000000
	WindGustKmph	cloudcover	humidity	precipMM	pressure
count	4018.000000	4018.000000	4018.000000	4018.000000	4018.000000
mean	12.506471	15.702091	40.311847	1.774888	1008.096565
std	4.637046	17.297730	18.704922	7.032324	7.366512
min	3.000000	0.000000	4.000000	0.000000	990.000000
25%	9.000000	2.000000	25.000000	0.000000	1002.000000
50%	12.000000	10.000000	38.000000	0.000000	1005.000000
75%	15.000000	24.000000	54.000000	0.500000	1015.000000
max	47.000000	94.000000	96.000000	226.100000	1025.000000

Fig. 1. Statistical summary of parameters

3 Assumptions of Multiple Linear Regression

Before implementing a multiple regression analysis on a selected dataset, it is important to satisfy the assumptions of multiple linear regression to ensure the validity, accuracy, and generalizability of the results to provide robust and reliable estimates of the regression coefficients. In this chapter, the following assumptions are taken into account:

– The dependent variable is measured on a continuous scale (i.e., an interval or ratio variable). If the dependent variables were scored on an ordinal scale, one would use ordinal regression instead of multiple regression.

- Observations should be independent (i.e., residuals should be separate), which can be easily verified using the Durbin-Watson statistic.
- The dependent variable is linearly related with each independent variable and the dependent variable is linearly related with all of the independent variables. There are several methods for determining whether these correlations are linear. Still, the authors suggest creating scatter plots and partial regression plots in SPSS Statistics and then visually examining them to determine if they are linear.
- The data must demonstrate homogeneity of variances, in which the variance along the line of best fit remains constant.
- Multicollinearity occurs when two or more independent variables are substantially associated. This results in difficulties in determining which independent variable contributes to the variation explained by the dependent variable and technical difficulties when computing a multiple regression model.
- There should be no significant outliers, high leverage points, or very impactful spots.
- The residuals (errors) are distributed normally. (a) a histogram (with a superimposed normal curve) and a Normal P-P Plot; or (b) a Normal Q-Q Plot of the standardized residuals are two standard techniques for testing this assumption.

These assumptions are essential because violating them can lead to biased or inefficient estimates of the regression coefficients, invalid conclusions, inaccurate predictions, and unreliable results. Therefore, checking these assumptions one by one before conducting a multiple linear regression analysis is important.

3.1 Dealing with Multi-collinearity

A correlation matrix can be used to identify multicollinearity between independent variables in a multiple linear regression analysis. Multicollinearity occurs when two or more independent variables are highly correlated, which can cause problems in the regression analysis, such as unstable and unreliable estimates of the regression coefficients and difficulties in interpreting the results. Correlation coefficients range from -1 to $+1$, with values closer to -1 or $+1$ indicating stronger correlations. The zero correlation coefficient indicates no correlation. If the variables are highly correlated between pairs of independent variables, as mentioned in Fig. 2, then this suggests the presence of multicollinearity.

In this case, removing one or more of the highly correlated independent variables from the analysis may be necessary to reduce the multicollinearity and improve the accuracy and reliability of the regression analysis as mentioned in Fig. 2b. After dropping highly correlated parameters, the linear regression analysis is conducted on the selected dataset by using the 'Data-Analysis' feature of MS-Excel and the obtained results are given in Table 1, wherein the $R-squared : cofficient of determination$ value, 0.616572 indicates low prediction power of the model.

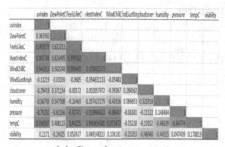

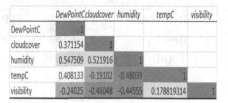

(a) Correlation matrix   (b) Updated Correlation matrix

Fig. 2. Correlation matrix before and after removing highly correlated parameters

Table 1. Regression Statistics

Multiple R	0.785221
R Square	0.616572
Adjusted R Square	0.616094
Standard Error	4.35724
Observations	4018

Statistical collinearity based on different parameters in a regression model is given in Table 2. In this table, the second and third columns show the unstandardized coefficients for each predictor variable, which represent the amount of change in the outcome variable associated with a one-unit change in that predictor variable. The fourth column shows the standardized coefficients, which allow to compare the relative importance of each predictor variable in the model. The standardized coefficients represent the change in the outcome variable associated with one-standard-deviation change in the predictor variable. The fifth column shows the t-values used to test the null hypothesis. A high t-value indicates that the coefficient is unlikely to be zero and is, therefore, statistically significant.

Table 2. Collinearity Statistics of parameters

	Unstandardized Coefficients		Standardized Coefficients	t	Sig.	Collinearity Statistics	
	B	Std. Error	Beta			Tolerance	VIF
(Constant)	221.784	34.121		6.500	.000		
UVindex	.026	.205	.007	.129	.898	.066	15.047
Dewpoint	−.215	.036	−.256	−5.916	.000	.105	9.537
Cloudcover	.101	.008	.248	12.899	.000	.534	1.874
Humidity	.166	.017	.442	9.835	.000	.098	10.255
Pressure	−.226	.033	−.237	−6.903	.000	.167	5.991
Temp	.053	.053	.062	.993	.321	.050	20.086

Table 3. ANOVA Test

	df	SS	MS	F	Significance F
Regression	5	122485	24497.01	1290.298504	0.000
Residual	4012	76169.97	18.98554		
Total	4017	198655			

Table 3 presents the results of an ANOVA (Analysis of Variance) test wherein the Regression row displays the results of the regression analysis, which examines the relationship between the independent and dependent variables of the model. The F-value is a test statistic that compares the variance unaccounted for with the variance explained by the model. The F-value in this instance is 1290.298504. The p-value is less than a predetermined level of significance (0.05 or 0.01). Therefore, the null hypothesis is rejected i.e., the regression model is statistically significant. The ANOVA table summarizes the variance components and indicates if the regression model is statistically significant.

Table 4. Regression coefficients of independent variables

	Coefficients	Standard Error	t Stat	P-value
Intercept	109.8253	2.116381	51.89296	0
DewPointC	0.063501	0.024737	2.566991	0.010294463
cloudcover	0.015091	0.004956	3.045242	0.002340029
humidity	−0.01467	0.011727	−1.25079	0.211084463
tempC	−1.1E-05	0.023528	−0.00047	0.999622135
visibility	−10.978	0.166528	−65.9229	0

The Table 4 provides information on the coefficients, standard errors, t-statistics, and p-values of each independent variable. The intercept coefficient is 109.8253, which means that when all the independent variables are zero, the predicted value of the dependent variable is 109.8253. The coefficients of the independent variables indicate the change in the dependent variable when the corresponding independent variable changes by one unit, holding all other independent variables constant. For example, the coefficient of DewPointC is 0.063501, which means that an increase of one degree Celsius in dew point temperature is associated with an increase of 0.063501 units in the predicted value of the dependent variable, holding all other independent variables constant. The standard errors provide a measure of the variability of the coefficient estimates. In this table, all the coefficients except tempC have p-values less than 0.05, which is commonly used as a threshold for statistical significance.

Table 5. Regression coefficients after resolving Multi-collinearity

Regression Statistics	
Multiple R	0.442059
R Square	0.195416
Adjusted R Square	0.194815
Standard Error	6.310253
Observations	4018

ANOVA

	df	SS	MS	F	Significance F
Regression	3	38820.38	12940.13	324.9712673	6.8E-189
Residual	4014	159834.6	39.81929		
Total	4017	198655			

	Coefficients	Standard Error	t Stat	P-value
Intercept	−6.2194	0.627228	−9.9157	6.51135E-23
cloudcover	0.11323	0.006769	16.72688	9.12411E-61
humidity	0.096285	0.007006	13.74296	4.95261E-42
tempC	0.069147	0.013635	5.071109	4.1336E-07

Table 5 shows regression statistics, ANOVA, and model coefficients. The regression statistics shows that the independent variables explain 19.54% of the dependent variable's variation. The model's multiple R-value is 0.442059, and its R-squared value is 0.195416, which is relatively low for a good regression model. The ANOVA table reveals that the regression is statistically significant. The coefficients of determination show that the independent variables are significantly related to the dependent variable. The second part of the table shows unstandardized coefficients (B), standard error, t-statistic, and p-value for each independent variable i.e. intercept, cloud cover, humidity and temperature. The coefficient of intercept is −6.2194 and significant at 1% level of significance.

Table 6. Collinearity Statistics after resolving Multi-collinearity

	Unstandardized Coefficients		Standardized Coefficients	t	Sig.	Collinearity Statistics	
	B	Std. Error	Beta			Tolerance	VIF
(Constant)	−6.219	.627		−9.916	.000		
Cloudcover	.113	.007	.279	16.727	.000	.723	1.383
Humidity	.096	.007	.256	13.743	.000	.577	1.733
Temp	.069	.014	.082	5.071	.000	.764	1.308

Table 6 presents the collinearity statistics after resolving multicollinearity in the multiple linear regression model, wherein all independent variables have significant coefficients (p-value < 0.05). The standardized coefficients (Beta) indicate that cloud cover has the highest impact on the dependent variable, followed by humidity and temperature. Moreover, the collinearity statistics indicate that the tolerance values are above 0.1 and the VIF values are below 10 for all variables, which indicates that multicollinearity is no longer an issue in the model. Table 6 also shows independent variable tolerance and variance inflation factor (VIF) collinearity statistics. Tolerance values lie between 0.577 and 0.764, while VIF values vary from 1.308 to 1.733. Overall, these results suggest that the multiple linear regression model with the resolved multicollinearity issue can be used to analyze weather data with improved accuracy.

3.2   Distribution Charts

To test the assumption that the residuals (errors) are normally distributed in a multiple linear regression analysis one standard techniques is Distribution Charts, If it appears to be approximately bell-shaped and the normal curve fits well over the histogram, then it suggests that the residuals are normally distributed as depicted in Figs. 3 and 4. Another way to assess normality is by using normal probability plots or QQ plots, which compare the distribution of the residuals to a normal distribution. If the points on the plot follow a relatively straight line, then it indicates that the residuals are normally distributed.

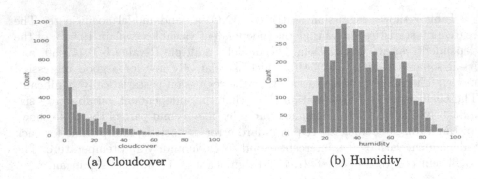

(a) Cloudcover   (b) Humidity

Fig. 3. Distribution plot of cloud and humidity parameter

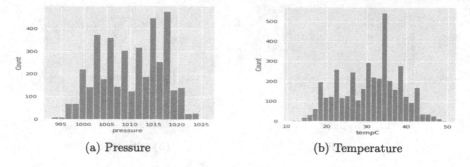

(a) Pressure   (b) Temperature

Fig. 4. Distribution plot of pressure and temperature parameter

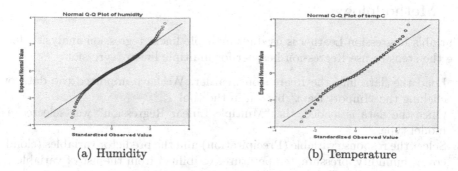

(a) Humidity   (b) Temperature

Fig. 5. Quartile-Quartile Plot of independent variables

3.3 Q-Q Plots

The univariate normality of a dataset can be inferred from its position on the Normal Q-Q plot as depicted in Fig. 5a, 5b.

The points are clustered around the 45-degree line as the data follows a normal distribution. In the context of statistical analysis, the normality assumption is often required for many statistical tests and models to be validate linear regression, etc. Therefore, a Q-Q plot is a useful tool to help assess whether the normality assumption is met, which is important for ensuring the validity and reliability of statistical inference.

3.4 Dealing with Outliers

Outliers are data points that are significantly different from the other data points in the dataset, and they can distort the analysis and interpretation of the data. The boxplot identifies the extremes of the data, which are the points that are furthest away from the median. These points are often the outliers and can be easily spotted in a boxplot as depicted in Fig. 6a and 6b.

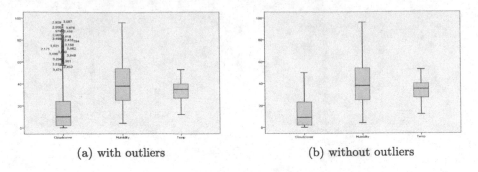

(a) with outliers   (b) without outliers

Fig. 6. Box-plot before and after resolving outliers

4   Methodology

Matlab's Regression Learner is used for multiple linear regression analysis. Here are the steps to use Regression Learner for multiple linear regression:

1. Load the data into the Regression Learner. We have imported the data by clicking the "Import Data" button in the tool.
2. Once the data is loaded, the "Multiple Linear Regression" was selected as model type.
3. Select the response variable (Precipitation) and the predictor variables (cloud-cover, humidity, pressure, temperature, visibility) from the list of variables.
4. Click the "Train" button to train the model on the data.
5. The Regression Learner will then display the results of the regression analysis, including the coefficients for each predictor variable, the intercept, the R-squared value, and other statistics which are discussed in the Sect. 5.
6. Then the trained model to make predictions on new data by clicking the "Predict" button and entering the new data is used.

The Regression Learner also provides tools for visualizing the results of the regression analysis, including scatter plots, residual plots, and diagnostic plots.

5   Numerical Computation

5.1   Determining How Well the Model Fits

The Model Summary Table 7 is the first one worth looking at, how well a regression model fits the data is determined by observing the values of the R, the modified R2, and the standard error of the estimate.

Table 7. Model Summary

Model	R	R Square	Adjusted R Square	Std. Error of the Estimate	Durbin-Watson
1	.389	.151	.151	6.481	1.386

In this Table 7, the R square value is 0.151, indicating that only 15.1% of the variance in the dependent variable can be explained by the independent variables in the model whereas the adjusted R square value is also 0.151, which means that adding independent variables did not improve the fit of the model. The last column shows the Durbin-Watson statistic, which is used to test for the presence of autocorrelation in the residuals (errors) of the model. The value ranges between 0 and 4, with values closer to 2 indicating no autocorrelation, values below 2 indicating positive autocorrelation, and values above 2 indicating negative autocorrelation. In this case, the value is 1.386, which suggests positive autocorrelation.

5.2   Statistical Significance

In Table 8, the Regression row indicates that the sum of squares for the regression is 30077.677, with 3 degrees of freedom. The mean square is 10025.892, and the F-value is 238.727. The p-value for the F-test is very small, indicating that the regression is significant at a high level of confidence. The Residual row shows that the sum of squares for the residuals is 168577.339, with 4014 degrees of freedom. The mean square is 41.997. The Total row shows that the sum of squares for the entire model is 198655.016, with 4017 degrees of freedom.

Table 8. ANOVA table

Model		Sum of Squares	df	Mean Square	F	Sig.
1	Regression	30077.677	3	10025.892	238.727	.000b
	Residual	168577.339	4014	41.997		
	Total	198655.016	4017			

5.3   Estimated Model Coefficients

When all of the other independent variables are held constant, unstandardized coefficients can be used to determine how much the dependent variable varies with one of the independent variables. In the Table 9, the coefficients represent the change in the outcome variable associated with a one-unit change in the predictor variable, holding all other predictor variables constant. The standardized coefficients allow for the comparison of the relative importance of each predictor variable in predicting the outcome variable.

Table 9. Estimated Model Coefficients

Model	Unstandardized Coefficients		Standardized Coefficients	t	Sig.
	B	Std. Error	Beta		
1 (Constant)	−6.754	.646		−10.456	.000
Cloudcover	.066	.009	.126	7.557	.000
Humidity	.129	.007	.343	18.165	.000
Temp	.072	.014	.085	5.071	.000

5.4   Statistical Significance of the Independent Variables

To determine the statistical significance of the independent variables in the above table, we need to look at the "Sig." column, which provides the p-value associated with each coefficient estimate. If the p-value is less than the significance level (usually 0.05), then we can conclude that the corresponding independent variable is statistically significant and has a significant effect on the dependent variable. Looking at the "Sig." column in the above Table 9, its observed that the three independent variables (Cloudcover, Humidity, and Temp) have p-values less than 0.05, which indicates that they are statistically significant and have a significant impact on the dependent variable.

6   Limitations

Based on the information provided in the Table 7, it has been observed that the R-squared value is relatively low at 0.151, indicating that the model explains only a small proportion of the variance in the dependent variable. This suggest that there may be other important factors affecting the weather data that are not captured by the multiple linear regression model used in the study. Additionally, the Durbin-Watson value of 1.386 suggests that there may be some autocorrelation in the data, which could limit the accuracy of the model's predictions. Also from Table 9, the model assumes that the relationships between the independent variables and the dependent variable are linear. However, this may not be the case in reality, and non-linear relationships could lead to inaccurate predictions. Also Non-linear relationships can be identified by testing the statistical significance of the coefficients of the independent variables. If the coefficients are statistically significant, then it suggests the presence of non-linearity in the model as depicted in the Table 9.

Further, to validate these limitations, the Regression Learner feature in MAT-LAB is employed to build and assess multiple linear regression models. The different tree models and different variants of linear regression models are tested on same data. The model training process involves adjusting the number of delay steps from 3 to 10 and comparing the performance of MAE, MSE, and RMSE

Table 10. Evaluation Metrics

Criteria	Description	Formula
MSE	Mean Absolute Error	$\sum_{i=1}^{D} \lvert x_i - y_i \rvert$
MAE	Mean Squared Error	$\sum_{i=1}^{D} (x_i - y_i)^2$
RMSE	Mean Squared Error	$\sqrt{\sum_{i=1}^{D} (x_i - y_i)^2}$
R^2	Coefficient of Determination	$1 - \frac{sumsquaredregression(SSR)}{totalsumofsquares(SST)}$

Table 11. Performance measures of Tree Models

	Tree Models		
	Fine Tree	Medium Tree	Coarse Tree
RMSE	5.4643	5.0649	5.1314
R-squared	0.19	**0.31**	0.29
MSE	29.859	25.653	26.331
MAE	1.8742	1.7894	**1.8176**

Table 12. Performance measures of Linear Regression Models

	Linear Regression Models			
	Linear	Interactions Linear	Robust Linear	Stepwise Linear
RMSE	5.3572	5.0605	6.3276	**5.0599**
R-squared	0.23	0.31	0.08	0.31
MSE	28.7	25.608	40.038	**25.602**
MAE	2.5452	1.9536	1.7251	1.9561

criteria, Table 10, using a 5-fold cross-validation approach. The results obtained from this analysis are presented in Tables 11 and 12.

As per the provided Table 11 and Table 12, the lower value of R-squared indicates the limitations of multiple linear regression models.

7 Alternative Approaches

Here are some recommendations and best practices to overcome the limitations and improve the accuracy of weather data analysis using multiple linear regression:

- Gather more data: Increasing the sample size can help to reduce the impact of outliers and improve the accuracy of the regression analysis. Collecting data over a longer period of time can also provide a more complete picture of the weather patterns.

- Consider non-linear relationships: Use scatterplots and residual plots to check for non-linear relationships between the independent variables and the dependent variable. If there is evidence of non-linearity, consider using polynomial regression or other non-linear regression techniques.
- Polynomial regression: This model allows for non-linear relationships between the independent and dependent variables. It can capture more complex relationships than multiple linear regression.
- Generalized linear models (GLMs): GLMs are a family of models that can handle non-normal and non-continuous dependent variables. They can be used to analyze weather data with non-normal distributions, such as rainfall.
- Time series models: These models are designed to analyze data with temporal dependencies, such as weather data. They can account for trends, seasonality, and autocorrelation in the data.
- Machine learning models: Machine learning algorithms, such as random forest and support vector machines, can be used to analyze weather data. They can capture complex relationships and interactions among variables and are robust to outliers and missing data.
- Validate the model: Validate the model using cross-validation or other techniques. This can help to ensure that the model is not overfitting to the data and can be used for predicting future weather patterns.
- Consider external factors: Consider external factors that may impact the weather patterns, such as climate change or urbanization. Including these factors in the model can help to improve the accuracy of the regression analysis.
- Use domain expertise: Seek the advice of domain experts, such as meteorologists or climatologists, to ensure that the variables included in the model are relevant and meaningful analysis.

By following these recommendations and best practices, you can improve the accuracy of weather data analysis using multiple linear regression and obtain more reliable insights into weather patterns.

8   Conclusion

this chapter explored the assumptions and limitations of multiple linear regression in analyzing weather data. The analysis found that the assumptions of linearity, normality, independence, and homoscedasticity should be examined when using multiple linear regression for weather data analysis. The limitations of multicollinearity, outliers, and model selection were also identified as potential challenges in using multiple linear regression. To evaluate the performance of the regression analysis, various performance measures such as the mean square error (MSE), rooted mean square error (RMSE), mean absolute error (MAE), and R-squared were used. Finally, some recommendations and best practices were suggested to improve the accuracy of weather data analysis using multiple (non)linear regression. By following these recommendations, different stakeholders can improve their weather data analysis and make more accurate predictions.

References

1. India meteorological department ministry of earth sciences government of India (2023). https://mausam.imd.gov.in/responsive/rainfall-statistics.php
2. Ahmed, M.M., Abdel-Aty, M., Lee, J., Yu, R.: Real-time assessment of fog-related crashes using airport weather data: a feasibility analysis. Accid. Anal. Prev. **72**, 309–317 (2014)
3. Ashley, W.S., Strader, S., Dziubla, D.C., Haberlie, A.: Driving blind: weather-related vision hazards and fatal motor vehicle crashes. Bull. Am. Meteor. Soc. **96**(5), 755–778 (2015)
4. Deshmukh, D., Lunge, H.: Trend assessment in climatic variables by Mann-Kendall and t-test: a case study of Yavatmal district in Vidarbha, India. Statistics **2**(5) (2013)
5. Fang, T., Lahdelma, R.: Evaluation of a multiple linear regression model and sarima model in forecasting heat demand for district heating system. Appl. Energy **179**, 544–552 (2016)
6. Gad, I., Hosahalli, D.: A comparative study of prediction and classification models on NCDC weather data. Int. J. Comput. Appl. **44**(5), 414–425 (2022)
7. Hassan, H.M., Abdel-Aty, M.A.: Predicting reduced visibility related crashes on freeways using real-time traffic flow data. J. Safety Res. **45**, 29–36 (2013)
8. Kavitha, S., Varuna, S., Ramya, R.: A comparative analysis on linear regression and support vector regression. In: 2016 Online International Conference on Green Engineering and Technologies (IC-GET), pp. 1–5. IEEE (2016)
9. Khavse, R., Deshmukh, R., Manikandan, N., Chaudhary, J., Kaushik, D., et al.: Statistical analysis of temperature and rainfall trend in Raipur district of Chhattisgarh. Curr. World Environ. **10**(1), 305–312 (2015)
10. Kumar, V., Yadav, V.K., Dubey, E.S.: Rainfall prediction using machine learning. Int. J. Res. Appl. Sci. Eng. Technol. (IJRASET) **10**(5) (2022)
11. Liyew, C.M., Melese, H.A.: Machine learning techniques to predict daily rainfall amount. J. Big Data **8**, 1–11 (2021)
12. Mahabub, A., Habib, A.-Z.S.B., Mondal, M.R.H., Bharati, S., Podder, P.: Effectiveness of ensemble machine learning algorithms in weather forecasting of Bangladesh. In: Abraham, A., Sasaki, H., Rios, R., Gandhi, N., Singh, U., Ma, K. (eds.) IBICA 2020. AISC, vol. 1372, pp. 267–277. Springer, Cham (2021). https://doi.org/10.1007/978-3-030-73603-3_25
13. Maulud, D., Abdulazeez, A.M.: A review on linear regression comprehensive in machine learning. J. Appl. Sci. Technol. Trends **1**(4), 140–147 (2020)
14. Mueller, A.S., Trick, L.M.: Driving in fog: the effects of driving experience and visibility on speed compensation and hazard avoidance. Accid. Anal. Prev. **48**, 472–479 (2012)
15. Pisano, P.A., Goodwin, L.C., Rossetti, M.A.: Us highway crashes in adverse road weather conditions. In: 24th Conference on International Interactive Information and Processing Systems for Meteorology, Oceanography and Hydrology, New Orleans, LA (2008)
16. Theofilatos, A., Yannis, G.: A review of the effect of traffic and weather characteristics on road safety. Accid. Anal. Prev. **72**, 244–256 (2014)
17. Trick, L.M., Toxopeus, R., Wilson, D.: The effects of visibility conditions, traffic density, and navigational challenge on speed compensation and driving performance in older adults. Accid. Anal. Prev. **42**(6), 1661–1671 (2010)

18. Valli, M., Sree, K.S., Krishna, I.V.M.: Analysis of precipitation concentration index and rainfall prediction in various agro-climatic zones of Andhra Pradesh, India. Int. Res. J. Environ. Sci. **2**(5), 53–61 (2013)
19. Vittal, B., Reddy, M.K.: Statistical analysis of rainfall moving trend in Telangana state. Int. J. Sci. Res. Math. Stat. Sci. **6**, 4 (2019)
20. Vlachogianni, A., Kassomenos, P., Karppinen, A., Karakitsios, S., Kukkonen, J.: Evaluation of a multiple regression model for the forecasting of the concentrations of NOX and PM10 in Athens and Helsinki. Sci. Total Environ. **409**(8), 1559–1571 (2011)

Sentiment Analysis of User-Generated Data Using CNN-BiLSTM Model

Mridul Rao$^{(\boxtimes)}$, Ashwini Kumar, and Vishu Tyagi

Graphic Era University, Dehradun, India
`mridulrao674385@gmail.com`

Abstract. With the availability of user-generated data, like reviews, it has become possible to gain valuable information that can help service providers to improve their services. There can be various methods to gain helpful information, including sentiment analysis of the reviews. Sentiment analysis is a popular method used to extract information from these reviews, but it can be challenging due to irregularities and ambiguities in the data. This chapter proposes a novel model architecture that enhances sentiment analysis and provides more accurate results than state-of-the-art technology. The proposed model takes advantage of the convolutional layer and Bidirectional long short-term layer (BiLSTM) coupled with max-pooling and a network of hidden layers. Regularizers are also incorporated to enhance the accuracy of the proposed model during training. The proposed model's main advantage is its ability to provide more accurate sentiment analysis results compared to previous models. In our chapter, we observed that the model overcomes the limitations of earlier models by improving the handling of irregularities and ambiguities in unstructured data (user-generated reviews) and providing valuable insights to service providers by accurately classifying reviews into positive and negative categories, enabling them to take appropriate actions based on customer feedback.

Keywords: Convolutional Neural Network · Bidirectional-Long short term memory · Sentiment Analysis

1 Introduction

Web 2.0 defines the current internet, and with its ascent, user data have been generated more than ever. The internet engages with the user, and users are encouraged to share experiences and data rather than view it. This aspect of the internet led to the transformation of social media, which allowed users to interact with each other and produce a tremendous amount of data daily. Facebook, Twitter, Instagram, and other blog websites have transformed how data is shared. One of the central aspects of this user-generated data is reviews that users post online, describing the services availed by the user.

Reviews posted online help in sharing the experience and showcase key features of the service, which can attract potential new customers. Moreover, the studies also provide insights into the aspects of the service which can be improved. Mining and

R. N. Shaw et al. (Eds.): ICACIS 2023, CCIS 1920, pp. 239–246, 2023.
https://doi.org/10.1007/978-3-031-45121-8_20

analyzing these reviews from various social media platforms have attracted different service providers' attention. Existing literature has focused on multiple application areas, such as the prediction of election results, healthcare service rating, and rating tourist places.

Opinion analysis is the most effective method to extract valuable information from textual data (customer's opinion/review) and use it to improve the services businesses offer. However, retrieving this helpful information from user-generated data has often proven difficult as there are possibilities of irregularities and ambiguities. Moreover, with the speed at which the data is being generated, keeping track of valuable information becomes practically impossible.

The main contribution of our chapter is that our novel model architecture, sentiment analysis of unstructured data(reviews), can be enhanced and provide more accurate results compared to state-of-the-art technology.

2 Literature Survey

Sentiment classification is crucial in gaining insights into the performance of services the public uses. The reviews provided by the users can be analyzed and classified into mainly two categories –positive and negative, enabling service providers to precisely identify positive or negative attitudes about their product or service and take appropriate actions if needed. However, labelling raw data can be tedious with the amount of raw data being generated daily. Therefore, there has been much work in recent years in creating deep learning models and using classical machine learning algorithms [8, 12, 13] to analyze reviews and classify them into positive or negative categories.

Kumar and Zymber [7] analyzed the effect of word embeddings on the review classification, suggested a CNN-based classification model, and used Twitter Airline Dataset. The accuracy of the proposed model compared with SVM (support vector machine) and several neural network architectures to map the tweet into positive and negative categories. Their research also used the Apriori algorithm to generate association rules for positive and negative sentiments associated with the reviews.

In the study by Jain et al. [6], a CNN-LSTM model was proposed for sentiment analysis on the US airline quality dataset with 75910 reviews and the US airline Twitter dataset with 14618 reviews. The authors compared the performance of the CNN-LSTM model with classical machine learning algorithms, including LR, DT, SVM, and LST, and reported that the proposed model achieved an accuracy rate of 91.3%.

In another study by Mahto et al. [9], a Glove-embedding[10] CNN-LSTM model and a Hierarchical Bidirectional-LSTM model were proposed for sentiment classification on the US airline Twitter dataset. The authors reported an accuracy of 93.25% in sentiment analysis using their proposed models. The categorical cross-entropy loss function was utilized to classify the tweet into one of the three possible classes, i.e., positive, negative, or neutral.

Our research aims to improve sentiment analysis of reviews in the Twitter Airline and US Airline Datasets. To achieve this, we propose a hybrid model with Convolutional Neural Network (CNN) and Bidirectional Long Short-Term Memory (LSTM) architecture. Our proposed model demonstrates superior performance compared to existing state-of-the-art methods. Further details on the model have been provided in Sect. 3.5.

3 Methodology

3.1 Problem Formulation

Given a review, we analyze the sentiment associated with the review and classify the analyzed sentiment under one of the two possible categories – Positive or Negative. The negative reviews can provide valuable feedback to the service providers on how they can improve their services. On the other hand, positive reviews can help highlight key features of the service that might attract new users.

3.2 CNN - Convolutional Neural Network

CNNs are neural networks specifically suited for processing spatial data, such as text. In CNNs, a convolutional window is moved across the input data (text) to produce a subset of the input data that contains local features of the input. Recent studies by Seo et al.[11] and Du et al. [2] have demonstrated the effectiveness of using CNNs for tasks such as text classification and other NLP tasks, yielding promising results.

3.3 LSTM - Long Short Term Memory

LSTM networks are a specific type of Recurrent Neural Network that can effectively learn long-range dependencies. Hochreiter and Schmidhuber [5] introduced this architecture in 1997, and LSTMs have shown exceptional performance in various applications due to their ability to overcome the long-term dependency problem that RNNs typically encounter. LSTMs consist of four robust neural networks that interact with each other. The fundamental concept of LSTMs revolves around the cell state, which can cautiously add or remove information controlled by structures known as gates. The gates consist of a dense layer with a sigmoid function and a Pointwise multiplication operation that protects and regulates the cell state.

3.4 Bidirectional-LSTM

A bidirectional LSTM neural network is a variation of the LSTM network that involves two LSTMs. In this arrangement, one LSTM processes the input data in a forward direction while the other processes it in a backward direction. In this LSTM architecture, the network can take advantage of information from both directions, which can improve the accuracy of the predictions. LSTM and BiLSTM are commonly used in natural language processing applications for various language understanding tasks.

3.5 Proposed Model

The proposed model is shown in Fig. 1. It consists of an embedding layer that uses Glove embeddings to convert each word into a fixed-length vector of a defined size. The benefits of using fixed-length vectors for the representation of sentences in language models were highlighted in [3]. The output of the embedding layer is then passed through the convolutional layer. The dropout layer is attached after the convolutional layer to

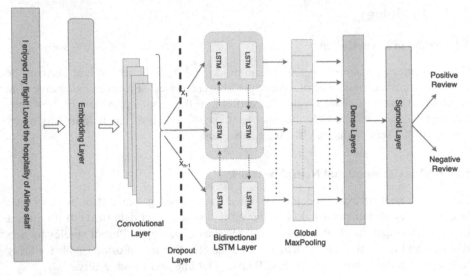

Fig. 1. Architecture of the proposed model

prevent overfitting by skipping random neurons. Then convolutional layer output, after being passed from dropout, is passed to the Bidirectional LSTM layer. The BiLSTM block helps retain the maximum amount of information extracted during training [1]. Next, the GloabalMax pooling layer is attached after the BiLSTM layer, downsampling the output of the BiLSTM layer, which is then passed to a network of hidden dense layers with ReLu activation. Finally, the output layer predicts the sentiment of the input. The model is compiled with Adam optimizer, and the loss function is binary cross-entropy to predict one output.

The CNN, BiLSTM, and network of hidden neural layers also contain regularizers that apply penalties on layer parameters or layer activity during optimization, thus helping in increasing the accuracy while training. All the hyperparameters for both models were determined using Grid Search, and the training was performed on a system with M1 CPU using TensorFlow v2.0.

4 Experiment

4.1 Dataset

Airline-quality sentiment dataset[1] – The dataset is collected from skytrax.com, which contains reviews of various British airlines. The dataset of processed reviews can be accessed from Kaggle. The dataset is made up of 17 columns, out of which only two columns are required for this chapter. The 'Customer Column" contains the review given by an airline customer, and the "Recommended" columns justify whether the customer recommends the airline. We have classified the customer recommendation as a positive

---

[1] https://www.kaggle.com/datasets/efehandanisman/skytrax-airline-reviews.

review and the customer nonrecommendation as a negative review. The dataset contains approximately equal positive and negative reviews and thus can be considered a balanced dataset for training the model.

Twitter Airline dataset[2] – The Twitter US airlines dataset was taken from Crowd-Flower's library. The dataset contains 15 columns, of which only the reviews and sentiment labels were used. Contributors of the dataset classified tweets as positive, negative, or neutral. We only considered the positive and negative tweets for our chapter.

More details of both the dataset, like size and average length of sentences, can be found in Table 1.

Table 1. Details of Dataset Used

Dataset	Metric	Training	Validation	Testing
Airline-quality Sentiment Dataset	Number of Samples	57897	11580	6433
	Avg. Length of Sentences	130	130	126
	Max Length of Sentences	365	365	320
Twitter Airline Dataset	Number of Samples	10386	2077	1155
	Avg. Length of Sentences	17	17	12
	Max Length of Sentences	30	30	25

4.2 Evaluation Metric Used

The performance of the proposed model is assessed using several metrics [4] such as accuracy, precision, recall, and F1 score, to ensure that the test dataset is correctly classified. The equations for these metrics are shown below, where TruePos represents the occurrences of true positive results, TrueNeg represents the occurrences of true negative results, FalsePos represents the occurrences of false positive results, and FalseNeg represents the occurrences of false negative results.

Accuracy – It measures the correct number of predictions from the entire predictions and general performance measures.

$$Accuracy = \frac{TruePos + TrueNeg}{TruePos + FalsePos + TrueNeg + FalseNeg} \tag{1}$$

Precision It measures the model's accuracy as it measures the ratio between true positive and all the positive (True Positive added with False Positive).

$$Precision = \frac{TruePos}{TruePos + FalsePos} \tag{2}$$

---

[2] https://data.world/crowdflower/airline-twitter-sentiment.

Recall - It measures the model's ability to identify true positives correctly. It is the ratio of true positive and true positive added with false negative.

$$Recall = \frac{TruePos}{TruePos + FalseNeg} \tag{3}$$

F1 Score - The F1 score is an accuracy measure in our binary classification model and evaluates the numerical average of precision and recall. In many deep learning tasks, we come across situations that require high precision or recall, but both cannot be high simultaneously. There is a trade-off between Precision and Recall. We use the F1 score as the perfect valuating measure in such cases.

$$F_1\ Score = 2 * \frac{Precision * Recall}{Precision + Recall} \tag{4}$$

5   Result

Table 2 summarizes the sentiment analysis results on the Airline-quality sentiment dataset. Our proposed model achieved an overall accuracy of **91.32%**, outperforming the current state-of-the-art methods. Similarly, Table 3 summarizes the sentiment analysis results on the Twitter Airline dataset, where our model outperformed the current state-of-the-art model with an overall accuracy of **91.67%**. Furthermore, the precision, recall, and F1 score of our proposed model consistently improved on both datasets, as shown in Tables 2 and 3, indicating the effectiveness of our novel architecture for accurate sentiment analysis tasks. Additionally, the accuracy and loss graph of our proposed model on the Airline-quality and Twitter Airline datasets can be seen in Figs 2 and 3, respectively.

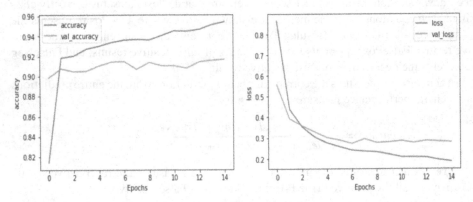

Fig. 2. Accuracy and Loss graph of the proposed model on Twitter Airline dataset

The results showcase that the CNN-BiLSTM model performs better in sentiment analysis of reviews than classical machine learning algorithms and other neural architectures like CNN, LSTM, and CNN-LSTM models.

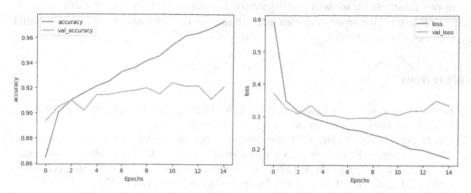

Fig. 3. Accuracy and Loss graph of the proposed model on Airline-quality sentiment dataset

Table 2. Accuracy, Precision, Recall and F1 Score for our proposed CNN-BiLSTM model on Airline-quality Dataset

Neural Networks	Accuracy	Precision	Recall	F1
CNN Network	85.0	83.2	81.1	82.3
LSTM Network	85.2	86.5	86.1	86.3
CNN-LSTM Network	90.2	87.8	87.0	87.6
Proposed CNN-BiLSTM Network	**91.32**	**94.64**	**89.19**	**91.83**

Table 3. Accuracy, Precision, Recall and F1 Score for our proposed CNN-BiLSTM model on Twitter Airline Dataset

Neural Networks	Accuracy	Precision	Recall	F1
CNN Network	87.1	83.0	81.1	82.5
LSTM Network	88.2	87.1	86.0	86.2
CNN-LSTM Network	91.3	87.8	87.0	87.5
Proposed CNN-BiLSTM Network	**91.67**	**93.32**	**96.03**	**94.65**

6 Conclusion

This chapter introduces a novel architecture that enhances sentiment analysis of user-generated data, particularly reviews. The chapter is concentrated on analyzing the sentiment associated with Airline-quality sentiment and Twitter Airline datasets. Our results indicate that the proposed model surpasses the current state-of-the-art model in sentiment analysis on these datasets. Additionally, the proposed model outperforms the state-of-the-art model in all evaluation metrics.

In our future work, we will investigate the impact of positional embedding on generating review vector representations and the impact of using attention as a sequential layer in the proposed model.

References

1. Bunk, T., Varshneya, D., Vlasov, V., Nichol, A.: Diet: lightweight language understanding for dialogue systems. arXiv preprint arXiv:2004.09936 (2020)
2. Du, J., Gui, L., Xu, R., He, Y.: A convolutional attention model for text classification. In: Natural Language Processing and Chinese Computing: 6th CCF International Conference, NLPCC 2017, Dalian, China, 8–12 Nov 2017, Proceedings 6. pp. 183–195. Springer (2018)
3. Gulli, A., Pal, S.: Deep Learning with Keras. Packt Publishing Ltd (2017)
4. Hemmatian, F., Sohrabi, M.K.: A survey on classification techniques for opinion mining and sentiment analysis. Artific. Intell. Rev. 52(3), 1495–1545 (2019)
5. Hochreiter, S., Schmidhuber, J.: Long short-term memory. Neural Comput. 9(8), 1735–1780 (1997)
6. Jain, P.K., Saravanan, V., Pamula, R.: A hybrid cnn-lstm: a deep learning approach for consumer sentiment analysis using qualitative user-generated contents. Trans. Asian Low-Resour. Lang. Inform. Process. 20(5), 1–15 (2021)
7. Kumar, S., Zymbler, M.: A machine learning approach to analyze customer satisfaction from airline tweets. J. Big Data 6(1), 1–16 (2019)
8. Lee, P.J., Hu, Y.H., Lu, K.T.: Assessing the helpfulness of online hotel reviews: a classification-based approach. Telematics Inform. 35(2), 436–445 (2018)
9. Mahto, D., Yadav, S.C., Lalotra, G.S.: Sentiment prediction of textual data using hybrid convbidirectional-lstm model. Mobile Inform. Syst. 2022 (2022)
10. Pennington, J., Socher, R., Manning, C.D.: Glove: global vectors for word representation. In: Empirical Methods in Natural Language Processing (EMNLP), pp. 1532–1543 (2014), http://www.aclweb.org/anthology/D14-1162
11. Seo, S., Kim, C., Kim, H., Mo, K., Kang, P.: Comparative study of deep learning-based sentiment classification. IEEE Access 8, 6861–6875 (2020)
12. Siering, M., Deokar, A.V., Janze, C.: Disentangling consumer recommendations: Explaining and predicting airline recommendations based on online reviews. Dec. Support Syst. 107, 52–63 (2018)
13. Tomar, A., Kumar, S., Pant, B., Tiwari, U.K.: Dynamic kernel CNN-LR model for people counting. Appl. Intell. 1–16 (2022)

Performance of Bayesian Networks Classification Models for Tuberculosis Patient Outcome Prediction with Imbalanced Dataset

Chun Yan Alvin Khoo[1] , Sau Loong Ang[2]([✉]) , Chia Yean Lim[3] ,
Arvindran Alaga[4] , and Wei Lian Willian Foh[1]

[1] UOW Malaysia KDU Penang University College, Penang, Malaysia
{0206002,0205930}@student.uow.edu.my
[2] Tunku Abdul Rahman University of Management and Technology, Penang Branch,
77, Lorong Lembah Permai 3, 11200 Tanjung Bungah, Pulau Pinang, Malaysia
angsl@tarc.edu.my
[3] Universiti Sains Malaysia, Penang, Malaysia
cylim@usm.my
[4] Hospital Sultanah Bahiyah, Alor Setar, Malaysia
arvindran_82@yahoo.com

Abstract. Tuberculosis (TB) is a long-existing disease that is still posing threats to human health. The challenge to end the widespread prevalence of TB has persisted for over a century. The research on predicting the no-show rate with machine learning is very limited. Hence, this study aims to classify TB patients accurately into two class values which are "follow-up for treatment" and "no follow-up for treatment". The study uses a dataset with 5036 instances and 12 attributes, which are used as nodes in the Bayesian Networks. The dataset underwent a pre-processing stage, including the use of the Classbalancer filter to address the class imbalance, and rebalanced the class distribution of instances to achieve the highest accuracy possible in the classification model. Several learning algorithms were employed in Bayesian Networks classification models. These algorithms include K2, Hill Climber, LAGD Hill Climber, Repeated Hill Climber, Simulated Annealing, and Tabu Search. The potential use of Bayesian networks in TB patient classification highlights the importance of applying machine learning in enhancing medical decision-making, which ultimately helps in lifesaving TB threats and planning strategies for arrogant patients who turn up to be "no follow-up" for TB treatment. A comparison study was conducted to evaluate the classification accuracy and other outcome indicators such as precision and recall. The study provides valuable insights into the use of machine learning in patient classification, emphasizing the potential for these technologies in revolutionizing healthcare decision-making based on each patient's classification outcome.

Keywords: Bayesian Network · Clinical Decision Support · Medical
Diagnosis · Learning algorithm

R. N. Shaw et al. (Eds.): ICACIS 2023, CCIS 1920, pp. 247–258, 2023.
https://doi.org/10.1007/978-3-031-45121-8_21

1 Introduction

Tuberculosis (TB) is a well-known disease that most often attacks and affects the human lungs and spreads to other parts of the body. At the beginning of the 19th century, it was the primary deadly cause of mortality globally, and eventually developed into a devastating epidemic. WHO developed a TB strategy for 2030, which envisions a world free of TB, with no deaths caused by TB, disease, or any suffering from TB [1]. In addition, the strategy ambitiously proposes to "end the global TB epidemic by 2035" [2–4]. Nevertheless, the progress on TB elimination still records the highest mortality among other diseases and infections worldwide with an alarming number of deaths reported. It even outnumbered HIV/AIDS, which caused 1.5 million deaths in 2018 [1]. The statistics on TB data do not meet the goal of eliminating TB, despite the efforts, investments, treatments, and research being made.

The recent rapid progress of artificial intelligence (AI) has sparked new interest in the field [5]. On tasks that were at the human level, AI produced outstanding outcomes. For instance, AI improves and synchronizes factors and data to improve medical records, collecting, and outcomes, which keeps track of the vital statistics data of patient records and provides real-time information to doctors and families. As a result, AI offers digital control toward precise diagnoses to boost the effectiveness of patient treatment, and decision-making, which aids in creating medical consultations based on the availability of data and the classification created [6].

AI has received a lot of attention in this advanced technology era because of its potential to give intelligent systems and devices useful functionality. Most people regard machine learning and deep learning to have the same presence, each representation stands for a distinct meaning and result. The goal of machine learning is to solve difficult issues with computational automation. It represents a system's ability to learn from specific problems based on training data and automate the analytics process without explicit scripting [7].

The data categorization model seeks to organize data into pertinent categories and to draw inferences based on the observed dataset or values. These aspects play a role in the process of organizing data. A classification model uses the input to attempt to anticipate potential outputs that could be used as labels on the dataset [8].

Bayesian networks which fall under the category of machine learning, a subset of AI, showed some promising results in classifying tuberculosis diagnosis and treatment outcomes [9]. Bayesian networks are believed to have significant potential in medical applications, particularly in disease diagnosis, predicting disease progression and treatment outcomes, and personalizing treatment plans. These models assist clinicians to make decisions based on complex patient data. It also helps them to make accurate diagnoses and treatment decisions.

2 Related Works

2.1 Medical Diagnosis

Machine learning has been playing an important role in medical diagnosis in recent years. Among the machine learning techniques used are convolutional neural network (CNN) and classification and regression tree (CART). In 2018, Zheng et al. [10] adopted

CNN for breast cancer diagnosis. In the same year, Wang et al. [11] used CART to detect liver fibrosis. Meanwhile, in 2021, Jiang et al. [12] built a deep learning-based model of CNN to predict the occurrences of hemorrhagic transformation after a stroke.

Some research findings found that the classification models showed great potential in TB diagnosis accuracy [13]. For example, Lee et al. [14] successfully developed a deep learning-based CNN model which could classify chest X-rays into two classes which are normal and abnormal. On the other hand, Li et al. [9] diagnosed liver disease by applying data such as symptoms, laboratory test results, and medical history into 3D convolution neural network (CNN) models. Lately, Misra et al. [15] also proposed a CNN model to evaluate chest X-ray images for screening for COVID-19. All the proposed models showed tremendous results with an accuracy of 94% [9, 14] and a specificity of 96.2% [15].

Besides predicting medical diagnosis, classification models could also predict treatment outcomes and suggest clinical decision makings [16, 17]. For example, A Bayesian Network model was applied in predicting the 2-year all-cause mortality of stage-4 or stage-5 chronic kidney disease patients [18]. The evaluation conducted by Velikzhanin [19] claimed that Bayesian network models were promising machine learning models to help in making wise decisions in healthcare. On the other hand, the comparison study between machine learning and conventional statistical models also discovered that machine learning outperformed statistical models in making better healthcare predictions in heart failure readmission and mortality [20]. These studies demonstrate the potential of machine learning and data analytics in medical diagnosis and highlight the importance of selecting appropriate algorithms and features for building accurate and efficient models [21, 22].

2.2 Bayesian Network

Bayesian networks are built into directed acyclic graphs based on the conditional probability generated from the variables in a dataset by implementing Bayes' Theorem [23]. The causal relationships between the variables in Bayesian networks provide insight views and knowledge in identifying critical uncertainties among the empirical data. Bayesian networks provide a reliable method for performing risk analysis based on probability obtained from the frequency of a dataset. It is a strong and fundamental tool in decision science, offering an advantage to a user [24].

As seen Eq. 1, is the fundamental equation based on Bayes Theorem,

$$P(A|B) = (P(B|A)P(A))/P(B) \tag{1}$$

where $P(A|B)$ is the posterior probability of an event A, given an event B, $P(B|A)$ is the likelihood probability, $P(A)$ is the prior probability of the event A, and the $P(B)$ is the marginal probability of the event B.

Besides, Bayesian network learning is divided into two stages, which are the stage of structure learning and the stage of parameter learning. Structure learning focuses on discovering the optimum approach to create a Bayesian network, while parameter learning emphasizes learning about conditional probability distributions [25]. Equation (2) shows the joint distribution over a set of n random variables which is labeled as $X = (X_1, \ldots, X_n)$ and the conditional probability of each variable given its parent, labeled as Pai for i = 1, 2, 3,…,n. This joint distribution allows for linking dependencies between nodes in a Bayesian network and creating a classifier that provides the posterior probability distribution of the variable given the conditional probability of other attributes based on the training data and variables [26].

$$P_B(X_1, \ldots, X_n) = \prod_{i=1}^{n} P(X_i | Pa_i) \qquad (2)$$

The Bayesian network uses these parameters to create a classifier that provides the posterior probability distribution of the variable given the conditional probability of other attributes based on the training data and variables [26]. The outcome can be represented by probabilities for various features, methods for making accurate decisions regarding risk assessments, and risk management [27]. Probabilistic classification is the process of finding the highest class value for the posterior probability of a class given a set of assigned attributes.

3 Proposed Method

This section outlines the proposed methodology, including the research purpose, flow, data pre-processing, algorithm implementation, dataset, and evaluation metrics.

3.1 Research Purpose

Tuberculosis (TB) is a very alarming public health issue, causing devastating impacts such as high death tolls, loss of money due to negligence of TB patients to seek treatment, and endless spread of TB infections [28]. Despite many efforts and progress made in halting the widespread of TB disease, to control TB disease, the threat remains at large, especially to human health with 1.5 million deaths globally recorded in 2018 [1].

In battling TB disease, WHO has poured in many initiatives and efforts in developing a global TB strategy for 2030. The organization aimed to end the global TB epidemic by 2035 as one of its ambitious goals.

To echo the urge of WHO, this study targets to implement Bayesian networks with various learning algorithms to classify TB patient outcomes. With the classification model in place, it is expected to help doctors, medical officers, and nurses to give the best advice and treatments to the infected patients.

This research is expected to assist in improving the accuracy of TB patient classification and lead to a decrease in TB-related morbidity and mortality rates with appropriate and precise treatment.

3.2 Dataset

The dataset used in this study was taken from a nationwide retrospective cohort study in South Africa. The cohort study assessed the impact of Gene Xpert MTB/RIF implementation on treatment initiation [29]. Gene Xpert MTB/RIF is a diagnostic test performed on a patient to detect TB and to test the patient whether he or she has drug-resistant TB. This test is highly accurate in assisting medical practitioners to prescribe treatments for TB patients.

MTB stands for Mycobacterium Tuberculosis, which causes TB disease. If one is detected with the presence of MTB, it indicates that he or she is infected with TB disease. RIF is known as Rifampicin, a first-line drug commonly used to treat TB disease. If a patient is found to be resistant to this drug via Gene Xpert MTB/RIF test, he or she cannot be treated with the usual first-line TB treatment but needs a treatment regime with a second-line TB treatment for up to 18 months.

The dataset classified the patients into two major groups "follow-up for treatment" or "no follow-up for treatment" after diagnosis via Gene Xpert MTB/RIF. The dataset revealed a large treatment gap for the patients who are resistant to RIF in South Africa. The dataset varied significantly across provinces, where an imbalance between classes is a common issue in medical datasets. The imbalanced dataset presents a challenge for machine learning during the training process, as the results are overwhelmed by the majority of instances. Dealing with imbalanced datasets is a challenging task in machine learning. When the number of instances in one class greatly exceeds the number of instances in another class, the classifier becomes biased toward the majority class, leaving poor classification results for the minority class.

The ClassBalancer filter in Weka [30] can be applied to address the imbalanced class distribution. This technique involves re-weighting the classes based on their frequencies and can improve the performance of classifiers even when the dataset is highly imbalanced. The classifier can achieve a more balanced classification performance, which is especially important in cases where the minority class is of particular interest [31]. There is a need to balance the class distribution in the dataset to ensure that the classifier is accurately capturing the patterns in both the majority and minority classes [32].

3.3   Research Flow

The research flow for this project involves several key steps. Firstly, the TB dataset, which comprises various patient attributes and follow-up results, is loaded into the project. The dataset is then pre-processed using Weka to remove columns with rows containing dummy values.

In addition, the ClassBalancer filter is implemented to make a balance between the two class values. The imbalance of class values tends to produce biased classification results. These pre-processing steps are very significant to determine the consistent performance of classification models to provide high-accuracy classification results.

The classification models based on Bayesian Networks with various learning algorithms will be evaluated based on two scenarios, which are the classification with the ClassBalancer filter, and the classification without the ClassBalancer filter.

In summary, this research flow ensures that the pre-processed dataset is effectively utilized to train a proficient model that can be utilized for accurate predictions and improve TB treatment outcomes.

3.4 Data Preprocessing

The dataset used in this study exhibited class imbalance, with one class having a significantly larger number of instances than the other. To address this issue, various data preprocessing techniques were employed, including removing redundant attributes and dropping rows with missing or unknown values. Despite these efforts, the class imbalance remained, with 3309 instances of the class "Yes" and only 1727 instances of the class "No". This imbalance can have a detrimental effect on the performance of machine learning models, as they may be biased toward the majority class, leading to poor performance in the minority class. Therefore, the ClassBalancer filter can be applied to increase the weight of the minority class to improve the performance of machine learning models trained on imbalanced datasets.

Table 1 shows the weight assigned to each class before balancing while Table 2 shows the weight assigned to each class after balancing the dataset, where the "Yes" class is from 4949 to 2518, while the "No" class is from 87 to 2518. The weight assigned is inversely proportional to the frequency of its class, since the "No" class is the minority class, its weight will be lower compared to the "Yes" class after balancing the dataset. The main reason for balancing the dataset is not to equalize the weights of each class, but rather to reduce the bias towards the majority class and improve the overall performance of the machine learning model. It helps to upgrade the performance of the machine learning model by balancing the class distribution in the dataset.

Table 1. Class distribution before ClassBalancer filter in Weka.

Class	Count	Weight
Yes	4949	4949
No	87	87
Total	5036	

Table 2. Class distribution after ClassBalancer filter in Weka.

Class	Count	Weight
Yes	4949	2518
No	87	2518
Total	5036	

3.5 Algorithm Implementation

Six algorithms are implemented for performance comparison of the Bayesian network-based classification model's learning algorithms: Hill Climber, Repeated Hill Climber,

LAGD Hill Climber, K2, Simulated Annealing, and Tabu Search [33, 34]. The parameters of the Bayesian Network were learned by using these algorithms, based on a set of training data. We defined the structure of the Bayesian Network using the attributes relevant to predicting patient outcomes and then used each algorithm to learn the conditional probabilities which are associated with each of the nodes in the network.

K2 is a heuristic algorithm that uses a score function to evaluate the quality of different network structures, while Hill Climber is a local search algorithm that gradually improves the quality of the current network structure by making small changes [35]. LAGD Hill Climber is a variant of Hill Climber that uses gradient descent to prevent the scenario of getting stuck in local optima. Repeated Hill Climber randomly restarts the search to avoid getting stuck in a local optimum [36], while Simulated Annealing serves as a global optimization algorithm that can escape local optima by allowing some uphill moves [37]. Tabu Search is another global optimization algorithm that uses a tabu list to avoid revisiting previously explored solutions [38].

Different learning algorithms can be applied to a Bayesian network-based classification model to find the most optimal structure of the network for a specific dataset. Each algorithm has its strengths and weaknesses, and the selection of the algorithm can affect the quality of the final model. For instance, K2 is a popular algorithm due to its speed and ability to handle a large number of nodes, while Hill Climbing is a simpler algorithm that can handle noisy data but may get stuck in local optima. Tabu Search is a more complex algorithm that can handle a wider range of datasets, but it requires more computational resources. By comparing the performance of different learning algorithms, researchers can determine which algorithm is most suitable for a specific dataset and optimize the classification model accordingly.

3.6   Evaluation Metrics

The ClassBalancer filter was used to correct the class imbalance following the TB patient dataset performed pre-processing. For the goal of evaluating the data, 10-fold cross-validation was applied to assess each algorithm. Precision, recall, accuracy, and F1 score as the evaluation measures that may be used to evaluate the effectiveness of the classification models [39]. The confusion matrix, on the other hand, is the most straightforward and popular evaluation metric [40]. The number of accurate and inaccurate predictions produced by the classification model will be tabulated in a confusion matrix. The true positives (TP), false positives (FP), true negatives (TN), and false negatives (FN) rates will be shown in tables to tabulate the classification model results, to compare and analyze the effectiveness of each technique. These proportions can be used to determine evaluation criteria like sensitivity, specificity, and the overall accuracy of the model.

Several metrics, such as precision, recall, accuracy, and F1-score, were seen to analyze the machine learning models' outputs. The confusion matrix, however, offers an outline of the performance of the model by displaying the number of true positives, true negatives, false positives, and false negatives. It is the most straightforward and often-used statistic.

Table 3 provides a tabular representation of predicted and actual class labels that helps in evaluating the performance. FP and FN represent cases that were wrongly classified, whereas TP and TN show the number of occurrences that were correctly classified. Other evaluation metrics like precision, recall, and F1-score can also be computed using the confusion matrix.

Table 3. Confusion Matrix.

	Predicted No Follow-up	Predicted Follow-up
Actual No Follow-up	TN (true negative)	FP (false positive)
Actual Follow-up	FN (false negative)	TP (true positive)

4 Experimental Results

Despite pre-processing the TB patient dataset, class imbalance persisted. The ClassBalancer filter using Weka was applied to mitigate the impact of class imbalance on the machine learning model, and the model was trained using Weka. To improve the accuracy of the classification model, rebalances the class distribution of instances, addressing the class imbalance in machine learning.

The class distribution of the datasets was tabulated to comprehend the differences between the original dataset and the dataset after applying the ClassBalancer filter. Before using the ClassBalancer filter, the class distribution revealed a major imbalance with a small percentage of patients needing follow-up treatment. The class distribution improved when the ClassBalancer filter was applied, with the minority class having a better representation in the dataset. In a real-world example, Javed et al. [41] used the ClassBalancer filter in their study to handle a class imbalance in a dataset for predicting credit card fraud. The results showed that using the ClassBalancer filter significantly improved the classification model's accuracy. This example highlights the importance of handling class imbalance in machine learning models and the potential impact it can have on the performance of the model.

Bayesian networks are useful in identifying the majority and minority classes in the dataset. They are specifically employed to handle class imbalance datasets due to their ability to capture the relationships between the attributes and the class variable. In other words, the Bayesian Networks help to identify the patterns in the data which are significant to determining the classification for the minority class.

Results of the experiment (refer to Tables 4 and 5) suggest that different machine learning algorithms may perform differently when dealing with class imbalance. Some algorithms may be more sensitive to class imbalance than others and may require additional techniques such as the ClassBalancer filter to achieve optimal performance. In the experiment, several machine learning algorithms are evaluated, including K2, Hillclimber, LAGDHC, Repeated Hillclimber, Simulated Annealing, and Tabu Search.

The results showed that some algorithms performed better than others and that the ClassBalancer filter was particularly effective in improving the accuracy of the models trained using K2 and Hillclimber.

Table 4. Distribution of TB Patient Data Before ClassBalancer Filter.

Learning algorithm	TP Rate	FP Rate	Precision	Recall	F-Measure	MCC	ROC Area	PRC Area
K2	0.972	0.576	0.977	0.972	0.975	0.330	0.946	0.986
HillClimber	0.973	0.622	0.977	0.973	0.975	0.308	0.947	0.985
LAGDHC	0.983	0.983	NA	0.983	NA	NA	0.884	0.982
RepeatedHC	0.973	0.622	0.977	0.973	0.975	0.308	0.947	0.985
Simulated Annealing	0.980	0.904	0.972	0.980	0.975	0.139	0.943	0.986
TabuSearch	0.974	0.610	0.977	0.974	0.976	0.326	0.948	0.985

Table 5. Distribution of TB Patient Data After ClassBalancer Filter.

Learning algorithm	TP Rate	FP Rate	Precision	Recall	F-Measure	MCC	ROC Area	PRC Area
K2	0.890	0.110	0.890	0.890	0.890	0.780	0.947	0.945
HillClimber	0.896	0.104	0.897	0.896	0.896	0.793	0.949	0.946
LAGDHC	0.894	0.106	0.896	0.894	0.894	0.791	0.884	0.860
RepeatedHC	0.896	0.104	0.897	0.896	0.896	0.793	0.949	0.946
Simulated Annealing	0.960	0.140	0.861	0.860	0.860	0.721	0.927	0.923
TabuSearch	0.902	0.098	0.905	0.902	0.902	0.806	0.951	0.947

The results of this study indicate how class imbalance can significantly affect the way that machine learning models its intended purpose. The TB patient dataset's initial distribution revealed a significant class imbalance, with the dominant class being over-represented. The classification models produced a biased result towards the majority class, as they tended to predict occurrences as belonging to the dominant class. However, the class distribution was balanced after using Weka to apply the ClassBalancer filter, leading to a better classification model.

One of the prominent methods for dealing with a class imbalance is machine learning models. It functions by adjusting the distribution of instances of a class to ensure either the majority class instances or the minority class instances are undersampled. This balances the class distribution and can improve the classification model's accuracy. As a result of using the ClassBalancer filter to balance the class distribution of the TB patient dataset in our experiment, the classification models' accuracy was significantly improved and balanced. The outcomes of our study emphasize how crucial it is for machine learning models to handle class imbalance distribution. Biased models can result from class imbalance since they frequently overestimate the majority class and underestimate the minority class. This can have serious consequences in real-world applications, such as in healthcare or finance, where accurate predictions are critical. The ClassBalancer filter is a useful technique for addressing class imbalance and can help to improve the accuracy of machine learning models.

5 Conclusion and Future Works

Based on the findings and outcomes shown, a conclusion can be made on the impact of extreme distribution for class values which caused imbalance and bias is great. For this dataset, a comparison performance is conducted based on Bayesian networks with different learning algorithms in TB patient classification. The results showed a gap in accuracy and other evaluation metrics between the dataset with the implementation of the ClassBalancer filter and without the ClassBalancer filter. The ClassBalancer filter played a significant role in determining the improvement of accuracy for the TB patient classification.

The application of the ClassBalancer filter in Weka not only helped to address the class imbalance issue but also improved the accuracy of the classification model for different learning algorithms applied on Bayesian networks as the model for TB patient classification. These findings are particularly relevant to real-world applications such as healthcare, where accurate predictions are critical. Future research can further explore the application of the ClassBalancer to other datasets and learning algorithms, as well as investigate other techniques for handling class imbalance.

In terms of future work, this research is planned to expand and collaborate with local authorities and hospitals to obtain datasets that are specific to the Malaysian context. It is believed that this research could have a significant impact in Malaysia, as there has been no similar research conducted in the country. This work highlights the potential for machine learning models to improve TB treatment and contribute to better healthcare outcomes.

References

1. Harding, E.: Who global progress report on tuberculosis elimination. Lancet Respir. Med. **8**(1), 19 (2020)
2. WHO: Consolidated guidelines on tuberculosis. Module 2: Screening – systematic screening for tuberculosis disease. World Health Organization, Geneva (2021)
3. WHO: Operational handbook on tuberculosis. Module 2: Screening – systematic screening for tuberculosis disease. World Health Organization, Geneva (2021)
4. WHO: Consolidated guidelines on tuberculosis. Module 3: Diagnosis – rapid diagnostics for tuberculosis detection 2021 update. World Health, Geneva (2021)
5. Aldahiri, A., Alrashed, B., Hussain, W.: Trends in using IoT with machine learning in health prediction system. Forecasting **3**(1), 181–206 (2021)
6. Charon, C., Wuillemin, P.H., Belmin, J.: Learning bayesian networks for the prediction of unfavorable health events in nursing homes. Challenges of Trustable AI and Added-Value on Health, pp. 147–148. IOS Press (2022)
7. Davenport, T., Kalakota, R.: The potential for artificial intelligence in healthcare. Future Healthcare J. **6**(2), 94–98 (2019)

8. Saravanan, R., Sujatha, P.: A state of art techniques on machine learning algorithms: a perspective of supervised learning approaches in Data Classification. In: 2018 Second International Conference on Intelligent Computing and Control Systems (ICICCS), pp. 945–949 (2018)
9. Li, X., Zhou, Y., Du, P., Lang, G., Xu, M., Wu, W.: A deep learning system that generates quantitative CT reports for diagnosing pulmonary tuberculosis. Appl. Intell. 51(6), 4082–4093 (2020)
10. Zheng, Y., Yang, C., Merkulov, A.: Breast cancer screening using convolutional neural network and follow-up digital mammography. Comput. Imaging III Int. Soc. Opt. Photon. 10669, 1066905 (2018)
11. Wáng, Y.X.J., et al.: A combined use of intravoxel incoherent motion MRI parameters can differentiate early-stage hepatitis-b fibrotic livers from healthy livers. SLAS Technol. Transl. Life Sci. Innov. 23(3), 259–268 (2018)
12. Jiang, L., Zhou, L., Yong, W., Cui, J., Geng, W., Chen, H.: A deep learning-based model for prediction of hemorrhagic transformation after stroke. Brain Pathol. 33, e13023 (2023)
13. Chen, J., Dai, X., Yuan, Q., Lu, C., Huang, H.: Towards interpretable clinical diagnosis with Bayesian network ensembles stacked on entity-aware CNNs. In: Proceedings of the 58th Annual Meeting of the Association for Computational Linguistics, pp. 3143–3153 (2020)
14. Lee, J.-G., et al.: Deep learning in medical imaging: general overview. Korean J. Radiol. 18(4), 570 (2017)
15. Misra, S., Jeon, S., Lee, S., Managuli, R., Jang, I.S., Kim, C.: Multi-channel transfer learning of chest X-ray images for screening of COVID-19. Electronics 9(9), 1388 (2020)
16. Pan, Y., Fu, M., Cheng, B., Tao, X., Guo, J.: Enhanced deep learning assisted convolutional neural network for heart disease prediction on the internet of medical things platform. IEEE Access 8, 189503–189512 (2020)
17. Mridha, K., et al.: Deep learning algorithms are used to automatically detection invasive ducal carcinoma in whole slide images. In: 2021 IEEE 6th International Conference on Computing, Communication and Automation (ICCCA), pp. 123–129. Arad, Romania (2021). https://doi.org/10.1109/ICCCA52192.2021.9666302
18. Tran, N.T.D., Balezeaux, M., Granal, M., Fouque, D., Ducher, M., Fauvel, J.P.: Prediction of all-cause mortality for chronic kidney disease patients using four models of machine learning. Nephrol. Dial. Transplant. Vol. 316 (2022)
19. Velikzhanin, A., Wang, B., Kwiatkowska, M.: Bayesian network models of causal interventions in healthcare decision making: literature review and software evaluation. arXiv preprint arXiv:2211.15258 (2022)
20. Shin, S., et al.: Machine learning vs. conventional statistical models for predicting heart failure readmission and mortality. ESC Heart Failure 8, 106– 115 (2021)
21. Ferdous, M., Debnath, J., Chakraborty, R.N.: Machine learning algorithms in healthcare: a literature survey. In: 2020 11th International Conference on Computing, Communication and Networking Technologies (ICCCNT), pp. 1–6 (2020)
22. Cascella, M., et al.: Bayesian network analysis for prediction of unplanned hospital readmissions of cancer patients with breakthrough cancer pain and complex care needs. Healthcare 10(10), 1853 (2022)
23. Fenton, N.E., Neil, M.: Risk Assessment and Decision Analysis with Bayesian Networks. CRC Press, Boca Raton (2019)
24. Aalders, I.: Modeling land-use decision behavior with Bayesian belief networks. Ecol. Soc. 13(1) (2008)
25. Ji, Z., Xia, Q. Meng, G.: A review of Parameter Learning Methods in Bayesian network. Lect. Notes Comput. Sci. 3–12 (2015)
26. Ang, S.L., Ong, H.C., Low, H.C.: Classification using the general Bayesian network. Pertanika J. Sci. Technol. 24(1), 205–211 (2016)

27. Marcot, B.G., Penman, T.D.: Advances in bayesian network modeling: integration of modeling technologies. Environ. Model. Softw. **111**, 386–393 (2019)
28. Global tuberculosis report 2022, World Health Organization. https://www.who.int/publicati ons/i/item/9789240061729. Accessed 27 April 2023
29. Cox, H., Dickson-Hall, L., Ndjeka, N., van't Hoog, A., Grant, A., Cobelens F., et al.: Delays and loss to follow-up before treatment of drug-resistant tuberculosis following implementation of Xpert MTB/RIF in South Africa: a retrospective cohort study. PLoS Med **14**(2), e1002238 (2017)
30. Frank, E., Hall, A.M., Witten, I.H.: The WEKA workbench. online appendix for data mining: practical machine learning tools and techniques, Morgan Kaufmann, Fourth Edition (2016)
31. Weiss, G.M.: Mining with rarity. ACM SIGKDD Explor. Newsl **6**(1), 7–19 (2004)
32. He, H., Garcia, E.A.: Learning from imbalanced data. IEEE Trans. Knowl. Data Eng. **21**(9), 1263–1284 (2009)
33. Chickering, D.M.: Learning bayesian networks is NP-complete. In: Fisher, D., Lenz, HJ. (eds.) Learning from Data. LNS, vol. 112. Springer, New York, NY (1996). https://doi.org/ 10.1007/978-1-4612-2404-4_12
34. Koller, D., Friedman, N.: Probabilistic Graphical Models Principles and Techniques. MIT Press, Cambridge, Mass (2012)
35. Cooper, G.F., Herskovits, E.: A bayesian method for the induction of probabilistic networks from data. Mach. Learn. **9**(4), 309–347 (1992)
36. Margaritis, D.: Learning Bayesian network model structure from data. Dissertation, Carnegie-Mellon Univ Pittsburgh Pa School of Computer Science (2003)
37. Kirkpatrick, S., Gelatt, C.D., Vecchi, M.P.: Optimization by simulated annealing. Science **220**(4598), 671–680 (1983)
38. Glover, F.: Future paths for integer programming and links to Artificial Intelligence. Comput. Oper. Res. **13**(5), 533–549 (1986)
39. Pierre, B., Soren, B.: Bioinformatics the Machine Learning Approach. Affiliated East-West Press P. Ltd, New Delhi (2003)
40. Sokolova, M., Lapalme, G.: A systematic analysis of performance measures for classification tasks. Inf. Process. Manage. **45**(4), 427–437 (2009)
41. Javed, Z., et al.: Policy gradient bayesian robust optimization for im-itation learning. In: International Conference on Machine Learning, pp. 4785–4796 (2021)

Development of Facial Emotion Recognition System Using Unimodal and Multimodal Approach

Shwetkranti Taware[1][✉] and Anuradha D. Thakare[2]

[1] Research Scholar, Department of Computer Engineering, Pimpri Chichwad College of Engineering, Pune, India
shweta.taware@gmail.com
[2] Department of Computer Science and Engineering (AI&ML), Pimpri Chinchwad College of Engineering, Pune, India
anuradha.thakare@pccoepune.org

Abstract. The lack of very precise emotion recognition in current human-computer interactions (HCI) is a technology gap. In their interactions with people, these systems are unable to adequately identify, express, and feel emotions. They continue to be less sensitive to human emotions. Facial emotion recognition attempts this gap by recognising emotions with help of different feature extraction techniques like local binary pattern, histogram of oriented gradients, Gabor filter and Scale-invariant feature transform. The feature technique has been evaluated on extended Cohn Kanade database (CK + 48). Nowadays deep learning used for facial emotion recognition due to increased size of dataset like FER 2013 and RAF-DB dataset. Convolution network has been evaluated on two mentioned datasets with highest accuracy. At last Convolution Neural Network (CNN) has applied on multimodal dataset i.e. Emotic to recognise emotion in context. It recognises almost categories of emotion. Compared to existing works the coverage of different emotions is increased by 5% in multimodal emotion recognition.

Keywords: Facial Emotion recognition (FER) · local binary pattern · histogram of oriented gradients · Gabor filter and Scale-invariant feature transform · Context Awareness

1 Introduction

Emotion has valuable information about human behaviour. The most recent studies prove that emotions are effective and increases contribution in decision making applications [1]. Perceiving emotions is ability to identify, interpret emotion from face images, audio etc. Emotions can be perceived through the different human non behaviour cues like facial expression, speech, physiological signals like EEG, ECG etc. Nowadays, Emotion recognition is primary focus of Human Computer Interaction researchers. Moreover, many human mental disorders like anxiety, depression relevant to emotions [2, 3]. Hence there is need of automatic emotion recognition techniques to communicate between human and machine. The unimodal emotion recognition systems usually explore independently the prominent features for the emotion of interest from one specific modality.

© The Author(s), under exclusive license to Springer Nature Switzerland AG 2023
R. N. Shaw et al. (Eds.): ICACIS 2023, CCIS 1920, pp. 259–268, 2023.
https://doi.org/10.1007/978-3-031-45121-8_22

The face is the most widely used cues of human nonverbal behaviour for emotion recognition [4]. As the face is visible in first sight, commands attention and location of all sense of organs. There are four kinds of face signal systems: static, slow, artificial, and rapid signs. Rapid signs give information about emotion and mood. There are two main methods to measure momentary facial movement (Expression).

1. Message Judgment approach
2. Sign Signal based Approach

In Sign Signal based Approach, three methods for measuring facial sign vehicles i.e. Manual Coding, Recognition of faces Electromyography (EMG) and Automatic facial analysis. Nowadays researcher made significant progress in facial emotion recognition domain.

Section 2 describes related work of the facial emotion recognition with different feature extraction technique. Section 3 Implementation of HOG (Histogram of oriented Gradients), Local Binary Pattern (LBP), SIFT (Scale-invariant feature transform) and Gabor filter on CK+ dataset. Section 3.2 describes the deep learning model for facial emotion recognition on FER2013 and RafDB dataset. Section 3.3 describes the context aware multimodal emotion recognition with two modals body posture and image on Emotic dataset.

2   Related Work

Cohn et al. [5] was among the earliest efforts towards automatic evaluation of depression through facial image analysis. Active Appearance Models (AAM) used with Support Vector Machines (SVM) On the Pittsburgh dataset, we achieved 79% overall accuracy for binary classification (depressed vs. non-depressed). Alghowinemet et al. [6] 128 statistical characteristics ("functional") were calculated in total. A distances between eyelids and eye corners with SVM for the classification and On the BlackDog dataset, we acquired 88.3% recall (i.e., sensibility) for the identical binary issue. A.Thakare et al. [17] proposed Word2Vec tool for establishing an expanded phrase list for depression, which backed up the study's recommendation of a preliminary screening algorithm for microblogs suspected of depression. It also recognised and indicated depression by collecting and evaluating social media data from microblogs of college students. According to experimental results on the microblog dataset of college students, the complete lexical technique exceeds the SDS questionnaire segmentation method in terms of screening accuracy, with a screening accuracy rate of 65.7%. Pampouchidou et al. [8] concentrated on dynamic facial expression descriptions, using Image of motion history merged with expression-based feature extraction techniques (local binary patterns, histogram of directed gradients) and optical geometric characteristics of groups created using deep learning networks by transfer learning and also compares proposed method on new dataset and AVEC. A.Thakare et al. [9] proposed method immediate access to EEG data and might quickly and accurately recognize depressed states in the absence of the need such as feature extraction either processing. The method proposed in this study outperforms prior methods with Depression is differentiated with 99.08% accuracy, 98.77% sensitivity, and 99.42% specificity. Pampouchidou et al. [10] centred on methodologies and techniques for optical feature extraction, reducing dimensionality, selection techniques for regression and classification methods, and various merging tactics for automated depression detection. Tackle unresolved challenges by developing automated, objective evaluation systems that may be used across research and clinical practise.

Subudhiray et al. [11] proposed a facial emotion recognition system based on K nearest neighbour algorithm. Facial features extracted based on pictures of faces by utilising Gabor filter, Local Binary Pattern (LBP), and Histogram Oriented Gradient (HOG). The Knn with Gabor filter method was able to achieve abest average accuracy of 94.8% but required more computational time for six basic emotions.

Hassan et al. [12] used facial image to detect emotions using graph data mining. Dlib is used to extract features from facial image. The features are classified to emotion using a binary classification. To find frequent subgraphs for emotion used the concepts of graph mining. The method based on graph mining gives the accuracy 90.00%.

Li et al. [13] proposed2D+3D multimodal face expression recognition approach based on features was put out. A vast number of automatically recognised landmarks are used to fully automate it. Comprehensive evidence is provided for the complementarities between 2D and 3D features. The technique has so far produced the highest accuracy on BU-3DFE databases.

Laxmi et al. [14] proposed, An innovative feature descriptor for face emotion detection suggested based on enhanced Local Binary Pattern (LBP) and Histogram of Oriented Gradients (HOG) feature descriptors. Extracted features are reduced with the help of deep stack autoencoder and passed to multi-class Support Vector Machine to classify and recognise the categorical emotion.

Mehendale [15] proposed two level facial emotion recognition based on convolution neural network (CNN). The method takes away the backdrop from images in first level and emotion recognised using CNN.

Ghosh et al. [16] proposed Late Hill Climbing and Memetic algorithm for selecting non redundant and relevant facial feature for emotion recognition. The algorithm used more effective local search by combining the concept of minimal Redundancy Maximal-Relevance and Local Hill-Climbing. The algorithms reduce the feature dimension and increase the accuracy of emotion recognition.

A.Thakare et al. [17] Suggested critical viewpoint Text data is encrypted, a semantic representation is produced, and the parameters are trained. The Weibo classification of negative emotions is implemented using the BiLSTM model, and the preferences are also modified. The MAML metalearner utilises machine gradient descent to examine the total losses through different training sessions and courses, then does a second gradient descent that adjusts the metalearner parameters. The improved metalearner is capable of quickly adapting to novel Weibo content classification issues.The proposed method gives 1.68%, 2.86%, and 2.27% the respective precision rate,recall rate and F1-score.

3 Proposed Facial Emotion Recognition System Using Unimodal and Multimodal Approach

3.1 Facial Feature Extraction Technique

In this section HOG, Gabor filter, LBP, and Scale-invariant feature transform (SIFT)-based feature extraction technique are explained and implemented on CK+48 [18] dataset.

3.1.1 Histogram of Oriented Gradients

HOG [19] is histogram of gradients for describing the texture based facial feature. It extracts contrast in different regions of images in feature vector. It takes face image, resize it. After that, its finds gradient (change in image intensity) in x and y direction in terms of magnitude and direction. It will be mapping these calculated values in bins (Angle values) for computing histogram. The final feature vector is produced by merging each cell's histograms. To extract HOG feature from CK+, 48* 48 Image dimensions are being taken to considerations. The final feature vectors were created after applying HOG feature descriptors to each face expression picture. Figure 1 shows the sample HOG facial descriptor.

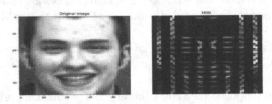

Fig. 1. HOG facial descriptor

To recognise emotion, sequential model has been applied on final feature vector generated by HOG as shown in Table 1.

The training accuracy of applied sequential model is 61.92% for the five number of epochs.

LBP [20] is a useful texture-based feature extraction technique. It takes intensities differences of middle pixel with surrounding pixels to capture the edge properties. With size of kernel 3 * 3, comparing eight surrounding pixels with middle pixel. If the result of distinction in between centre pixels and all of the adjacent pixels was more than zero, if yes than 1 was assigned; otherwise 0. Middle pixel represented by LBP code. The final feature vectors were produced by applying LBP feature descriptors to each face expression picture. Figure 2 shows the sample LBP facial descriptor.

To recognise emotion, sequential model as described in Table 1 has been applied on final feature vector generated by LBP.The training accuracy is 68.52% for the five number of epochs.

SIFT [21] is has a vast majority of applications in computer vision. It extracts SIFT descriptors on seven selected key points. It Includes 4 points around the lips at different

Table 1. Sequential Model

Layer (type)	Output Shape	Param #
conv2d (Conv2D)	(None, 48, 48, 6)	156
max_pooling2d (MaxPooling2D)	(None, 24, 24, 6)	0
conv2d_1 (Conv2D)	(None, 24, 24, 16)	2416
max_pooling2d_1 (MaxPooling2	(None, 12, 12, 16)	0
conv2d_2 (Conv2D	(None, 10, 10, 64)	9280
max_pooling2d_2 (MaxPooling2	(None, 5, 5, 64)	0
flatten (Flatten)	(None, 1600)	0
dense (Dense)	(None, 128)	204928
dropout (Dropout)	(None, 128)	0
dense_1 (Dense)	(None, 7)	903

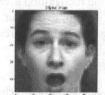 

Fig. 2. LBP facial descriptor

location on lip, 1 point at the centre of each eye, 1point on the nose base.Feature vector is achieved by concatenating the SIFT descriptor extracted on these points. To recognise emotion sequential model described in table 1 has been applied on final feature vector generated by SIFT.The training accuracy is 79% for the five number of epochs.Fig. 3 shows the sample SIFT facial descriptor.

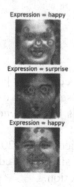 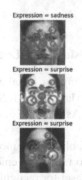 

Fig. 3. SIFT Filtered feature.

A popular frequency-based feature descriptor is the Gabor filter. [22]. The Gabor filter is primarily concerned with detecting the existence of explicit frequency information in a specific direction inside an area that is relevant or focused region related to the centre of attention in the picture. It is also scale, rotation, and translation insensitive. After applying Gabor filter on CK+images, one of the following sample Gabor filtered image shown in Fig. 4.

Fig. 4. Gabor Filtered Image.

To recognise emotion sequential model has been applied on final feature vector generated by Gabor filter. The training emotion recognition accuracy is 86% for the five number of epochs. At the last without any feature extraction, a model achieves 83% accuracy for emotion recognition. Following table shows the result of feature extraction techniques on CK+48 dataset (Table 2).

Table 2. Comparison of Feature Extraction Techniques

Filter	Accuracy%(5 epochs)
HOG	61
LBP	69
SIFT	79
GABOR	86
Without any Feature extraction tech	83

3.2 Facial Emotion Recognition Using Deep Learning

Nowadays researchers use deep learning for facial emotion recognition [23–26]. CNN has been applied on FER2013 [27] dataset. FER2013 dataset consist of test dataset (3591) and training dataset (28221).As the size of dataset is high, it's not feasible to apply feature extraction filters.

Following training described in Table 3.CNN model applied on FER2013 train data. It results in 91% training accuracy to recognise emotion. It also achieved accuracy of 87.21% on RAF-DB dataset [28] dataset for recognising emotion.

Table 3. CNN model

Layer (type)	Output Shape	Param #
conv2d_1 (Conv2D)	(None, 48, 48, 32)	320
conv2d_2 (Conv2D)	(None, 48, 48, 64)	18496
batch_normalization_1	(Batch (None, 48, 48, 64)	256
max_pooling2d_1 (MaxPooling2	(None, 24, 24, 64)	0
dropout 1(Dropout)	(None, 24, 24, 64)	0
conv2d_3(Conv2D)	(None,24, 24, 128)	73856
conv2d_4 (Conv2D)	(None, 22, 22, 256)	295168
batch_normalization_2	(Batch (None, 22, 22, 256)	1024
dropout 2(Dropout)	(None, 11, 11, 256)	0
flatten_1 (Flatten)	(None, 30976)	0
dense_1 (Dense)	(None, 1024)	31720448
dropout_3 (Dropout)	(None, 1024)	0
dense_2 (Dense)	(None, 7)	7175

3.3 Emotion Recognition with Context Awareness

The emotion recognition system does not consider context awareness or not able to detect emotion in dynamic conversation. Also, the current ones work about the identification of emotions based on Ekman's six basic emotion. Facial emotion recognition was trained to classify very few discrete categories like anger, happy, disgust, sad, surprise and fear. The FER should consider dataset with context awareness and classify more emotion categories like in Plutchik wheel of emotions [29]. To address this challenge taken Emotic [30] dataset for multimodal facial emotion recognition. Emotic dataset contains annotated images with 26 emotion categories and 3 dimensional categories like valence, arousal and dominance. After applying CNN to both modal body and image. The result is shown in for one sample imageshown in Fig. 5 and Average precision (AP) is shown in Table 4.

Table 4. AP for emotion category

Emotion Category	APs	Emotion Category	APs	Emotion Category	APs
Affection.........	26.01	Embarrassment	3.08	Pleasure.........	48.65
Anger............	11.29	Engagement.......	86.27	Sadness..........	19.29
Annoyance.........	16.39	Esteem............	18.58	Sensitivity......	8.94
Anticipation......	58.99	Excitement.......	78.54	Suffering.........	17.6
Aversion.........	9.56	Average..........	28.33	Surprise.........	21.96
Confidence.......	81.09	Fatigue..........	10.31	Sympathy.........	15.25
Disapproval......	16.28	Fear.............	16.44	Yearning.........	9.01
Disconnection....	21.25	Happiness.........	55.21		
Disquietment......	20.13	Pain.............	10		
Doubt/Confusion...	33.57	Peace............	22.94		

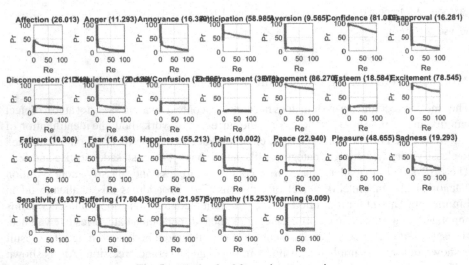

Fig. 5. AP plot for 26 emotion categories

4 Conclusion

In this paper, we have focussed identification of facial emotions from facial expression images using 4 feature extraction techniques -HOG, LBP, SIFT and Gabor filter. As can be seen, feature extraction using Gabor filters produces results that are superior to those produced by other approaches. However, it should also be noted that CNNs without any feature extraction methods also produce results that are superior to those produced by methods like HOG, LBP, and SIFT. As training samples increased for getting more accurate result, Deep learning models must be used for face emotion identification. The multimodal emotion recognition approach can recognize the more emotions of Plutchik wheel and outperforms as compared to unimodal approach. Compared to existing works the coverage of different emotions is increased by 5% in multimodal emotion recognition.

References

1. Kołakowska, A., Landowska, A., Szwoch, M., Szwoch, W., Wróbel, M.R.: Emotion recognition and its applications. In: Hippe, Z., Kulikowski, J., Mroczek, T., Wtorek, J. (eds.) Human-Computer Systems Interaction: Backgrounds and Applications 3. AISC, vol. 300. Springer, Cham (2014). https://doi.org/10.1007/978-3-319-08491-6_5
2. Al-Kaysi, A.M., et al.: Predicting tDCS treatment outcomes of patients with major depressive disorder using automated EEG classification. J. Affect. Disorders **208**, 597–603 (2017)
3. Bocharov, A.V., Knyazev, G.G., Savostyanov, A.N.: Depression and implicit emotion processing: an EEG study. Clin. Neurophysiol. **47**(3), 225–230 (2017)
4. Harrigan, J., Rosenthal, R., Scherer, K. (eds.): The New Handbook of Methods in Nonverbal Behavior Research. Oxford University Press (2008). https://doi.org/10.1093/acprof:oso/978 0198529620.001.0001
5. Cohn, Jeffrey F., et al.: Detecting depression from facial actions and vocal prosody. In: 2009 3rd International Conference on Affective Computing and Intelligent Interaction and Workshops. IEEE (2009)
6. Sharifa, A., et al.: Eye movement analysis for depression detection. In: 2013 IEEE International Conference on Image Processing. IEEE (2013)
7. Kumar, A., et al.: Identification and classification of depressed mental state for end-user over social media. Comput. Intell. Neurosci. **2022**, 10 p., 8755922 (2022)
8. Pampouchidou, A., Pediaditis, M., Kazantzaki, E., et al.: Automated facial video-based recognition of depression and anxiety symptom severity: cross-corpus validation. Mach. Vision Appl. **31**(4), 1–19 (2020). https://doi.org/10.1007/s00138-020-01080-7
9. Thakare, A., Bhende, M., Deb, N., Degadwala, S., Pant, B., Kumar, Y.B.: Classification of bioinformatics EEG data signals to identify depressed brain state using CNN Model. BioMed Res. Int.
10. Pampouchidou, A., et al.: Automatic assessment of depression based on visual cues: a systematic review. IEEE Trans. Affect. Comput. **10**(4), 445–470 (2019). https://doi.org/10.1109/TAFFC.2017.2724035
11. Swapna, S., et al.: Comparative analysis of histograms of oriented gradients and local binary pattern coefficients for facial emotion recognition. In: 2021 8th International Conference on Computing for Sustainable Global Development (INDIACom). IEEE (2021)
12. Hassan, A.K., Mohammed, S.N.: A novel facial emotion recognition scheme based on graph mining. Defence Technol. **16**(5), 1062–1072 (2020)
13. Li, H., et al.: An efficient multimodal 2D+ 3D feature-based approach to automatic facial expression recognition. Comput. Vis. Image Understand. **140**, 83–92 (2015)
14. Lakshmi, D., Ponnusamy, R.: Facial emotion recognition using modified HOG and LBP features with deep stacked autoencoders. Microprocess. Microsyst. **82**, 103834 (2021)
15. Mehendale, N.: Facial emotion recognition using convolutional neural networks (FERC). SN Appl. Sci.s **2**(3), 1–8 (2020). https://doi.org/10.1007/s42452-020-2234-1
16. Soumyajit, S., et al.: Feature selection for facial emotion recognition using cosine similarity-based harmony search algorithm. Appl. Sci. **10.**8, 2816 (2020)
17. Bhende, M., Thakare, A., Pant, B., Singhal, P., Shinde, S., Dugbakie, B.N.: Integrating multiclass light weighted BiLSTM model for classifying negative emotions. Comput. Intell. Neuroscie.

18. Patrick, L., et al.: The extended cohn-kanade dataset (ck+): a complete dataset for action unit and emotion-specified expression. In: 2010 IEEE Computer Society Conference on Computer Vision and Pattern Recognition-Workshops. IEEE (2010)
19. Swati, S., Singh, R., Misra, A.K.: Efficient facial expression recognition using histogram of oriented gradients in wavelet domain. Multimedia Tools Appl. **77**, 28725–28747 (2018)
20. Zhao, H., et al.: Local binary pattern-based adaptive differential evolution for multimodal optimization problems. IEEE Trans. Cybern. **50**(7), 3343–3357 (2019)
21. Tony, L.: Scale invariant feature transform, p. 10491 (2012)
22. Grigorescu, S.E., Petkov, N., Kruizinga, P.: Comparison of texture features based on Gabor filters. IEEE Trans. Image Process. **11**(10), 1160–1167 (2002)
23. Yu, Z., et al.: Spatio-temporal convolutional features with nested LSTM for facial expression recognition. Neurocomputing **317**, 50–57 (2018)
24. Rawat, R., Mahor, V., Chirgaiya, S., Shaw, R.N., Ghosh, A.: Sentiment analysis at online social network for cyber-malicious post reviews using machine learning techniques. In: Bansal, J.C., Paprzycki, M., Bianchini, M., Das, S. (eds.) Computationally Intelligent Systems and their Applications, pp. 113–130. Springer Singapore, Singapore (2021). https://doi.org/10.1007/978-981-16-0407-2_9
25. Liang, D., et al.: Deep convolutional BiLSTM fusion network for facial expression recognition. Visual Comput. **36**, 499–508 (2020)
26. Kalpana Chowdary, M., Nguyen, Tu.N., Jude Hemanth, D.: Deep learning-based facial emotion recognition for human–computer interaction applications. Neural Comput. Appl. 1–18 (2021). https://doi.org/10.1007/s00521-021-06012-8
27. Zahara, L., et al.: The facial emotion recognition (FER-2013) dataset for prediction system of micro-expressions face using the convolutional neural network (CNN) algorithm-based Raspberry Pi. In: 2020 Fifth International Conference on Informatics and Computing (ICIC). IEEE (2020)
28. Li, S., Deng, W., Du, J.: Reliable crowdsourcing and deep locality-preserving learning for expression recognition in the wild. In: Proceedings of the IEEE Conference on Computer Vision and Pattern Recognition (2017)
29. Melissa, D.: Plutchik's wheel of emotions—2017. Update (2017)
30. Ronak, K., et al.: EMOTIC: emotions in context dataset. In: Proceedings of the IEEE Conference on Computer Vision and Pattern Recognition Workshops (2017)

Author Index

A

Abhishek, Bavanasi   II-210
Alaga, Arvindran   I-247
Al-banaa, Akram   II-138
Alfred, Quazi Mohmmad   II-179
Ali, Jabir   II-138
Ali, Shakir   II-231
Ang, Sau Loong   I-247, II-168
Ashwini Reddy, C.   II-210

B

Balusamy, Balamurugan   I-212
Banerjee, Avishek   II-219
Bansal, Savita   I-221
Bera, Rabindranath   II-179
Bhati, Mohak   I-13
Bhatlawande, Shripad   I-188, II-32
Bhuvana Sri, Gorrela   II-12

C

Chandrappa, S.   I-1, I-49
Chatterjee, Santanu   I-140, II-45, II-120
Chauhan, Deepa   I-201
Chidrawar, Sairaj   II-1

D

Das, Sanjoy   II-138, II-161
Dasgupta, Anurag   II-219
De, Sudip Kumar   II-219
Deshmukh, Sumit   II-1
Dhamankar, Bhushan   II-1
Dharwal, Mridul   I-201

F

Faheem, Muhammad   II-271
Foh, Wei Lian Willian   I-247

G

Gaur, Chintan   II-161
Ghosh, Ankush   I-140, II-45, II-120, II-219
Ghosh, Enakshmi   I-140, II-45, II-120
Gowthami, S.   II-23
Goyal, Anjali   I-71
Goyal, Himanshu Rai   II-97
Grover, Veena   I-212

H

Haque, Merazul   I-26
Haque, Mustafizul   I-26, II-231
Hemalatha, K.   II-23

J

Jadhav, Hritika   I-117
Jha, Mayank   II-32
Johri, Ishita   I-212
Jyotsna, Gottumukkala Sai Naga   II-12

K

Kamble, Sanchi   I-117
Kangule, Rohit   II-1
Kapoor, Chirag   II-97
Khoo, Chun Yan Alvin   I-247
Kiran, J.   I-1
Kotgire, Anuradha   I-117
Kotiyal, Arnav   I-1, I-49
Kulkarni, Subhash S.   I-39
Kumar, Arun   I-80
Kumar, Ashwini   I-59, I-239, II-161
Kumar, D. K. Santhosh   I-1, I-49
Kumar, Santosh   I-59
Kumar, Satyam   I-90

L

Lahari, P. L.   I-127
Lakshmi Kumari, P. D. S. S.   II-12
Lathika, D.   II-109
Lim, Chia Yean   I-247, II-168

R. N. Shaw et al. (Eds.): ICACIS 2023, CCIS 1920, pp. 269–271, 2023.
https://doi.org/10.1007/978-3-031-45121-8

Printed in the United States
by Baker & Taylor Publisher Services